THE MAP AND
THE TERRITORY

By the Same Author

The Age of Turbulence

ALAN GREENSPAN

The Map and the Territory

Risk, Human Nature, and the Future of Forecasting

ALLEN LANE
an imprint of
PENGUIN BOOKS

ALLEN LANE

Published by the Penguin Group
Penguin Books Ltd, 80 Strand, London WC2R 0RL, England
Penguin Group (USA) Inc., 375 Hudson Street, New York, New York 10014, USA
Penguin Group (Canada), 90 Eglinton Avenue East, Suite 700, Toronto, Ontario, Canada M4P 2Y3
(a division of Pearson Penguin Canada Inc.)
Penguin Ireland, 25 St Stephen's Green, Dublin 2, Ireland (a division of Penguin Books Ltd)
Penguin Group (Australia), 707 Collins Street, Melbourne, Victoria 3008, Australia
(a division of Pearson Australia Group Pty Ltd)
Penguin Books India Pvt Ltd, 11 Community Centre, Panchsheel Park, New Delhi – 110 017, India
Penguin Group (NZ), 67 Apollo Drive, Rosedale, Auckland 0632, New Zealand
(a division of Pearson New Zealand Ltd)
Penguin Books (South Africa) (Pty) Ltd, Block D, Rosebank Office Park, 181 Jan Smuts Avenue,
Parktown North, Gauteng 2193, South Africa

Penguin Books Ltd, Registered Offices: 80 Strand, London WC2R 0RL, England

www.penguin.com

First published in the United States of America by The Penguin Press,
a member of Penguin Group (USA) LLC 2013
First published in Great Britain by Allen Lane 2013
001

Copyright © Alan Greenspan, 2013

The moral right of the author has been asserted

Printed in Great Britain by Clays Ltd, St Ives plc

A CIP catalogue record for this book is available from the British Library

ISBN: 978–0–241–00359–6

www.greenpenguin.co.uk

MIX
Paper from
responsible sources
FSC
www.fsc.org   FSC™ C018179

Penguin Books is committed to a sustainable
future for our business, our readers and our planet.
This book is made from Forest Stewardship
Council™ certified paper.

FOR MY BELOVED ANDREA

CONTENTS

THE MAP AND
THE TERRITORY

INTRODUCTION

I t was a call I never expected to receive. I had just returned home from indoor tennis on the chilly, windy Sunday afternoon of March 16, 2008. A senior official of the Federal Reserve Board was on the phone to alert me of the board's just-announced invocation, for the first time in decades, of the obscure but explosive section 13 (3) of the Federal Reserve Act. Broadly interpreted, section 13 (3) empowered the Federal Reserve to lend nearly unlimited cash to virtually anybody.[1] On March 16, it empowered the Federal Reserve Bank of New York to lend $29 billion to facilitate the acquisition of Bear Stearns by JPMorgan.

Bear Stearns, the smallest of the major investment banks, founded in 1923, was on the edge of bankruptcy, having run through nearly $20 billion of cash just the previous week. Its demise was the beginning of a six-month erosion in global financial stability that would culminate with the Lehman Brothers failure on September 15, 2008, triggering possibly the greatest financial crisis ever. To be sure, the Great Depression of the 1930s involved a far greater collapse in economic activity. But never before had short-term financial markets, the facilitators of everyday commerce, shut down on so global a scale. The drying up of deeply liquid markets, literally overnight, as investors swung from euphoria to fear, dismantled vast financial complexes and led to a worldwide contraction in economic activity. The role of human nature in economic affairs was never more apparent than on that fateful day in September and in the weeks that followed.

On the face of it, the financial crisis also represented an existential crisis for economic forecasting. I began my postcrisis investigations, culminating in this book, in an effort to understand how we all got it so wrong, and what we can learn from the fact that we did. At its root, then, this is a book about forecasting human nature, what we think we know about the future and what we decide we should do about it. It's about the short term and the long term, and perhaps most important, about the foggy place where the one turns into the other. We are at this moment faced with a number of serious long-term economic problems, all in a sense having to do with underinvesting in our economic future. My most worrisome concern is our broken political system. It is that system on which we rely to manage our rule of law, defined in our Constitution (see Chapter 14). My fondest hope for this book is that some of the insights my investigations have yielded will be of some use in bolstering the case for taking action now, in the short term, which is in our long-term collective self-interest despite the unavoidable short-term pain it will bring. The only alternative is incalculably worse pain and human suffering later. There is little time to waste.

THE FORECASTING IMPERATIVE

As always, though we wish it were otherwise, economic forecasting is a discipline of probabilities. The degree of certainty with which the so-called hard sciences are able to identify the metrics of the physical world appears to be out of the reach of the economic disciplines. But forecasting, irrespective of its failures, will never be abandoned. It is an inbred necessity of human nature. The more we can anticipate the course of events in the world in which we live, the better prepared we are to react to those events in a manner that can improve our lives.

Introspectively, we know that we have a limited capability to see much beyond our immediate horizon. That realization has prompted us, no doubt from before recorded history, to look for ways to compensate for this vexing human "shortcoming." In ancient Greece, kings and generals sought out the advice of the oracle of Delphi before embarking on political or military ventures. Two millennia later, Europe was enthralled by the cryptic prognostications of Nostradamus. Today, both fortune-tellers and stock pickers continue to make a passable living. Even repeated forecasting failure will not deter the unachievable pursuit of prescience, because our nature demands it.

ECONOMETRICS

A key plot point in the history of our efforts to see the future has been the development over the past eight decades of the discipline of model-based economic forecasting. That discipline has embraced many of the same mathematical tools employed in the physical sciences, tools used by almost all economic forecasters, both in government and in the private sector, largely to build models that "explain" the past, and perhaps, as a consequence, make the future more comprehensible.

I was drawn to the sophistication of the then-new mathematical economics as a graduate student at Columbia University in the early 1950s. My professors Jacob Wolfowitz and Abraham Wald were pioneers in mathematical statistics.[2] But my early fascination was increasingly tempered over the years by a growing skepticism about its relevance to a world in which the state of seemingly unmodelable animal spirits is so critical a factor in economic outcomes.

John Maynard Keynes, in his groundbreaking 1936 opus, *The General Theory of Employment, Interest and Money,* set the framework for much of modern-day macromodeling. The Keynesian model, as it came to be known, to this day governs much government macroeconomic policy. Keynes's model was a complete, though simplified version of how the major pieces of a market economy fit together. The class of models that today we still call Keynesian is widely employed in the public and private sectors, especially to judge the impact of various governmental policies on the levels of GDP and employment.

Keynes's approach was a direct challenge to classical economists' belief that market economies were always self-correcting and would, when disturbed, return to full employment in relatively short order. By contrast, Keynes argued that there were circumstances in which those self-equilibrating mechanisms became dysfunctional, creating an "underemployment equilibrium." In those circumstances, he advocated government deficit spending to offset shortfalls in aggregate demand. Remarkably, more than seventy-five years later, economists continue to debate the pros and cons of that policy.

Economic forecasting of all varieties, Keynesian and otherwise, has always been fraught with never-ending challenges. Models, by their nature, are vast simplifications of a complex economic reality. There are literally millions of relationships that interact every day to create aggregate GDP, even for a relatively simple market economy. Because only a very small fraction of these interactions can be represented in any model, economists are continually seeking sets of equations that, while few in number, nonetheless are presumed to capture the fundamental forces that drive modern economies.

In practice, model builders (myself included) keep altering the set of chosen variables and equation specifications until we get a result that appears to replicate the historical record in an economically credible manner. Every forecaster must decide which relative handful of "equations" he or she believes most effectively captures the essence of an economy's overall dynamics.

For the most part, the modeling of the nonfinancial sectors of market economies has worked tolerably well. Vast amounts of research have increasingly enhanced our understanding of how those markets function.[3] Finance, however, as we repeatedly learn, operates in a different leveraged environment where risk is of a significantly larger magnitude than in the rest of the economy. Risk taking and avoiding is at the root of almost all financial decisions. Nonfinancial business is more oriented to engineering, technology, and management organization.

Nonfinancial businesses do factor risk into all their capital investment and other decisions, but their principal concern concentrates on, for example, how many transistors can be squeezed onto a microchip and how to ensure bridges can safely carry the traffic load they are built to carry. But that is the application of quantum mechanics and engineering, where risk has been largely, though not wholly, removed from decision making. Synthetic derivative trading and other new activities in our financial sector have levels of risk many multiples greater than exist in the physical sciences, the critical body of knowledge that supports nonfinancial business. Human nature has no role to play in how subatomic particles interact with one another.[4] Our propensities related to fear, euphoria, herding, and culture, however, virtually define finance. Because finance importantly guides a nation's savings toward investment in cutting-edge technologies, its impact on overall economic outcomes, for good or ill, is far greater than its less than 10 percent share of GDP would suggest. Moreover, financial imbalances are doubtless the major cause, directly or indirectly, of modern business cycles. Finance has always been the most difficult component of an economy to model.

Spurred in the 1960s by the apparent success of the forecasting models of the Council of Economic Advisers (CEA) under Presidents Kennedy and Johnson, econometrics, as it came to be known, moved from the classroom to the forefront of economic policy making. By the late 1960s, econometric models had become an integral part of government and private policy making, and remain so to this day.

But the road forward for forecasters has been rocky. Simple models do well in the classroom as tutorials, but regrettably have had less success in the world beyond. No sooner had Keynes's paradigm gained wide acceptance within the economics profession than the American economy began to behave in a manner that contradicted some of the core tenets of the so-called Keynesian models, including the thesis that a rise in unemployment reflected increased slack in the economy that would in turn lower the rate of inflation. For much of the 1970s, the unemployment rate rose, but the inflation rate remained stubbornly elevated—a malady dubbed stagflation at the time.

The forecasting tools that had made government economists seem so prescient a decade earlier now appeared flawed. Milton Friedman of the University of Chicago gained intellectual traction by arguing that our inflationary economic policies, most notably the rapid expansion of the money supply, were raising inflation expectations that overcame the disinflationary effect of slack in the labor market. Friedman and his followers developed a theory, monetarism, and a forecasting tool based on the growth in money supply that, for a while, appeared to forecast the developments of the late 1970s far more accurately than any of the variations of the Keynesian model. By the end of the 1970s, the weekly issuance by the Federal Reserve of its money supply figures soon drew as much attention as today's unemployment numbers.

By the 1980s, with inflation under control—thanks, in part, to the Federal Reserve's restraint of money supply growth—a rejuvenated but somewhat chastened Keynesianism, with a stagflation fix to reflect the importance of inflation expectations, reemerged. Such models worked reasonably well for the next two decades, largely as a consequence of an absence of any serious structural breakdown in markets. The model constructed by Federal Reserve staff, combining the elements of Keynesianism, monetarism, and other more recent contributions to economic theory, seemed particularly impressive, and was particularly helpful to the Fed's Board of Governors over the years of my tenure.

THE WORLD CHANGED

But leading up to the almost universally unanticipated crisis of September 2008, macromodeling unequivocally failed when it was needed most, much to the chagrin of the economics profession. The Federal Reserve Board's highly sophisticated forecasting system did not foresee a recession until the crisis hit. Nor did the model developed by the prestigious International Monetary Fund, which concluded as late as the spring of 2007 that "global economic risks [have] *declined* since . . . September 2006. . . . The overall U.S. economy is holding up well . . . [and] the signs elsewhere are very encouraging."[5] JPMorgan, arguably America's premier financial institution, projected on September 12, 2008—three days before the crisis hit— that the U.S. GDP growth rate would be accelerating into the first half of 2009.

Most analysts and forecasters, both public and private, agreed with the view expressed by the *Economist* in December 2006 that "market capitalism, the engine that runs most of the world economy, seems to be doing its job well." As late as the day before the crash, September 14, 2008, the outlook was still sufficiently equivocal that I was asked on ABC's Sunday morning show *This Week* if "the chances of escaping a recession [were] greater than fifty percent."[6] With the crisis less than twenty-four hours away, conventional wisdom had not yet coalesced around even the possibility of a typical recession, to say nothing of the worst economic crisis in eight decades.

Moreover, even after the crash, in January 2009, the unemployment rate, then at 7.8 percent, was forecast by the chairman designate of the President's Council of Economic Advisers to fall to 7.0 percent by the end of 2010 and to 6.5 percent by the end of 2011.[7] In December 2011, the rate was 8.5 percent.

What went wrong? Why was virtually every economist and policy maker of note so off about so large an issue?

My inquiry begins with an examination of "animal spirits," the term John Maynard Keynes famously coined to refer to "a spontaneous urge to action rather than inaction, and not as the [rational] outcome of a weighted average of quantitative benefits multiplied by quantitative probabilities."[8] Keynes was talking about the spirit that impels economic activity, but we now amend his notion of animal spirits to include its obverse, fear-driven risk aversion. I had long been aware of such "spirits" and their quirkiness; in 1959, as a young economist, I had my first taste of being impressively wrong in a public prediction when I worried in the pages of *Fortune* magazine of investors' "over-exuberance" at what would prove to be very far from the top of a roaring bull market.[9, 10] The point isn't that I and other economic forecasters didn't understand that markets are prone to wild and even deranging mood swings that are uncoupled from any underlying rational basis. The point is rather that such "irrational" behavior is hard to measure, and stubbornly resistant to any reliable systematic analysis.

But now, after the past several years of closely studying the manifestations of animal spirits during times of severe crisis, I have come around to the view that there is something more systematic about the way people behave irrationally, especially during periods of extreme economic stress, than I had previously contemplated. In other words, this behavior can be measured and made an integral part of the economic forecasting process and the formulation of economic policy.

In a change of my perspective, I have recently come to appreciate that "spirits" do in fact display "consistencies" that can importantly enhance our ability to identify emerging asset price bubbles in equities, commodities, and exchange rates—and even to anticipate the economic consequences of their ultimate collapse and recovery.

In Chapter 1 in particular, I seek to identify specific behavioral imperatives—spirits—such as euphoria, fear, panic, optimism, and many more—and explore how they, and the cultures they foster, interact with rational economic behavior and spur important market outcomes. This isn't to say that we should throw *Homo economicus* out with his dirty bathwater: Despite ample evidence of persistent irrational market behavior, the data indicate that over the long run, rational economic judgments still guide free economies. But, of course, the long run can, famously, take a *very* long time.

Nonetheless, it is essential to take both a long-term and a short-term perspective when we examine the roots of the 2008 crisis and the tepid recovery that followed. The rise and fall from 1994 to 2008 of two asset price bubbles, the data indicate, did reflect in part real improvements in productivity, but the bubbles were also carried by a wave of irrational exuberance and bubble euphoria. Those waves, when they inevitably collapsed, produced widespread fear that disabled markets.

It is important to recognize, however, that not all bubbles, when they collapse, wreak the degree of havoc experienced in 2008. As I detail in Chapter 2, the crashes of 1987 and 2000 had comparatively minimal negative effect on the economy. The severity of the destruction caused by a bursting bubble is determined not by the type of asset that turns "toxic" but by the degree of leverage employed by the holders of those toxic assets. The latter condition dictates to what extent contagion becomes destabilizing. In short, debt leverage matters—as we see in Chapter 2.

This book touches on many related issues of importance to our economic future. Writing it has taken me into some uncharted waters—some that might, because of the nature of some of my concerns about the course we are now on, prove to be uncomfortably warm. But I did not write this book in a spirit of criticism, or of pessimism. My interest in writing it was not to establish what I now think but what I now believe I can demonstrate with some reasonable degree of assurance.

Coming out of World War II, the United States was at the top of its game. Productivity was growing rapidly. Household and business savings rates were close to 10 percent, and capital investment and residential building were booming. Moreover, even after funding our burgeoning capital investment, we still had enough savings to spare to invest beyond our borders.

After securing our place of leadership in the economic world, we turned magnanimously to ensure that the least well off in our society shared in the good fortune of the nation as a whole. After many years of Social Security and lesser programs, such "government social benefits to persons" totaled 4.7 percent of GDP. But starting in 1965, with the additions of Medicare and Medicaid, and shortly thereafter a major increase in Social Security through benefit inflation indexation, we embarked on a truly bipartisan unprecedented four-decade rise in outlays averaging nearly 10 percent per year. The unfortunate consequence of our magnanimity, as I demonstrate in later chapters, is that these benefits have been crowding out private savings almost dollar for dollar. That loss of funding for capital investment led to slowed productivity growth, a phenomenon that would have been even worse if we had not turned to borrowing so heavily from abroad. Moreover, to fund our generosity we have foraged into every corner of our federal budget to meet the rise in social benefit spending. We are eating our seed corn, and damaging the very engine of America's comparative strength in the world. We desperately need a change in direction. We have done it before—many times, in fact.

A NOTE TO READERS

Where applicable in the chapters that follow, I have included appendices in support of my conclusions, with additional explanatory text, tables, charts, and regression analyses, the most widely used statistical procedure to assist in judging economic cause and effect.[11] Statistics first appear in Chapter 2 and I have accompanied that chapter's appendix with a short primer on the interpretation of the results of regression analysis. For those uninterested in these metrics, appendices can readily be bypassed. I trust my written commentary will carry the line of reasoning of the appendices' equations.

A significant part of the statistical analysis in our exhibits rests on the National Income and Product Accounts of the Bureau of Economic Analysis (BEA). Shortly before we went to press, the BEA published a major revision of those accounts. While there are significant changes in the levels of many series, none importantly alter any conclusions in the forthcoming chapters.

ONE

ANIMAL SPIRITS

I n my early years, I lived a cloistered life, traveling only rarely outside the confines of New York City. When, in my mid-to-late teens, I was first exposed to the rest of the world, I was amazed at how similarly all varieties of people behaved. They may have hailed from different cultures and spoken different languages, but their interactions and behavior were quite familiar to a boy brought up in the canyons of New York City. As I began to travel widely, I became fascinated when businesspeople in Norway, tribal leaders in South Africa, and Chinese musicians all had remarkably similar emotional reactions to day-to-day events. They all smiled and laughed, for example, as a sign of pleasure. They all expressed fear and euphoria in a similar manner.

As the years rolled on, I observed generation after generation of teenagers all exhibiting similar insecurities, awkwardness, and aspirations. The novels of Jane Austen, written in early nineteenth-century Britain, depicted to me a playing field of social intercourse quite familiar to everyone alive today. We humans appear to be a truly homogenous species.

But at root, what are we? We like to describe ourselves as fundamentally driven by reason to an extent not matched by other living creatures. This is doubtless true. But we are far from the prototype depicted by neoclassical economists: that of people motivated predominantly by considerations of rational long-term self-interest. Our thinking process, as behavioral economists point out, is more intuitive than syllogistic. In the end, of course, all intellectual and hence material progress requires verification by a systematic logical process, but that is rarely the way we think day by day.

The economics of animal spirits, broadly speaking, covers a wide range of human actions, and overlaps with much of the relatively new discipline of behavioral economics. The point is to substitute a more realistic version of behavior than the model of the wholly rationality-driven "economic man" so prominent for so long in economics courses taught in our universities.[1] This more realistic view of the way people behave in their day-by-day activities in the marketplace traces a path of economic growth that is somewhat lower than would be the case if people were truly "rational" economic actors. Most of the time this issue is of little more than academic interest because all of our statistical observations and forecasts are already based on decisions that people *actually* made, not what those decisions would have been had people been acting more rationally. While it's true that if people acted at the level of rationality presumed in the standard economics textbooks I was brought up with, the world's standard of living would be measurably higher; but, in fact, they do not. From the perspective of a forecaster, the issue is thus not whether behavior is rational but whether it is sufficiently repetitive and systematic to be numerically measured and predicted.

Can we better identify and measure those quick-reaction judgments on which we tend to base much, if not all, of our rapid-fire financial market and related decisions—"fast thinking," in the words of Daniel Kahneman, a leading behavioral economist? I think so.

THE LONGER PERSPECTIVE

Consider the insights that brought us the steam engine and the electric motor, the railroad, the telegraph, atomic energy, and the integrated circuit. It was those innovations, and more, that over the past two centuries propelled civilization to the highest material standards of living ever achieved. They were all the result of human reasoning. As the seventeenth-century French mathematician Blaise Pascal is said to have put it, "Man's greatness lies in his power of thought." It's Kahneman's "slow thinking."

To be sure, great innovators often explain their insights as epiphanies, or intuition. But those epiphanies seem to happen only to those who have laboriously accumulated the knowledge relevant to such awakenings.[2] I rank the revolution of the eighteenth century, the Enlightenment, particularly in the works of John Locke, David Hume, Adam Smith, and their followers, as the critical intellectual root of the twenty-first century's elevated standard of living. The radical ideas of such men led to the political upheaval that changed societies previously ruled by the divine right of kings, often in complicity with the Church. Many countries reorganized under a rule of law that protected individual rights, especially property rights. By engaging our competitive self-interest, we fostered the innovations that changed the world after millennia of economic stagnation. Those were all acts of human intelligence from which the historical roots of modern capitalist economies have arisen. But that human intelligence has always existed side by side with a large strain of human irrationality.

As the nineteenth century progressed and populations moved from self-sufficient farming to the increasingly complex and interactive urban-dominated economies of the modern world, the industrial business cycle emerged. It demonstrably was driven by the animal spirits we currently observe at the core of speculative booms. But because agriculture, diminishing in importance but still prominent into the 1950s, was largely dependent on weather rather than animal spirits, it was out of sync with the business cycle of nonagricultural industries and thus assuaged the ebb and flow of economic activity as a whole.

On occasion in this book I try to supplement standard forecasting models to capture what we have always known about financial market disruption but have never integrated into those models. As I mentioned, I had always viewed animal spirits as the human propensities driven largely by *random* irrationalities not readily integrated into formal models of the way market economies function. September 2008 was a watershed moment for forecasters, myself included. It has forced us to find ways to incorporate into our macromodels those animal spirits that dominate finance.

All such spirits, as I observe later, are tempered by reason to a greater or lesser degree, and hence I more formally choose to describe such marketplace behavior as "propensities." The technologies that have driven productivity since the Enlightenment were, at root, reasoned insights. Random irrationality produces nothing. If reason were not ultimately prevailing, we could not explain the dramatic improvements in standards of living that the world has achieved in the past two centuries.

As I will demonstrate, these reason-tempered animal spirits significantly affect *macro*economic decision making and outcomes. Newly popular behavioral economics is forcing forecasters to evaluate economic data in the context of a more complex model than that to which most of us had become accustomed.

BEHAVIORAL ECONOMICS

Behavioral economics is not a substitute for conventional economics, nor is it claimed to be. Daniel Kahneman, in discussing his latest book, noted that "much of the discussion . . . is about biases of intuition. However, the focus on error does not denigrate human intelligence. . . . Most of our judgments and actions are appropriate most of the time."[3]

As Colin Camerer and George Loewenstein aptly put it a decade ago:

> At the core of behavioral economics is the conviction that increasing the realism of the psychological underpinnings of economic analysis will improve economics *on its own terms.* . . . It does not imply a wholesale rejection of the neoclassical approach to economics based on utility maximization, equilibrium, and efficiency. . . . [Behavioral] departures are not radical . . . because they relax simplifying assumptions that are not central to the economic approach. For example, there is nothing in core neoclassical theory that specifies that people should . . . weight risky outcomes in a linear fashion, or that they must discount the future exponentially at a constant rate.[4]

IDENTIFICATION

Because human beings demonstrate similar characteristics, most, if not all, inbred propensities can be inferred by introspection and observation by every one of us. Fear, euphoria, competitive drive, and time preference, for example, are both introspectively self-evident and readily recognizable in others. Other propensities, such as inbred herding and home bias, we infer mainly by observing the behavior of others. (All of these separate propensities will be discussed shortly.)

In classifying propensities, I do not pretend to know which are truly inbred and which just have statistical regularities that are tantamount to being inbred. I classify propensities as "inbred"—herd behavior, for example—more for convenience than insight. I use the term "inbred" to cover both truly inbred propensities and those consistencies of behavior that enable model builders to operate on that assumption. I do not contend to have covered all of the economically relevant spirits or propensities, but I do hope that I have addressed the most important of them. My ultimate purpose is defining a set of economic stabilities of human actions that are statistically measurable and hence capable of being modeled. I am fully aware that in the process I am delving into disciplines with which I have little experience, and have tried to temper my conclusions accordingly.

PROPENSITIES

Fear and Euphoria

We all directly experience threats to our self and our values (fear) and the sense of well-being or elation (euphoria) triggered in the course of our pursuit of our economic interests. Fear, a major component of animal spirits, is a response to a threat to life, limb, and net worth. That emotion is decidedly inbred—no one is immune to it. But people respond to fear in different ways, and the differences are part of what defines the individuality of people. We are all alike fundamentally, but it is our individuality that makes for differences in values and our position in the hierarchy of society. Moreover, it is our individuality that creates markets, division of labor, and economic activity as we know it.

Risk Aversion

Risk aversion is a complex animal spirit crucial to forecasting. It reflects the ambivalent attitude people exhibit to the taking of risk. That we need to act to obtain food, shelter, and all the necessities of life is evident to all, as is the fact that we can't necessarily know in advance how successful our actions will be. The process of choosing which risks to take and which to avoid determines the relative pricing structure of markets, which in turn guides the flow of savings into investment, the critical function of finance (an issue I address in Chapter 5).

If risk taking is essential to living, is more risk taking better than less? If more risk were better than less risk, demand for lower quality bonds would exceed demand for riskless bonds, and high-quality bonds would yield more than low-quality bonds. They do not, from which we can infer the obvious: Risk taking is a necessary part of living, but it is not something the vast majority of us actively seek. Finding the proper balance of risks is critical to all of us in our day-to-day lives and perhaps manifests itself most obviously in finance in the management of portfolio risk.

The extremes of zero and full risk aversion (or its obverse, full and zero risk taking) are outside all human experience. Zero risk aversion—that is, the absence of any aversion to engaging in risky actions—implies that an individual does not care about, or cannot discriminate among, objective states of risk to life and limb. Such individuals cannot (or do not choose to) recognize life-threatening events. But to acquire the staples of life requires action, that is, the taking of risks, either by an individual or by others, such as parents taking risks on a child's behalf.

We live our lives day by day well within these outer boundaries of risk aversion and risk taking, which can be measured approximately by financial market yield spreads with respect to both credit rating and maturity. Those boundaries are critical to forecasting. The turn in stock prices in early 2009 following the crash of 2008 was a sign of the level of human angst approaching its historical limit (see Chapter 4). The limits of angst are also evident in credit spreads, which exhibit few or no long-term historical trends. Prime railroad bonds of the immediate post–Civil War years, for example, reflect spreads over U.S. Treasuries that are similar to our post–World War II experience, suggesting long-term stability in the degree and spread of human risk aversion.

I calibrate how people respond to risk in nonfinancial markets, both rationally and emotionally, with a measure I have employed for years—the share of liquid cash flow that management *chooses* to commit to illiquid, especially long-term, capital investments. That share is a measure of corporate managers' degree of uncertainty and hence their willingness to take risks. In 2009, it had fallen to its lowest peacetime level since 1938. The equivalent measure of risk aversion for households is the share of household cash flow invested in homes. This measure reached its lowest postwar level in 2010. That collapse in investment, especially in long-lived assets, explains most of the recent failure of the American economy to follow a path of recovery similar to the other ten post–World War II recoveries (see Chapter 7, "Uncertainty Undermines Investment").

Throughout this book I delve into the role of risk aversion and uncertainty as critical determinants of economic activity. I conclude that stock prices are not only an official leading indicator of business activity but are also a major cause of that activity (see Chapter 4). Uncertainty has many of the characteristics of peering into fog. Heavy discounting of the future is tantamount to having difficulty perceiving clearly beyond a certain point, and progressively less well as distance (risk) increases. The lessening or the end of uncertainty is like the lifting of the fog.

Time Preference

Time preference is the self-evident propensity to value more highly a claim to an asset today than a claim to that same asset at some fixed time in the future. A promise delivered tomorrow is not as valuable as that promise conveyed today. That many buyers of Apple's immensely popular iPhone 5 (released in September 2012) would have paid for immediate delivery to bypass a waiting list is a clear reflection of time preference. We experience this phenomenon mainly through its most visible counterpart: interest rates and savings rates (see Box 1.1). The stability of time preference over the generations can be demonstrated; indeed, in fifth-century-BC Greece, interest rates exhibited levels similar to what we see in today's markets.[5] The Bank of England's official policy rate for the years 1694 to 1972 ranged between 2 percent and 10 percent. It surged to 17 percent during the inflationary late 1970s, but it has since re-turned to its single-digit historical range. It is reasonable to conclude that time preference, too, has no evident long-term trend.

Such inferences of the stability of time preference are also con-sistent with behavioral economics. A famous experiment, conducted in 1972 and 1990 by Stanford psychologist Walter Mischel, concluded that the ability of children between the ages of four and six to forgo immediate gratification[6] was reflected years later by the high SAT scores of those who deferred gratification as children compared with those who could not. A follow-up study of the same individuals in 2011 confirmed the response, indicating a *lifelong* inbred propensity to a specific level of time preference, though not the same for each individual. To forgo short-term gratification for greater rewards in the future is generally consistent with higher intelligence.

Real (inflation expectation adjusted) market interest rates, I as-sume, are continually converging toward a stable time preference, though we cannot be sure because time preference is rarely directly visible.

BOX 1.1: TIME PREFERENCE AND SAVINGS

The extent that we discount the future (time preference) must obviously affect our saving propensity. A high preference for immediate consumption would diminish the propensity to save while a high preference for saving for retirement, for ex-ample, would diminish the propensity to consume. But through most of history, time preference could not have had a major determining role in the level of savings. Prior to the late nineteenth century, almost all production had to be dedicated to keeping the population alive. There was little to save even if our inbred propensities were inclined in that direction.

Western Europe's population, for example, was able to grow only 0.2 percent annually between 1000 and 1820, following stagnation in the previous millennium.* It is only when innovation and productivity growth freed generations from the grip of chronic starvation that time preference could emerge as a significant economic force. Since 1880, the gross private savings rate in the United States has been remarkably stable, ranging mostly between 10 and 20 percent of GDP. Gross domestic savings averaged somewhat higher, and as can be seen from Exhibit 9.5, the savings rate rose sharply after 1834.

Savings is a measure of the extent of abstaining from consumption. Investment is a measure of the particular assets to which those savings are applied. Savings and investment, as I note in Box 9.3, are alternate measures of the same transactions, *ex post.*

Culture reflects a country's degree of abstinence. People acting rationally would tend to save in their early years to create provisions for years of retirement. ("Retirement," incidentally, is only a twentieth-century phenomenon.) But our less rational propensities are too often evident in a failure to always do so.

What is remarkable is how, in the United States, we have managed to exhibit so stable a private savings rate for more than a century. Time preference, judging from the historical

---

*Angus Maddison, *The World Economy: A Millennial Perspective.* Development Centre of the OECD, 2001, p. 28.

data on the long stability of real riskless interest rates, apparently remained stable, and doubtless sets the upper limits to the proportion of income that people are willing to save, if they are able to do so at all. It has only been when human ingenuity brought production levels beyond the needs of raw survival that time preference became a factor in the rate of savings.

Herd Behavior

There is a universally observed human trait to follow or emulate a leader of some sort. It is driven by most people's need to achieve the security (emotional and physical) of belonging to a group. It is arguably one of our most important propensities, second only to fear, and a significant driver of economic activity. Herd behavior exaggerates speculation and the business cycle as it distracts us from the facts of markets and draws us to the less relevant views of other people. It captures consumer behavior known by the idiom "keeping up with the Joneses," also known as "conspicuous consumption," the term coined by Thorstein Veblen in 1899.[7, 8]

I would argue that this behavior accounts for the long-term stability we see in household spending and saving patterns from one generation to the next. Personal savings as a share of disposable personal income during peacetime has held in a relatively narrow range of 5 percent to 10 percent almost all of the time since 1897 (see Exhibit 1.1). With the very large rise in average real household incomes over the generations, why does the average savings rate not rise as a consequence? As I noted in *The Age of Turbulence* (pages 269–70), happiness depends far more on how people's incomes compare with those of their perceived peers, or even those of their role models, than how they are doing in any absolute material sense. When graduate students at Harvard were asked awhile back whether they would be happier with $50,000 a year if their peers earned half that, or $100,000 if their peers doubled that, the majority chose the lower salary. When I first saw the story, I chuckled and started to brush it off. But it struck a chord, and ultimately brought back a long-dormant memory of a fascinating 1947 study by Dorothy Brady and Rose Friedman.[9]

Brady and Friedman presented data that showed that the share of income an American family spends on consumer goods and services is largely determined not by the level of family income but by its level relative to the nation's average family income. Their study suggests that a family with the nation's average income in 2000 would be expected to spend the same proportion of its income as a family with average family income in 1900, even though in inflation-adjusted terms that 1900 income was only a minor fraction of that of 2000. I reproduced and updated their calculations and confirmed their conclusion.[10] Consumer behavior has not much changed over the last century and a quarter.

Herding is a different type of propensity from all the rest in that it refers not only to individuals' copycat propensity but also to the principles of group behavior and thus has implications for the economy overall. Fear and euphoria, for example, are contagious processes exaggerated by herding.[11] It can be difficult to parse, however, why individuals seek to emulate one group rather than another and what it takes to wean them away from one "crowd" to join another. The emergence of modern social media has only accelerated herd behavior.

Herd behavior is a key driver and an essential characteristic of speculative booms and busts. Once the speculative herd-driven propensity arrives at a state in which the vast majority of market par-ticipants have become committed to the bull market, the market becomes highly vulnerable to what I dub the Jessel paradox (see Chapter 3), and the market breaks. While the Jessel paradox explains the upside of speculative booms, an analogy to how the downside plays out, both literally and figuratively, is the extreme form of herd-ing, the dreaded stampede—a term borrowed from the cattle drives of our Old West.

Dealing with day-to-day reality requires a level of detailed deci-sion making that most adults, to a greater or lesser extent, perceive as beyond their ken.[12] For most of us, the comfort of guidance is sought in religion, and all of us are drawn to following the directions or emulating the actions of our peers or leaders.

Those who believe, rightly or wrongly, that they know the direc-tion that their society should take compete for leadership. Cliques or political parties arise, from which the ultimate leaders emerge, sometimes by grasping the levers of military power. In democratic societies at least, who the leaders turn out to be, for good or ill, is heavily influenced by herd behavior.

Few if any social groups have flourished without some hierarchy of leadership. Communal groups that make collective decisions by strict consensus—especially those attempting to live communally to the extent of holding income and wealth in common—almost always collapse. People have a propensity to form emotional bonds to a larger group, but when these bonds demand an equal sharing of in-come or status in a pecking order, they tend to break down, floun-dering on the inbred self-centered nature of our species. Our propensity for competition invariably produces the jockeying for leadership that has persistently undermined communal societies.

People in every society seek to improve their status in the peck-ing order of any organization. Even those who deem themselves unaffected by the opinions of others conform to the customs and culture of their societies. Albert Einstein, for example, however intellectually self-generating, followed many of the social norms of his day. Ayn Rand, the most independent person I have ever known, followed many of the trivial dress customs of her society.

Dependency

Our sense of mutual dependency leads us to search for the companionship and approval of people we perceive as our peers. Instead of living as self-sufficient hermits, people almost universally choose to live in groups and gain from companionship and a division of labor.[13] And, of course, if we did not harbor an inbred biological imperative to procreate, none of us would be here. But a sense of dependency by definition places "dependents" in a constant state of uncertainty. To assuage the uncertainty, people's inbred sense of self-worth asserts itself and we challenge authority. Our nature also requires us to seek a measure of independence. Dependency in one form or another is a necessary but not necessarily a pleasurable state. Children under the restrictive guidance of elders often revolt against parental apron strings. Many children, at one time or another, in extremis, leave home in an assertion of independence, only to return when the reality of their dependence becomes all too real.

The Interaction

Time preference, coupled with risk aversion and herd behavior, governs the pricing of all income-producing assets and, since the nineteenth century, sets the proportion of income that households seek to save over the long run. The real (inflation-adjusted) interest rate is anchored by time preference, and it fluctuates according to the balance of saving and investment in an economy and the degree of financial intermediation. Bond yields measure risk aversion in two dimensions: by credit rating and maturity. Herd behavior will often skew an individual's risk aversion judgment toward the mean of a group: other investors, family, or pundits. Stock prices can be thought of as the sum of the expected future earnings per share, tempered by a rate of discount applied to those earnings. That discount rate is the rate of return that investors require to hold such risky assets. The equity premium is the rate of return that investors expect, less the real rate of return on riskless assets, a proxy for time preference. The capitalization of rental returns on real estate properties is similarly calculated.

Home Bias

Home bias is the propensity to deal with the familiar: with people and things geographically close to home and familiar in terms of culture, language, and interests. This is especially evident in trade data, both foreign and domestic, even allowing for savings in transportation costs. Canada and Mexico, for example, accounted for 29 percent of our total international trade in 2011, far more than their share of global non–U.S. GDP. And my family's favorite pharmacy sells the vast majority of its wares to patrons who live within a mile of its location.

Aside from any direct or indirect barriers, people seem to prefer to invest in familiar local businesses. The United States has no barriers to interstate investment, and the states share a common currency, culture, language, and legal system. Yet studies have shown that individual investors and even professional money managers have a slight preference for investments in their own communities and states. Trust, so crucial an aspect of investing, is most likely to be fostered by the familiarity of local communities.

A propensity related to the comfort and familiarity of trading with partners close to home is the emotional comfort we all sense in personal relationships that become familiar and predictable. The uncertainty that arises with strangers imparts a certain, if minor, stress that subsides with familiarity. Personal relationships that build over months and years are a major reason why people born and brought up in a particular locale tend to stay put, often for a lifetime, even when they have accumulated the physical resources to move elsewhere and have ample reason to do so. The familiarity of home is the source of the angst we feel after leaving, namely homesickness.

Competition

More complex, and battling with our sense of dependency, is our introspectively self-evident propensity to be competitive. Its consequences range over a much broader spectrum than most propensities. Competition as it plays out in markets is, of course, indispensable to the efficient functioning of our economies, as has been emphasized by economists for more than two centuries. The degree of competitiveness has a broad sway in defining our culture and its indirect effect on economic events.

We compete whether on a ball field or during a dinner conversation. When we view a familiar competitive sport, even though we may begin by having no preference for either competitor, we usually find ourselves rooting within a matter of minutes for one or the other. If not, we lose interest. It is our nature. And when we combine this propensity with copycat herd behavior and our home bias propensity, we develop overwhelming support for local teams against "foreign" competitors. Spectator sports are effectively morality plays: stylized views of the type of competition in which we all engage in our day-to-day activities with respect to both economic and noneconomic relationships. The specific spectator sport is irrelevant—all that is required is that there is competitive "combat" and that there are winners and losers to gain our attention.

I suspect, but cannot prove, that this propensity is driven by the fact that competition is, in a Darwinian sense, necessary for survival. Unless we successfully compete in the taking of risk, we perish. War appears to be an ugly extension of this propensity. War is competition raised to a level of mortal combat in which there are ultimate winners and losers. Since war has been a part of the human condition as far back as history allows, I assume this propensity is inbred. This is one of many ambivalences that arise with animal spirits.

Code of Values

No human being can avoid the imperative of judging right from wrong. What we feel is right and just reflects our own deep-seated code of values. We rationally codify our introspective view of how our actions will further our values and, therefore, what set of actions we believe, rightly or wrongly, will nurture our lives. The value systems of most people are rooted in religion and culture and are heavily inculcated at an early age by our parents and, later in life, by our peers.

What is perceived by people as right or wrong is not preordained and requires that each of us fill in the blanks by drawing on our own value systems. Herd behavior, not surprisingly, is apparently a major factor in individuals' choices, and people's value hierarchy can and does change over time. Moreover, we cannot help applying our own standards to judge the actions of others.

This propensity is the source of our sense of "fairness" in economic matters. Most people act as though a particular sense of fairness is self-evident. It is not. It is rather one's most deeply imbedded hierarchy of values that most people have difficulty expressing, or even identifying in some instances. Most commentators take it as self-evident that taxing the wealthy at a higher rate than lower income groups is "fairer." But that implies that somehow upper income taxpayers have not "earned" their income, a view that rests on the belief that in a division of labor of society, all income is produced jointly. The alternate view is that even though output is produced collectively in a free, competitive market, each individual's income reflects that person's marginal contribution to total output. Either view can be, and has been, rationally held, but neither can claim self-evidence. "Ability to pay" is a pragmatic view that also rests on the premise that income is not "earned."

Most people in a society or country tend to hold similar standards of fairness. This, in democratic societies, ultimately determines what is legally "just," the basis of our set of laws. Such fundamental beliefs are the major glue that holds societies together. In the United States, for example, the pact with respect to public issues is our Constitution. We are governed by a rule of law anchored by the protection of those "fundamental" individual rights. That constitution has existed with relatively few amendments since 1789. But that stability in the governing law of our land has periodically come under strain over the generations and indeed broke down on the set of issues, slavery first among them, that led to the Civil War. That the break did not come sooner is surprising given the inherent contradiction between the Declaration of Independence's assertion that "all men are created equal" and the existence of slavery.

Optimism

Another propensity is people's bias toward optimism rather than realism—a propensity to assume that success in all actions is more likely than the objective probabilities. We wouldn't take risks if we were certain of failure. The mentality behind widespread gambling, for example, is that one can beat the odds, even as they are objectively stacked against us. This is especially the case in a lottery where pure chance prevails. As Kahneman observed, "We also tend to exaggerate our ability to forecast the future, which fosters optimistic overconfidence. In terms of its consequences for decisions, the optimistic bias may well be the most significant of the cognitive biases."[14] Of greater economic relevance, the propensity toward "hope" encourages entrepreneurial initiatives. That probably assures greater successes, but certainly more failures as well.

Bias to Value Relatives

The evidence is unequivocal that people have an inbred propensity to value relatives, especially children, over others. This perpetuates the concentration of inherited wealth and the distribution of income from one generation to the next.

Self-interest

We direct our actions to achieve those values, material and otherwise, that are required by our nature to survive and thrive. If we fail, we perish. In the realm of economics, the vast majority of our actions are driven by self-interest relative to the interests of others. If self-interest were not the primary determinant in economic activity, how do we explain the universal evidence that demand curves have downward slopes and supply curves trend upward—that is, that buyers will buy more and suppliers will supply less if prices fall? It is that, plus its obverse, that creates uniquely determined prices in all types of markets. Upward-sloping demand curves are a rare phenomenon.[15] Profit as a motive necessarily narrows choice. But even here there are trade-offs that pit long-term benefits against immediate gratification. All human beings harbor an inbred propensity to value human life. Even though there are clearly qualifications, that inbred propensity is the source of our feelings of empathy, charity, and in extreme cases, self-sacrifice. This is also the motive behind a father risking his own life to rescue his drowning child. Thus, much beyond narrowly focused economic self-interest has significant economic implications. In crisis, we seek to help one another as we all seek a common outcome. We saw such behavior in the London blitz of 1940 and, more recently, in Boston after the horror of the Boston Marathon bombings.

Self-esteem

All human motivation appears to have a basis in our never-ending quest to achieve self-esteem. Self-esteem is an inbuilt human requirement, and one that demands continued nurturing—almost all human actions in one form or another are arguably directed at bolstering self-esteem. Mark Twain put it less stentoriously: "A man cannot be comfortable without his own approval." People perpetually seek a reaffirmation of self-worth, often through the approval of others and the gratitude of those whom we have assisted. Unless our self-esteem is nurtured, most of us fall into depression.

PROPENSITIES: PLUSES AND MINUSES

Some of our human propensities have both positive and negative effects on economic activity. On the positive side, an inbred propensity to compete engages the forces of self-interest and self-esteem that direct resources to their highest valued uses, as judged by the value preferences, on average, of a society as a whole. And copycat herd behavior shapes trends for goods and services that spread improvements in our quality of life. The herd propensity leads to enhanced mass production and lower real unit costs of many consumer goods and services (as well as copycat capital investments), all supporting growth of productivity and living standards. On the negative side, competitiveness at its extreme, as I noted earlier, can morph into ugliness, and even violence.

RATIONALITY

Most human responses to daily economic events fall into the category of intuitive or "fast" thinking. These so-called knee-jerk decisions arise from the way our mind detects familiar patterns in new situations. A virtually instantaneous first cut of analysis yields the conclusions that come to us intuitively without having to access their sources. Given time and conscious appraisal, we often revise our less thoughtful initial reactions and sometimes completely reject them.

As our experience in a field deepens, our intuitions regarding that field become ever more perceptive. I say this with some caveats. From my own introspections and those of my acquaintances whom I have queried, I conclude that we are not consciously aware of the way our mind's "black box" or frontal lobe works: We pour information into our mind and, with a delay, out pop epiphanies. Albert Einstein, an intellectual tower of the twentieth century, when queried about the source of his insights, described the process: "A new idea comes suddenly and in a rather intuitive way. But intuition is nothing but the outcome of earlier intellectual experience."[16] Not surprisingly, important innovative intuitions occur only to those whose mental databanks are sufficiently endowed.

Most human responses to economic events are in the end rational, or largely so, as much of animal spirits are heavily tempered by rational oversight. Markets, even in their most euphoric or fear-driven state, do not expect global stock market averages to double or triple overnight, or wheat prices to fall to five cents a bushel.

Animal spirits nonetheless cannot readily be classified as either rational or irrational. These are terms from the world of free choice, not the world of the hardwired determinism of inbred reactions. But to the extent that any human action is at least partially driven by "spirits," the material outcomes are less satisfactory (in purely economic terms) than they would be under the hypothetical presumption that animal spirits did not exist and that human beings' economic behavior was wholly rational. A fundamental insight of classical economics is that wealth and standards of living are maximized when market participants seek their own long-term self-interests. Anything short of that, by definition, is suboptimal. If the maximum growth in output per hour in the developed world over fifteen-year periods has been 3 percent (see Chapter 8) under an economy significantly affected by animal spirits, then the hypothetical growth rate of output per hour without animal spirits, of necessity, would have been much higher. If the difference were only one half of a percentage point a year, the cumulative level over, say, a fifty-year span would be more than a fourth higher at the end of that time span. Clearly the substituting of animal spirits for the hypothetical model based on rational long-term self-interest is not likely to be a trivial quantity. Knowing what the human race could do if it were fully rational at least gives us the upper bounds of possible economic achievement.

TWO

THE CRISIS BEGINS, INTENSIFIES, AND ABATES

I first became fully aware of the seriousness of the developing global financial crisis with the disclosure on August 9, 2007, that BNP Paribas, a major French bank, was holding significant quantities of defaulting securitized American subprime mortgages. That disclosure was followed later that day by a massive injection of reserves by the European Central Bank (ECB). On August 10, the ECB was joined by the central banks of the United States, Japan, Australia, and Canada in the first globally coordinated action by central banks since 2001. I was stunned. Such coordination, in my experience, was implemented only when central banks perceived the risk of imminent and serious financial or economic disruption.

For a while the official concerns were largely confined to the financial and housing sectors. In early 2007, the composition of the world's nonfinancial corporate balance sheets and cash flows appeared in as good a shape as I can ever recall.[1] After the S&P 500 closed at record highs on July 19, stock prices fell sharply in the weeks following as lackluster data on new home sales; a dismal outlook from Countrywide Financial, the largest mortgage lender; and a handful of disappointing earnings reports compounded growing fears of problems in the housing and mortgage markets.

The markets nonetheless quickly shook off the bad news and stock prices recovered all of their losses and more, peaking at an all-time high on October 9, 2007. But the cracks were already appearing. As the crisis widened, stock prices turned down and proceeded to decline for the eleven months leading up to the Lehman failure. By the time of the Lehman default on September 15, 2008, global losses in publicly traded corporate equities stood at $16 trillion. But losses more than doubled in the weeks following the Lehman default, bringing the cumulative drop in global equity values to almost $35 trillion, a decline of more than half. Added to that were trillions of dollars of losses of equity in homes ($7 trillion in the United States alone) and losses of nonlisted corporate and unincorporated businesses that brought the global aggregate equity loss close to $50 trillion, equivalent to a staggering four fifths of 2008 global GDP.

LIQUIDITY EVAPORATION

The period of deep financial trauma began with the wholly unanticipated evaporation of the global supply of short-term credit in the immediate wake of the Lehman Brothers failure. Such a breakdown on so global a scale was without historical precedent.[2] A run on money market mutual funds, heretofore perceived to be close to riskless, was under way within hours of the announcement of Lehman's default,[3] followed within days by a general withdrawal of trade credit that set off a spiral of global economic contraction.[4] Meanwhile, the Federal Reserve had to move quickly to support the failing U.S. commercial paper market. Even the fully collateralized repurchase agreement market encountered severe and unprecedented difficulties as the quality of debt collateral was severely undermined by the collapse in the value of the counterparties' equity buffer. With a severely diminished global equity buffer, debt burdens became oppressive. Finance was in the grip of the most dreaded of animal spirits: a fear-induced stampede.

Particularly hard hit were the investment banks that were prone to the type of run by their creditors that had often been experienced by commercial banks prior to the onset of deposit insurance in 1933. Not only did short-term funding collapse, but, as I note in Chapter 5, customer collateral that was subject to recall fled. The institutions were led astray by the mistaken belief that the tight bid-ask spreads in financial markets at the top of the boom were an indication of a persistent availability of liquidity. That in fact was not the case. As I point out later, liquidity is a function of the state of risk aversion, and when risk aversion rises sharply, liquidity evaporates.

While commercial banks had their share of failures,[5] many of the most complex dangers emanated from the so-called shadow banking system—the set of financial institutions that do not accept insured deposits and hence heretofore had been largely unregulated. But not all shadow banking was devastated. Unaffiliated hedge funds, by and large, weathered the storm.* To my knowledge, none of the larger funds failed. To be sure, many of them had to liquidate after severe losses, but none defaulted on their debt.

---

*Some affiliated funds, however, did run into trouble.

SHADOW BANKING

Shadow banking is a form of financial intermediation whose funding is not supported by the traditional banking safety nets—in the United States, deposit insurance and access to central bank funding. Shadow banking includes the activities of investment banks, hedge funds, money market funds, structured investment vehicles (SIVs), and other credit intermediaries acting outside the regular banking system. Those institutions have developed in recent decades into a very substantial part of international finance and have been heavy traders in derivatives, including synthetic collateralized debt obligations and credit default swaps. Although shadow banking activities lie outside the banking system, many of these activities have been conducted by regulated banks. For example, most SIVs were organized by commercial banks. The expansion of SIVs and other off-balance-sheet conduits moved significant amounts of assets and liabilities off bank balance sheets, thereby ostensibly creating more robust capital levels. But as the crisis loomed, SIVs that carried the name and reputation of their originating banking entities were absorbed (with their risk) back onto the banks' balance sheets.

The shadow banking system globally grew at an astonishing pace in the years leading up to the crisis, and appears to have changed little since. According to a November 2012 report by the Financial Stability Board,[6] assets of shadow banking institutions globally grew from $26 trillion in 2002 to $62 trillion in 2007, and following a decline in 2008, reached $67 trillion by the end of 2011. As a share of total financial intermediary assets, shadow banking consistently accounted for 23 percent to 27 percent during that time frame. Of course, the assets of commercial banks grew at a nearly proportional rapid pace, and thus the shadow banking system remained slightly more than half the size of the regular banking system throughout the 2002 to 2011 period. Still, they were very large players on the financial landscape. In the United States alone, shadow banking constituted $23 trillion in assets at the end of 2011, by far the largest constituent of the global network of nonbank credit intermediaries.

BANK CAPITAL BUFFERS

Banking has always involved inducing depositors, or in earlier centuries note holders, to fund bank assets. In the 1840s, for example, U.S. (state) banks had to maintain a capital buffer in excess of 50 percent of assets in order to create willing holders of their notes (Exhibit 2.1). In the century that followed, the necessary capital buffer declined with the increasing consolidation of specie reserves following the Civil War. That consolidation occurred as improved rail transportation facilitated the movement of specie, and telegraphed money transfers grew as correspondent bank links expanded. Finally, in later years, the emergence of various government safety nets reduced the need for capital.

Systemic risk in the United States is almost exclusively generated by the risks posed by financial institutions and financial markets—the concern especially being that defaults of those institutions could dismantle the financial system and, with it, the broader economy. The systemic risks posed by nonfinancial companies are far less daunting. The default of an individual nonfinancial corporation will affect its creditors, suppliers, and some of its customers, but rarely does it have an effect much beyond that. Nonfinancial corporate defaults do not have the broad contagious effect that is associated with the default of a financial institution. Moreover, nonfinancial businesses hold a much higher ratio of equity to assets than do financial institutions, typically one third to one half of the value of assets, compared with only 5 percent to 15 percent for highly liquid financial firms.

TOO BIG TO FAIL

The perceived systemic effect of the failure of large financial institutions is the genesis of the "too big to fail" (TBTF) or the "too big to liquidate quickly" problem. For years I have been concerned about the ever larger size of our financial institutions. More than a decade ago, I noted that "megabanks being formed by growth and consolidation are increasingly complex entities that create the potential for unusually large systemic risks in the national and international economy should they fail."[7] Federal Reserve research had been unable to find economies of scale in banking beyond a modest-sized institution.[8] I often wondered as the banks increased in size throughout the globe prior to the crash and since: Had bankers discovered economies of scale that Fed research had missed?

One highly disturbing consequence of the TBTF-bailout problem is that it is going to be difficult to convince market participants henceforth that a large financial institution in trouble should be allowed to fail. The implicit subsidy to these large institutions that such notions spawn insidiously impairs the efficiency of finance and the allocation of capital. I will address this important issue in Chapters 5 and 11.

In retrospect it is now evident to all that the level of capital that commercial banks and especially investment banks accumulated prior to 2008 as crisis protection was inadequate. The marked increase in risk taking of a decade ago could have been guarded against wholly by increased capital. Regrettably, that did not occur and the accompanying dangers were not fully appreciated, even in the commercial banking sector. For example, in 2006, the Federal Deposit Insurance Corporation (FDIC), speaking for all U.S. bank regulators, judged that "more than 99 percent of all insured institutions met or exceeded the requirements of the highest regulatory capital standards."[9] Newly acquired capital additions accordingly remained modest.

RISK MANAGEMENT FAILS

But why did the large array of fail-safe buffers that were supposed to counter such developing crises fail? We had thought that we depend on our highly sophisticated global system of financial risk management to contain market breakdowns. How could these systems have failed on so broad a scale? The risk management paradigm that had as its genesis the work of several Nobel Prize winners in economics—Harry Markowitz, Robert Merton, and Myron Scholes (and Fischer Black, who would have received the award had he lived)—was so thoroughly embraced by academia, central banks, and regulators that by 2006 it had become the core of the global bank regulatory standards known as Basel II. Global banks were authorized, within limits, to apply their own company-specific risk-based models to judge their capital requirements. Most models estimated their parameters based on the last quarter century of observations. But even a sophisticated number-crunching model that covered the last five decades would not have anticipated the crisis that loomed.

Mathematical models that calibrate risk are surely better guides to risk assessment than the "rule of thumb" judgments of a half century earlier. To this day it is hard to find fault with the *conceptual* framework of our models, *as far as they go*. The elegant options-pricing model of Black and Scholes is no less valid or useful today than when it was developed in 1973. In the growing state of euphoria in the years before the 2008 crash, private risk managers, the Federal Reserve, and other regulators failed to ensure that financial institutions were adequately capitalized, in part because we all failed to comprehend the underlying magnitude and the full extent of the risks that were about to be revealed as the post–Lehman crisis played out. In particular, we failed to fully comprehend the size of the expansion of so-called tail risk. Tail risk is financial jargon that risk managers employ to identify the class of investment outcomes that occur with very low probabilities—but that are accompanied by very large losses when they materialize (see Box 2.1). For decades, a number of unusual "once in a lifetime" phenomena were occurring much too often to be credibly described as owing purely to chance. A defining moment for me was the wholly unprecedented stock price crash on October 19, 1987, that propelled the Dow Jones Industrial Average down more than 20 percent in that single day. There was no simple probability distribution from which that event could be inferred. Accordingly, the negative "tail" was thought to be fat. But when those previously unvisited areas of investment outcome distributions were filled in subsequent to the Lehman default, the fat tails turned out, in fact, to be morbidly obese. As a consequence of an underestimation of these risks, risk managers failed to anticipate the amount of additional capital that would be required to serve as an adequate buffer when the financial system was jolted.

BOX 2.1: TAIL RISK

If people acted solely to maximize their own self-interest, their actions would produce a long-term growth path consistent with their ability to increase productivity. But lacking omniscience, the actual outcomes of their risk taking would reflect random deviations from their long-term trend. And those deviations, with enough observations, would tend to be distributed in a manner similar to successive coin tosses, following what economists call a "normal" distribution (a bell curve with tails that rapidly taper off as the probability of occurrence diminishes).

If we introduce the realism of behavioral economics and add our propensities of euphoria and fear, we produce the business cycle that shifts observations of risk-taking outcomes from the middle parts of the distribution toward its tails. But as I demonstrate in Chapter 4, fear is a far more potent propensity than euphoria. The adjusted real-world probability distribution that emerges exhibits a tail of positive outcomes that is barely discernible, but a negative tail that is both highly visible and large.

The 2008 financial collapse has provided reams of new data to identify the shape of the critical, heretofore unknown tails of investors' "loss functions"; the challenge will be to use the new data to develop a more realistic assessment of the range and probabilities of financial outcomes, with an emphasis on those that pose the greatest dangers to the financial system and the economy. One can hope that in a future deep financial crisis—and there will surely be one—we will be more informed as to the way fat-tail markets work.

CREDIT-RATING AGENCIES FAIL

Another important source of the failure of risk management was the almost indecipherable complexity of the broad spectrum of new financial products and markets that developed as number-crunching and communication capabilities soared.[10] Investment managers subcontracted an inordinately large part of their task to the "safe harbor" risk designations of the credit-rating agencies, especially Moody's, Standard & Poor's, and Fitch. Most investment officers believed no further judgment was required of them because they were effectively held harmless by the judgments of these government-sanctioned rating organizations. Especially problematic were the triple-A ratings bestowed by the credit-rating agencies on many securities that in fact proved highly toxic. Despite decades of experience, the analysts at the credit-rating agencies proved no more adept at anticipating the onset of crisis than the investment community at large, and their favorable ratings of many securities offered a false sense of security to a great many investors.

REGULATION FAILS

Even with the breakdown of our sophisticated risk management models and the failures of the credit-rating agencies, the financial system would likely have held together had the third bulwark against crisis—our regulatory system—functioned effectively. But it, too, failed for many of the same reasons that risk management and the credit-rating agencies failed: an underappreciation of the risks faced by the financial system and an increasing complexity that made effective oversight especially difficult. Along with the vast majority of market participants, regulators did not anticipate the onset of crisis. Not only did regulators in the United States fail, but abroad, the heavily praised U.K. Financial Services Authority was unable to anticipate and prevent the bank run that threatened one of that country's largest commercial banks, Northern Rock, the first such run in Britain in a century. Moreover, the Basel Committee on Banking Supervision, representing regulatory authorities from the world's major financial systems, promulgated a set of capital rules (Basel II) that did not foresee the rapidly rising capital needs of the institutions under their purview.

It was not a lack of regulatory depth that was at fault. U.S. commercial and savings banks are extensively regulated; despite the fact that for years our ten to fifteen largest banking institutions have had permanently assigned on-site examiners to oversee daily operations, many of these banks still were able to take on toxic assets that brought them to their knees. Bank regulators had always relied on the thought that "prompt corrective action" would be a key weapon to be wielded against default; weak institutions would be shut down well before they ran out of capital, thereby preventing losses to the FDIC's reserves and ultimately to taxpayers. In the event, and contrary to every expectation of regulatory practice, the FDIC has had to charge off well upward of a half trillion dollars since the Lehman default.

THE SHORTFALL OF CAPITAL

One of my very first experiences as Federal Reserve chairman was at a staff meeting where I naively asked, "How do you determine the appropriate level of capital?" I was surprised at the lack of response. I soon realized that such fundamental issues are taken as a given and rarely addressed other than in the aftermath of a crisis. And through all of the years of my tenure at the Fed, bank capital had always seemed adequate to regulators. (See, for example, the 2006 FDIC statement quoted earlier in this chapter.) I have since regretted that we regulators never pursued the issue of capital adequacy in a timely manner.

No regulatory structures anywhere in the developed world required all of the major global financial institutions to maintain adequate capital buffers. And there can be little doubt that had capital levels of banks and other financial intermediaries worldwide been high enough to absorb all of the losses that surfaced after the Lehman default, no contagious defaults could have occurred and the crisis of 2008 would have been contained. In the normal course of banking, unexpected adverse economic events diminish a bank's capital, but in almost all cases, the buffer (provision for loan losses plus capital) remains adequate to fend off default. And with time, the flow of undistributed earnings and newly raised equity replenishes the depleted bank capital.

However, as 2008 starkly demonstrated, not all such events end so benignly. On rare occasions enough capital is breached, or wiped out, setting off an avalanche of serial defaults in which the suspension of payments by one firm throws its often highly leveraged financial counterparties into default. Those cascading defaults lead cumulatively to a full-blown crisis. Default contagion has many of the same characteristics of a snow avalanche, where a small breach in snow cover progressively builds until the surface tension breaks and a whole hillside of snow collapses.

For the same reasons that it is difficult to determine when a small crack in the snow cover will trigger a full-blown avalanche, it has proved difficult to judge in advance what will trigger a full-blown financial crisis, especially on the scale of September 2008.

DEBT MATTERS

Still, the question remains: Why did the bursting of the housing bubble set off an avalanche of financial failure when the deflation of the dot-com bubble in 2000 left so mild an imprint on the financial system and on the macroeconomy? To be sure, a recession followed the stock market bust, but the recession was one of the mildest on record and was relatively short-lived. Real GDP and employment in that downturn exhibited scarcely anything close to the savage contraction that followed the bursting of the housing bubble six years later. Reaching even further back, despite the (still) record one-day destruction of stock market wealth on October 19, 1987, there was virtually no mark left on overall economic activity.

Because the U.S. economy had so readily weathered the dot-com and 1987 bubbles, I had hopes at the outset of the 2008 crisis that the reaction to the housing bubble collapse would be similar. I did raise an early caution flag before a Federal (Reserve) Open Market Committee meeting in 2002 when I asserted that "our extraordinary housing boom . . . financed by very large increases in mortgage debt, cannot continue indefinitely." It did—for four more years. And I thought its effect could be contained. It wasn't.[11]

The critical reason for the much more severe outcome in the wake of the bursting of the housing bubble is that debt matters. In retrospect, and as I discuss in detail in Chapter 3, there can be little doubt that escalating defaults of securitized subprime mortgages were the trigger of the recent financial crisis. However, even after financial subprime problems arose in August 2007, there was little awareness of what was on the horizon.[12] When defaults of the underlying collateral for mortgage pools (primarily of privately issued subprime and Alt-A mortgage-backed securities) became widespread in

2007, the capital buffers of many banks (commercial and shadow) were dangerously impaired.[13] And as the demand in the United States for homeownership collapsed and home prices fell, widespread defaults of mortgage-backed securities saddled banks and other highly leveraged financial institutions with heavy losses, both in the United States and Europe.

In contrast, on the eve of the dot-com stock market crash of 2000, highly leveraged institutions held a relatively small share of equities, and an especially small share of technology stocks, the toxic asset of that bubble. Most stock was held by households (who were considerably less leveraged at that time than they became as the decade progressed) and pension funds. Their losses, while severe, were readily absorbed without contagious bankruptcies because the amount of debt held to fund equity investment was small. Accordingly, few lenders went into default and an avalanche was avoided. A similar scenario played out following the crash of 1987.

One can imagine how the crisis would have played out if the stocks that fell sharply in 2000 (or 1987) had been held by leveraged institutions in the proportions that mortgages and mortgage securities were held in 2008. The U.S. economy almost certainly would have experienced a far more destabilizing scenario than in fact occurred.

Alternatively, if mortgage-backed securities in 2008 had been held in unleveraged institutions—defined contribution pension funds (401ks) and mutual funds, for example—as had been the case for stocks in 2000, those institutions would still have suffered large losses, but bankruptcies, triggered by debt defaults, would have been far fewer.

Whether the toxic assets precipitating the bubble collapses of 1987, 2000, and 2008 were equities or mortgage-backed securities probably mattered little. It was the capital impairment on the balance sheets of financial institutions that provoked the crisis. Debt securities were the problem in 2008, but the same effect would have been experienced by the financial system had the dollar amount of losses incurred by highly leveraged financial institutions in the wake of the collapsing housing bubble been in equity investments rather than mortgage-backed securities.

Had Bear Stearns, the smallest of the investment banks, been allowed to fail, it might merely have advanced the crisis by six months. Alternatively, had the market absorbed the Bear failure without contagion, Lehman Brothers might have been put on notice, with ample time, to aggressively lower its high-risk profile. We will never know. But I assume that, seeing a successful Bear Stearns rescue, Lehman concluded that all investment banks larger than Bear would have been judged "too big to fail," offering the prospect of a similar rescue to Lehman had it been necessary. That scenario conceivably dulled Lehman's incentive to take (costly) precautionary actions to augment its capital.

IDENTIFYING TOXIC ASSETS

A related obstacle for forecasting and policy setting is that we seek to identify *in advance* which assets or markets could turn toxic and precipitate a crisis. It was not apparent in the early 2000s, as many commentators retroactively assume, that subprime securities were headed toward being the toxic asset that in 2007 they turned out to be. AAA-rated collateralized debt obligations based on subprime mortgages issued in 2005, for example, were bid effectively at par through mid-2007. They were still bid at over 90 percent of par just prior to the crisis. By March 2009, six months after the crisis erupted, they had fallen to 60 percent of par.[14]

Bankers, like all asset managers, try to avoid a heavy concentration of related assets in highly leveraged portfolios in order to avoid the risk that they will all turn sour simultaneously. Nonetheless, such a concentration of assets—securitized mortgages—did end up on the balance sheets of innumerable banks, both in the United States and abroad. At the time, presumably knowledgeable bankers judged the assets, at acquisition, sufficiently sound to leverage them. For most it was only in retrospect that they were able to differentiate good assets from bad. Securitization conveyed a false sense of financial well-being. Large bundles of seemingly diversified mortgages appeared a lot less risky than stand-alone mortgages. The problem was that if all those mortgages were vulnerable to the same macroshock (a decline in house prices), there was in the end more risk and less diversification than mortgage investors realized.

Regulators, in my experience, are no better qualified to make such judgments than the initiators of the investments. This is the reason I have long argued that regulators should let banks buy (within limits) whatever they choose, but impose large *generic* equity capital requirements as reserve against losses that will happen, but which cannot be identified in advance.[15] As I demonstrate in Chapter 5, regulations whose effectiveness relies heavily on regulators' forecasts of the future credit quality of the portfolios they regulate have almost always proved ineffective.

BEWARE OF POLICY SUCCESS

All speculative bubbles have a roughly similar trajectory and time frame over which the expansion leg of a bubble takes place.[16] Bubbles often emerge from growing expectations of stable long-term productivity and output growth combined with stable prices.

The near quarter century from 1983 to 2007 was a period of very shallow recessions and seemingly extraordinary stability. But protracted economic stability is precisely the tinder that ignites bubbles. All that is necessary is that a modest proportion of market participants view the change as structural. A quarter century of stability is rationally intoxicating. Herd behavior then takes over to enhance the uptrend.

Central banks have increasingly been confronted by the prospect that their success in achieving stable prices has laid the groundwork for asset price bubbles. This issue has concerned me for years. I expressed my discomfort in a Federal Open Market Committee meeting in May 1995. "The disequilibrium that is implicit in this [current] forecast is an asset price bubble . . . I am not sure at this stage that we know how, or by what means, we ought to be responding to that, and whether we dare . . . I almost hope that the economy will be a little less tranquil, buoyant, and pleasant because the end result of that [has] not [been] terribly helpful."[17]

How to deal with this prospect remains a challenge without a simple solution, at least to date. As copycat herd behavior converts "skeptical" investors to "believers," stock prices, capital investment, and the economy are thought to have nowhere to go but up. With different assets and actors, the numerous bubbles of the last century have followed similar paths.

HISTORY REPEATS

Nonetheless, given the repetitiveness of history, I could never get beyond the general notion that as the years of only modestly interrupted economic expansion rolled on, we would eventually be assaulted by disabling financial crises. As I put it in 2000, "we do not, and probably cannot, know the precise nature of the next international financial crisis. That there will be one is as certain as the persistence of human financial indiscretion."[18] The evidence was compelling that these episodes, though only occurring once or twice in a century, were nonetheless too recurrent and eerily similar in nature to be wholly sui generis.

In the chapters ahead, I will delve more deeply into the causes of the current crisis and its aftermath, and evaluate the tools that we economists have created to peer into the future, parsing the major policy disagreements that have plagued the economics profession in recent years. Every policy initiative reflects both a forecast of the future and a paradigm of the way an economy works. The current debates are part of an ongoing evolution of economic forecasting.

REGRESSION PRIMER

REGRESSION ANALYSIS

Astronomers have the capacity to forecast when the sun will rise outside my bedroom window exactly six months from now. Economists have no such capabilities. We seek instead to infer what history tells us about our future by disaggregating the "causes" of our economic past and assuming they will prevail in the future. In short, we endeavor to learn what caused, for example, capital investments to behave as they did in the past, and where they will settle if those forces are replicated in our future. To assist in that daunting task, economists rely heavily on the discipline of regression[19] analysis—statistical techniques whose roots lie in probability analysis, a discipline well known to all who play games of chance.

The raw material of business forecasting is the extensive body of time series that trace, for example, retail sales, industrial production, and housing starts. We seek to understand the economic factors determining monthly single-family housing starts, for example, and hope to forecast them. As a result of conversations with home builders, I might initially choose home prices and household formation as plausible explanatory variables. We call the time series being analyzed the dependent variable, and those explaining it—home prices and household formation—the independent variables. Regression analysis, then, statistically seeks out how a change in each independent variable impacts housing starts. The cleverness of such a filtering process is that it infers the relative statistical weights—coefficients—that, when applied to both home prices and household formation, yield a "fitted" time series that most closely approximates the history of actual housing starts.

With these data we can measure the fraction of the fluctuations (variance) of the dependent variable that is "explained" by the fluctuations of the independent variables in the model. That fraction is what we call the multiple regression coefficient (R^2). The higher the R^2, the closer the fitted time series is to the actual historical series. At 1.0, it exactly predicts the actual data series and explains all of the variance in the dependent variable.

But the reliability of the results rests on a number of mathematical conditions required of the regression variables. For example, the independent variables have to be completely uncorrelated with one another—that is, home price must not be correlated with household formation. In addition, the residuals of the regression, the difference between actual housing starts and their fitted (calculated) value in each period, cannot be "serially correlated"—that is, the residual in one period cannot influence the residual in the next.

In the real world, these conditions are almost never met. So statisticians have devised ways to measure and partially correct the extent to which the assumptions fall short. For instance, the Durbin-Watson statistic (D-W) measures the extent to which the sequential residuals are serially correlated. The D-W ranges between 0 and 4.0. A D-W of 2.0 indicates that the residuals are uncorrelated while a D-W of less than 2.0 indicates positive serial correlation, a bias that creates an overestimation of the statistical significance of the independent variables (see discussion of the t-statistic and statistical significance below).[20] Serial correlation is a characteristic of virtually all economic time series because the previous quarter's residual, in reality, does economically impact that of the current quarter. Converting the level of a time series to its absolute change will decrease serial correlation in a regression, but such a transformation will eliminate important information contained in the level form of the data. In my analyses, I prefer to live with serial correlation.

The t-statistic is a measure of the "statistical significance" of an independent variable—that is, the probability that its coefficient is different from zero.[21] The higher the t-statistic, the higher the probability that the relationship between an independent variable and the dependent variable is real, not merely the product of chance. Economists usually require a t-statistic, whether positive or negative, to be higher than 2.0 before we accord an independent variable credibility as a "cause" of variations of the dependent variable. The Newey-West estimator measures the extent of bias in the t-statistic owing to serial correlation and resets the t-values so that they more truly reflect the actual probabilities.

Another prominent bias in many economic correlations results from two time series that are only slightly related, if at all, but nonetheless exhibit a high R^2 when regressed against each other because both series reflect population growth. This bias can be largely eliminated by expressing the dependent and independent variables on a per capita basis.

Exhibit 7.3 is a typical example of regression analysis. The dependent variable is capital investment as a share of cash flow for nonfinancial corporations. We collect quarterly observations not only for the dependent variable, but also for the three independent variables[22] from 1970 to date. The dependent variable is regressed against the three independent variables and we create a fitted estimate of capital investment's share of cash flow. With an R^2 of .76, we have in effect "explained" three fourths of the variation in the share. As can be seen from the associated chart, the fitted series closely follows the actual share. The Newey-West–adjusted t-values are well in excess of 2.0 and hence the probability that the relationships are wholly the result of chance can be dismissed. The Durbin-Watson measure of serial correlation is only 0.57, suggesting there is still significant serial correlation. But as can be seen from the chart, it has not prevented the independent variables from following the dependent variable through boom and bust. Moreover, if we split the forty-three-year regression period into two equal halves, the results of the regressions for the two smaller periods are similar to those of the full regression. This is a useful test of whether the independent variables' impact on the dependent variable has changed over the forty-three years. The results here suggest not.

Exhibit 7.3

Dependent Variable (Time Period: Q1 1970–Q4 2012, 172 obs.)		
ln [US Nonfinancial Corporate Business: Capital Expenditures / Cash Flow]		
Independent Variable(s)	**Coefficient**	**t-Statistic***
ln [1 + (**Cyclically Adjusted U.S. Federal Deficit / GDP)] (1 quarter ago)	−4.208	−12.327
Nonfarm Operating Rate (Seasonally adjusted, %) (1 quarter ago)	0.0527	9.640
**Deficit & Cyclically Adjusted U.S. Treasury Spread: ***30yr–5yr (% p.a.) (1 quarter ago)	−0.0844	−6.977
Adjusted R-sq	**Durbin-Watson**	
0.722	0.825	

*t-statistic calculated using Newey-West HAC standard errors and covariance.
**Adjusted to decrease multicollinearity between independent variables.
***20yr Treasury substituted for 30yr Treasury prior to Q2 1977.

Source: U.S. Department of Commerce; Federal Reserve Board; author's calculations.

A POINT OF CAUTION

We must be careful to distinguish correlation (which regression analysis can measure) and causation (which it cannot). A high R^2 and high t-statistics are not necessarily, in themselves, a credible measure of causation. Regression analysis has turned out to be one of the most effective tools for divining economic cause and effect. But we must always keep in mind that correlation or association is not the same as causation. It must be backed up with a credible *economic* explanation of the association.

Regression equations as well as economic identities (see Box 9.3) are the most prominent inputs of our macroeconomic models. Regression analysis became widespread only with advances in computational capability. Back in the 1950s, it took me hours, if not days to estimate a regression using the desk calculators of the time. With today's computers and software, I need press only a small number of keys to produce an almost instantaneous final result.

THREE

THE ROOTS OF CRISIS

The toxic securitized U.S. subprime mortgages were the immediate trigger of the financial crisis, but the origins of the crisis reach back to the aftermath of the Cold War.[1] The fall of the Berlin Wall in 1989 exposed the economic ruin produced by the Soviet bloc's economic system. East Germany, touted as a strong competitor to West Germany, turned out to have achieved little more than one third the productivity levels of West Germany after four decades of rivalry. Most Western analysts, including those at some of the most vaunted intelligence agencies of the Western democracies, had estimated levels of productivity in East Germany that were 75 to 80 percent of the levels reached in West Germany.[2] They were shocked by the reality of the situation.

Competitive markets quietly but rapidly displaced much of the discredited central planning so prevalent in the Soviet bloc and in much of the Third World. India, a longtime bastion of Fabian socialism, initiated significant reform in 1991. Under Finance Minister Manmohan Singh (later India's prime minister), it opened markets and reduced the heavy burden of extensive regulation (though admittedly much of the bureaucratic apparatus remains intact in India). China, with its highly collectivized economy and with the Cultural Revolution only fifteen years in its past, embarked on what turned out to be a major embrace of free markets, though the Chinese economy continues to be plagued by too-frequent instances of crony capitalism that make its system a far cry from textbook capitalism.

China, and a large segment of the erstwhile Third World nations that followed suit, replicated the successful export-oriented economic model of the so-called Asian Tigers (Hong Kong, Singapore, South Korea, and Taiwan): Fairly well-educated, low-cost workforces, joined with developed-world technology, unleashed explosive economic growth.[3] Between 2000 and 2007, the real GDP growth rate of the developing world was almost double that of the developed world. The International Monetary Fund (IMF) estimated that by 2005 more than eight hundred million members of the world's labor force were engaged in export-oriented competitive market activities, an increase of five hundred million since the fall of the Berlin Wall.[4] Additional hundreds of millions engaged in domestic-oriented competitive markets, especially in the former Soviet Union.

Because consumption in the developing world was restrained, perhaps by culture, inadequate access to consumer finance, or in response to the aftermath of the Asian financial crisis, it did not keep up with the surge of income. As a consequence, the savings rate of the developing world soared from 23 percent of nominal GDP in 1999 to 33 percent by 2007, far outstripping its rate of investment. With investment elsewhere in the world slow to take up the slack, the result was a pronounced fall from 2000 to 2005 in global long-term interest rates, both nominal (Exhibit 3.1) and real.[5] Of course, whether it was a glut of intended saving or a shortfall of investment intentions is of interest primarily to economists. The conclusion is the same either way: Real long-term interest rates had to fall, and they did.

Long-term interest rates in all developed economies and the major developing economies had by 2006 converged to single digits.[6] Equity premiums (the excess rate of return required by investors in risky stocks over the return available on sovereign debt) and real estate capitalization rates were inevitably pressured lower by the fall in global long-term real interest rates. Asset prices, particularly home prices, accordingly moved dramatically higher.

The *Economist*'s surveys of nearly twenty individual countries document the striking global nature of the rapid ascent of home prices during the decade.[7] Japan, Germany, and Switzerland (for differing reasons) were the only important exceptions. At their peak increases, U.S. home price gains were no more rapid than the global average.[8]

In short, geopolitical events ultimately led to a fall in long-term interest rates and the mortgage interest rates to which they were tied. That led, with a lag, to a global boom in home prices. In the United States the change in the thirty-year mortgage interest rate tends to lead the monthly *change* in home prices (in the opposite direction) by three months (Exhibit 3.3).[9]

The subprime mortgage market that developed in the 1990s was a small but generally successful market of largely fixed-rate mortgages. It served mainly those potential homeowners who could not meet the down payment requirement of a prime loan but still had income adequate to handle the monthly payments of a fixed-rate mortgage. But when home prices accelerated after 1996 (Exhibit 3.4), subprime lending became increasingly attractive to investors. That said, subprime mortgages still constituted only 7 percent of total originations by 2002, and only a modest amount of those had been securitized.

SECURITIZATION OF SUBPRIMES: THE CRISIS STORY UNFOLDS

Belatedly drawn to the growing market for subprimes, many major financial firms, starting in late 2003, began to accelerate the pooling and packaging of subprime mortgages into securities (Exhibit 3.5). Leading the pack of securitizers were Countrywide Financial and Lehman Brothers—firms that were ultimately brought down by their involvement with these instruments. Combined, they issued more than a fifth of securitized subprimes in 2004.[10] The firms clearly had found receptive buyers. Heavy demand from Europe,[11] in the form of subprime mortgage-backed collateralized debt obligations, was fostered by attractive yields and a foreclosure rate on the underlying mortgages that, since late 2000, had been in decline for almost three years. The securitizers pressed subprime mortgage lenders such as Ameriquest, New Century, and Countrywide to originate mortgages and sell them to securitizers. This reversed the conventional sequence of mortgage banks, assisted by brokers, originating mortgages and *then* deciding to sell them to securitizers.

But a far heavier demand was driven by the need of Fannie Mae and Freddie Mac, the major U.S. government-sponsored enterprises (GSEs), to meet the expanded "affordable housing goal" requirements of the Department of Housing and Urban Development.[12]

Given the GSEs' expanded commitments, they had few alternatives but to invest, wholesale, in subprime securities.[13] As a consequence, by 2004, the GSEs accounted for nearly half of all newly purchased subprime mortgage securities retained on investors' balance sheets (Exhibit 3.6).[14] That was more than five times their esti-mated share in 2002. To meet this demand, securitizers began to purchase and securitize much of the billions of dollars of subprime whole mortgages not already pooled to back outstanding mortgage securities. But that source was nowhere near enough to meet the GSEs' needs, and at this point, securitizers unwisely prodded sub-prime mortgage originators to increase their scale of originations. But the number of potential homeowners seeking subprime fixed-rate mortgages was small. The originators therefore chose to reach out to a wholly new segment of potential homeowners who could meet neither the down payments of a prime loan nor the monthly debt-servicing requirements of fixed-rate subprime mortgages. The only available option to entice new, but risky, buyers was to offer adjustable-rate mortgages (ARMs) to subprime borrowers with ini-tially lower monthly payments. As a result, the share of ARMs in the total value of first mortgages subprime originations soared to nearly 62 percent by the second quarter of 2007.[15] The mortgage arrears of subprime ARMs almost immediately began to rise, and many bor-rowers failed to make even the first mortgage payment. Delinquen-cies of more than ninety days began to mount.[16]

By the first quarter of 2007, owing to pressure on the securitizers to meet the demand for subprime securities from the GSEs, virtually all subprime mortgage originations (predominantly ARMs) were being securitized, compared with less than half in 2000.[17] Also by the end of March 2007, more than $800 billion, or more than 80 per-cent of total outstanding subprime mortgages, was in pools support-ing outstanding subprime mortgage securities.[18] That $800 billion figure was almost seven times its level at the end of 2001.

Subsequent to 2003, the securitizers, profitably packaging this new source of adjustable-rate mortgage paper into mortgage pools and armed with what turned out to be grossly inflated credit ratings, were able to sell seemingly unlimited amounts of these securities into what appeared to be a vast and receptive global market. But this proved to be a mirage.

By 2005 and 2006, subprime mortgage originations had swelled to 20 percent of all U.S. home mortgage originations, almost triple their share in 2002.[19] We at the Federal Reserve were aware earlier in the decade of incidents of some highly irregular subprime mortgage underwriting practices. But, regrettably, we viewed it as a localized problem subject to standard prudential oversight, not the precursor of the securitized subprime mortgage bubble that was to arise several years later. On first being told in the early months of 2005 by Fed staff of the quarterly data for 2004, I expressed surprise given that our most recent official Fed data—those of the Home Mortgage Disclosure Act (HMDA) compilations for 2003—exhibited few signs of problems. I had never heard of the private source *Inside Mortgage Finance* before. But in retrospect those data turned out to be right.

But even had we had the hard official data from 2005 at that time (it was eventually published in the 2006 HMDA report by the Federal Reserve in December 2006), there was little the Fed could have done to contain the rise in home prices.

Some academics favored an incremental defusing of the bubble through a gradual tightening of monetary policy, but such incremental policies have never appeared to have worked in the real world. The Federal Reserve's incremental tightening in 1994 in the face of the inchoate dot-com boom, in retrospect, may well have fostered the bubble rather than contained it.[20] Policy makers confront nonmarket problems all the time, a large majority of which are readily resolved. We can spot bubbles as they inflate, but we are not able to forecast their complex resolution and collapse and, as I note later, perhaps never will. In responding to such issues, policy makers have to choose whether to clamp down on and prohibit a wide variety of market practices and accordingly accept the inevitable constraints on economic growth that that often implies.

SIZE OF THE PROBLEM CLOAKED

The true size of the American subprime problem was hidden for years by the defective bookkeeping of the GSEs. Fannie Mae was unable to get its books certified and had to stop reporting publicly between November 2004 and December 2006, pending an often delayed clarification of their accounts. Freddie Mac had had similar problems earlier. Not until the summer of 2007 did the full magnitude of the subprime problem begin to become apparent. Fannie's third-quarter write-offs almost quadrupled relative to the second quarter. Moreover, the source of loss did not become fully evident until September 2009, when Fannie Mae very belatedly disclosed a significant reclassification of loans, from prime to subprime, dating back to loans that it had made and held in 2003 and 2004. More important, those revelations helped to explain how what was thought to be a relatively sound portfolio of prime conventional mortgages in mid-2007 could generate the huge losses Fannie and Freddie had been reporting.[21] It is doubtful, however, even had such data been available in a timely manner, that regulators would have been able to head off the crisis, especially given our experiences with monetary tightening during the dot-com boom.

The role of Fannie and Freddie in the American financial system has been highly controversial at least since 2003, when the Federal Reserve raised serious questions about the potential systemic risk that these institutions might pose down the road. As I put it in testimony before a Senate committee in early 2004, "we see nothing on the immediate horizon that is likely to create a systemic problem.

But to fend off possible future systemic difficulties, which we assess as likely if GSE expansion continues unabated, preventive actions are required sooner rather than later."[22] Our problems with the GSEs had been simmering for years.

I recollect getting a call in late October 2008 from Henry Waxman, a senior House Democrat, inquiring whether I agreed with the position that the housing bubble's primary cause was the heavy demand by the GSEs for subprime mortgages and securities, as some House members had argued. (The housing market had peaked and fallen in 2006.) I responded that I thought the GSEs did contribute to the crisis, but that their holdings of subprime securities did not seem sufficiently large to account for the size of the bubble. With the new disclosures, it was obvious that Fannie and Freddie played a far more important role—perhaps even a key role—in the momentum that developed behind the housing bubble than many had theretofore recognized.

Had Fannie and Freddie not existed, a housing bubble could still have taken hold. But had such a bubble developed, it is likely that in and of itself, it would not have wreaked such devastation in late 2008. The paths of Canada and Australia's house price gains, for example, were in fact quite similar to those of the United States. Yet in retrospect, those gains did not have the destabilizing bubble characteristics experienced by Americans. Their financial systems were not breached and neither experienced a severe financial crisis.

Analysis of such crises is subject to considerable uncertainties, and I have little doubt that longtime political supporters of Fannie and Freddie will continue to advance potential explanations other than that which I have just offered. Many still claim the buildup of mortgage assets during 2003 and 2004 was simply a business decision on the part of the GSEs to regain lost market share (they are, after all, private corporations) and had little to do with the issue of affordable housing. But as Fannie Mae in December 2006, in political-speak, acknowledged, "We have also relaxed some of our underwriting criteria to obtain goals-qualifying mortgage loans and increased our investments in higher-risk mortgage loan products that are more likely to serve the borrowers targeted by HUD's goals and subgoals, which could increase our credit losses."[23] They sure did.

A CLASSIC EUPHORIC BUBBLE TAKES HOLD

The housing surge of the last decade had all the hallmarks of a classic euphoric bubble. Financial bubbles occur from time to time, and usually with little or no forewarning. The sources of bubbles and the markets in which they occur are quite varied, but patterns these bubbles trace have very common features. As the top of a speculative boom in stocks, homes, or commodities is approached, there obviously still must be a preponderance of buyers over sellers bidding up those already high prices. For were it otherwise, those prices could never have reached so high a tipping point. In fact, only if a vast majority of investors expect prices to move higher, and are fully committed, can prices break sharply. At that point, as buyers finally become sated, bids disappear, only sellers are left, and prices plunge.

JESSEL'S PARADOX

I was first exposed to this bull market paradox as a young teenager when George Jessel, a well-known comedian of the time, told the story of a skeptical investor who decides reluctantly to invest in stocks. He started by buying one hundred shares of a rarely traded fly-by-night company. And surprise, the prices moved from $10 per share to $11 per share. Encouraged that he had become a wise investor, he bought more. Finally, when he had bid the price up to $30 per share, he decided to cash in. He called his broker to sell out his position. The broker hesitated and then responded: "To whom?" I call it Jessel's paradox.

In an extension of Jessel's paradox, each "skeptical" buyer gradually becomes a committed bull. The cumulative process of conversion of bears to bulls propels prices ever higher, driven in part by herd behavior. In the simple case, at the market top everyone has turned into a believer and is fully committed. There are no unconverted skeptics left to buy from the first new seller.

I am not sure whether my subsequent insights years later added much to the Jessel story. But as a measure of how far the appetite for "Jessel" risk taking beyond the securitized mortgage market had gone in the mid-2000s, long-sacrosanct debt covenants were eased as a classic euphoric global bubble took hold.[24] By 2007, yield spreads in debt markets overall had narrowed to a point where there was little room for further underpricing of risk. A broad measure of credit risk, the yield spread between "junk" bonds rated CCC or lower and ten-year U.S. Treasury notes, fell to an exceptionally low level in the spring of 2007 (Exhibit 3.7). Almost all market participants of my acquaintance were aware of the growing risks but were also cognizant that risk often remained underpriced for years.

Financial firms were thus fearful that should they retrench too soon, they would almost surely lose market share, perhaps irretrievably.[25] Their fears were given expression in Citigroup Chairman and CEO Charles Prince's now-famous remark in 2007, just before the onset of the crisis, that "when the music stops, in terms of liquidity, things will be complicated. But as long as the music is playing, you've got to get up and dance. We're still dancing."[26]

The financial firms accepted the risk that they would be unable to anticipate the onset of crisis in time to retrench. However, they believed that those risks were limited because when a crisis was clearly at hand, the seemingly insatiable demand for their array of exotic financial products would dissipate sufficiently slowly to enable them to sell almost all of their portfolios without loss. They were mistaken. They failed to recognize that market liquidity is largely a function of the degree of risk aversion of investors, clearly the most dominant animal spirit that drives financial markets. Leading up to the onset of crisis, the lessening in the intensity of risk aversion among investors had produced increasingly narrow bid-asked credit spreads, backed by heavy volumes (the measure of liquidity) creating the illusion of being able to sell almost anything. But when fear-induced market retrenchment set in, that "liquidity" disappeared literally overnight as buyers pulled back and offers hit progressively lower bids. In fact, in many markets, at the height of the crisis of 2008, bids virtually disappeared.

As I noted in Chapter 2, some bubbles burst without severe economic consequences—the dot-com boom and the rapid run-up of stock prices in the spring of 1987, for example. Others burst with severe deflationary consequences. The more pernicious class of bubbles, as Carmen Reinhart and Kenneth Rogoff demonstrate, appears to be a function of the degree of leverage in the financial sector, particularly when the maturity of debt is less than the maturity of the assets it funds.[27]

Even given the excesses of the GSEs, had the share of financial assets funded by equity been significantly higher in September

2008, arguably the deflation of asset prices would not have fostered a default contagion, if at all, much beyond that of the dot-com boom.

WHY DID THE BOOM REACH SUCH HEIGHTS?

Aside from the excesses of Fannie, Freddie, and of much of the financial sector, why did the 2007 bubble reach century-rare euphoria? The answer, I believe, lies with the dot-com and 1987 bubbles, which, as I noted in Chapter 2, burst with very little footprint on U.S. and global GDP. These two episodes led many in the economics profession and many a sophisticated investor to believe that future contractions would also prove no worse than a typical postwar recession.

The need for large-bank capital buffers appeared increasingly less pressing during the period of great moderation, the years 1983 to 2007, when cyclical volatility shrunk perceptibly. The banking regulations adopted internationally under Basel I did induce a modest increase in capital requirements well before the crisis arose. But the debates in Basel that I attended over the pending global capital accord—so-called Basel II—were largely focused on whether to keep bank capital requirements unchanged or to *reduce* them. Leverage accordingly ballooned.

As I discussed in the Introduction, outsized leverage and financial intermediation in general collapsed on September 15, 2008, engendering possibly the greatest *financial* crisis ever. Five months later, with the carnage of global economic activity still under way, I reviewed the forces at play during the previous months before the Economic Club of New York. I quote extensively from that speech because it conveys the contemporaneous fear and yet the emerging critical paths to recovery as the selling climax in global equity prices was only weeks away.

We tend to think of fluctuations in stock prices in terms of "paper" profits and losses somehow not connected to the real world. But the evaporation of the value of those "paper claims" can have a profoundly deflationary effect on global economic activity. . . .

Of course, it is not simple to disentangle the complex sequence of cause and effect between change in the market value of assets and economic activity. If stock prices were wholly reflective of changes in economic variables, movements in asset prices could be modeled as endogenous and given little attention. But they are not. A significant part of stock price dynamics is driven by the innate human propensity to intermittently swing between euphoria and fear, which, while heavily influenced by real economic events, nonetheless has a partial life of its own. And in my experience, such episodes are often not mere forecasts of future business activity but are an important cause of that activity.

Stock prices are governed through most of the business cycle by profit expectations and economic activity. They appear to become increasingly independent of that activity at turning points. That is the meaning of being a leading indicator, the conclusion of most business cycle analysts.

When we look back on this period, I very much suspect that the force that will be seen to have been most instrumental to global economic recovery will be a partial reversal of the $35 trillion global loss in corporate equity values that has so devastated financial intermediation. A recovery of the equity market driven largely by a receding of fear may well be a seminal turning point of the current crisis.

The key issue, of course, is when. Certainly by any historical measure, world stock prices are cheap. But as history also counsels, they could get a lot cheaper before they turn. What is undeniable is that stock market prices today are being suppressed by a degree of fear not experienced since the early twentieth century (1907 and 1932 come to mind). But history tells us that there is a limit to how deep, and for how long, fear can paralyze market participants. The pace of economic deterioration cannot persist indefinitely.[28]

Shortly thereafter, the market found its bottom and began its ascent. The role of equity markets in shaping the dynamics of the broader economy is the subject of the next chapter.

FOUR

STOCK PRICES AND
EQUITY STIMULUS

I t was one of those episodes of childhood you never forget: my thirty-four-year-old stockbroker father trying to explain the intricacies of stock market forecasting to his increasingly befuddled ten-year-old son. As I remember it, he was very patiently trying to instruct me about how certain patterns of stock pricing behavior foretold future movements of the Dow Jones Industrial Average. I couldn't wait for the tutorial to end so I could get back to perusing numbers I cared about: the batting averages of my favorite baseball heroes—the stalwarts of the New York Yankees. Many years later I still cared about batting averages, but my father's passion finally stirred my interest. I now appreciate the challenge of short-term investing as I have grown to recognize the chart-pricing signals my father used in the 1930s—"head and shoulders," "descending channel," and "trading breakouts"—in many of the postwar stock market chartist services that, to this day, attract a large audience.

Over my more than six decades of intensive interest, I have encountered very few consistently successful stock price forecasting
techniques. Many appeared to work for a time but subsequently
failed. But are there any guideposts that at least raise the probability
of investment success? Short-term investing is complex, and for
guidance I defer to chartists (my father would be pleased) who argue
with some validity that market momentum ebbs and flows in de-
finable patterns. Longer-term strategies, especially "buy and hold,"
however, are much more promising because stocks have risen from
generation to generation almost without exception.[1]

The S&P 500 composite stock price index has averaged nominal
annual increases of nearly 7 percent from the end of World War II
through 2007, and almost never failed to log gains over any ten-year
time frame. Moreover, prices exhibited no tendency, even during our
most dramatic post–World War II bear market (2008), to fall back to
even the stock price *highs* of 1929, and during the stock market
depths of early 2009, prices were still higher than during the early
years of the dot-com boom. If bear markets never fully retrace all
bull markets (which they do not), it necessarily means an ever increasing part of capital gains becomes quasi-permanent.

Why do stock prices rise so persistently? The bottom line is that
over the long run, stock price-to-earnings ratios, and hence their in-
verse, earnings-to-stock price ratios, have no discernible trend going
back to at least 1890 (Exhibit 4.1). The equity yield peaked in 1949 at
16 percent and ranges between 5 percent and 10 percent for most
years. The reason for this relative historical stability is that these ratios are tied to interest rates that reflect our inbred stable time preference (see Chapter 1).[2] Corporate earnings are tied to gross corporate
product, or more generally, GDP. But GDP over the long run can be
reasonably proxied by the product of the civilian labor force, produc-

tivity, and, since 1933, inflation—all of which have persistently grown. Thus, earnings per share and stock prices rise with nominal GDP. Implicit in these relationships is that common stocks, in addition to being an investment in corporate performance, act as a hedge against inflation as well. Since 1921, for example, nominal stock prices have risen by 6.0 percent annually, the product of a 2.6 percent annual inflation rate (in prices of core personal consumption expenditures) and a 3.3 percent annual rate of increase in inflation-adjusted earnings.

The equity risk premium, calculated as the earnings yield less the real riskless long-term interest rate, is a measure of the compensation spread that investors require to hold equity rather than riskless bonds (Exhibit 4.2). It is often used to assess the degree of risk perceived in holding equities. These data recommend an investment strategy of concentrating purchases when equity premiums are in the upper bound of their range (that is, when stocks become "cheap" relative to their earnings and to bonds). Such mechanical trading strategies, if rigorously followed, displace "intuition" or "gut" trading, which demonstrably is biased by fear and hence is rarely as successful as buy and hold. Even experienced investors and/or speculators have difficulty in overcoming our ingrained aversion to risk, which is a far more emotionally gripping propensity than its obverse, euphoria.[3]

But not all professional traders are undermined by the biases of stock fund investors. There are a handful of professional investors who have had considerable success in amassing large fortunes by, for example, shorting the British pound sterling, American subprime mortgage securities, or some exotic derivatives. It is not a trading strategy for the faint of heart.

FEAR AND RISK AVERSION ARE DOMINANT PROPENSITIES

But suppressing fear is easier said than done. It is perhaps no accident that professionally managed equity funds have difficulty doing as well as "unemotional" index funds that avoid the biases of human judgment.[4] Fear, even when introspectively recognized, can undermine rational investment behavior. I recall many seasoned investors confessing to me that they sold near the bottom of the record one-day stock price decline of October 19, 1987, even though they understood that, given history, it was the wrong strategy. The *physical* pain they felt in seeing their net worth evaporate led them to seek relief by disengaging from the market.

THE UPSIDE

The momentum of euphoria-driven stock price booms, egged on by herd behavior, appears to have been remarkably similar through the past century, though at an increasingly dampened pace. In the five years preceding the peak of the most recent boom (October 2007), for example, stock prices rose at a 12 percent annual rate. In the five years preceding the peak of the dot-com boom (2000), stock prices rose at a 22 percent annual rate. The five-year boom that preceded the peak of 1987 produced an average rise of 24 percent, and the boom prior to the 1929 crash, an average annual gain of 28 percent. The pace of the rise in bull markets in earlier decades appears more erratic, but on average, somewhat smaller than the pace of the past eight decades.

This is probably as close as we can get to measuring the pace of the systematic buildup of euphoric herd-driven behavior. In less liquid markets we should expect the degree of tenacity and effectiveness of herd behavior to be smaller, and hence should anticipate a slower rate of euphoric growth. However, to my surprise, the average annual rate of home price increase in the five years leading up to the peak of the housing price bubble, at 12 percent, matched the concurrent pace of advances in equity prices.

THE DOWNSIDE

The inevitable contraction following all bull stock markets initiated and governed by fear has been far greater, more diverse, and less predictable than the rate of gain during bull markets. Fear, judging solely by the way markets react, is certainly a far more intense human propensity than euphoria.[5]

The *degree* of fear and euphoria is measured reasonably well by yield spreads, both with respect to credit risks and maturity. The longer the expected life of a prospective investment, the more uncertain the return and hence the greater the rate of discount applied to income from such assets. Disregarding credit risk, that discount rate should reflect the riskless yield of government bonds of the same maturity. And the difference between the yield on the thirty-year Treasury obligation and that on a five-year Treasury obligation[6] indicates how severely discounting increases with maturity. The effect of heavy discounting of long-lived assets, primarily buildings, is discussed in Chapter 7.

The variance of risk on capital investment (see "From Gut to Reason," page 85) can be proxied by the probability of default indicated by the yield spread between marginal junk bonds (S&P ten-year BB+ interest rates) and ten-year riskless U.S. Treasury notes. As can be seen in Exhibit 4.3, the spread slipped to 2 percent during the euphoric stock price and housing booms, only to soar to near 9 percent at the height of the post–Lehman crisis. Equally important, both fear and euphoria can also be measured by equity risk premiums.

THE LITTLE GUY

Fear plays an especially dominant role for investors with modest means. The risk-averse small investor confronts the bias of a gambler who has a small stake and knows if he loses it, he is out of business. His appetite for risk taking is limited. It is only when an investor's stake is large that he, or she, can suffer substantial losses with relative equanimity. In addition, an investor with large accumulated capital has the resources to disregard periodic market crashes, and indeed usually employs such opportunities to build up his or her stock portfolio.

ASSET PRICES

Only after many years of involvement with Wall Street did I become aware of how significant a role stock prices, or more generally, asset values, play in overall economic performance. The economic collapse of 2008 reinforced what previous experience had clearly shown me: Stock prices are not merely a leading indicator of business activity but a major contributor to changes in that activity.

... AND THE REAL ECONOMY

Stock price gyrations have a profound effect not only on financial markets and financing but on the real economy as well. Capital gains and losses are key factors in the ups and downs of the business cycle. Most pronounced is their effect on consumer spending. Over the past six decades, the market value of all stocks held by American households and nonprofit organizations directly or indirectly through equity holdings of pension and mutual funds, insurance companies, and other financial intermediaries has risen in value by nearly $20 trillion. The historical data strongly support the view that a rise in the market value of stocks held, for example, in 401k pension funds through contributions or quasi-permanent capital gains will induce households to spend part of their gains on personal consumption expenditures.[7] The empirical results developed in the appendix suggest that approximately 2.1 cents of every dollar in the equity holdings of households (on average during a year), 3.0 cents of every dollar of market value of equity in owner-occupied homes, and 2.0 cents of assets accumulated otherwise are spent, during that year, on personal consumption expenditures (Exhibit 4.4). These data do not do much to clarify whether, as many analysts believe, a dollar in home equity gains has a greater effect on consumption expenditures than a dollar of stock market capital gains. The Federal Reserve has long argued that there is no significant difference. My result does indicate a higher propensity to spend out of home equity than stock equity—but the difference is only marginally significant. In fact, data for the years 1953 to 2012 indicate that, on average, 12 perccent of personal consumption expenditures were determined by increases in net worth. The remaining 88 percent were determined by the level of disposable personal income and short-term savings rates (see Exhibit 4.5).[8] Nonetheless, analysts, myself included (in this book), still measure the rate of savings of a household as a percent of income only. Before econometricians discovered these important relationships, I, and I assume others as well, assumed that only disposable income determined personal consumption expenditures.

Moreover, changes in prices of owner-occupied homes affect not only expenditures by households on goods and services, but along with long-term mortgage rates, are a major factor in the decision of homebuilders to construct new homes.[9] Homebuilding, however, does not appear to be significantly affected by stock prices, with the possible exception of the stock price of a homebuilder's own company.

GOVERNMENT RESPONDS TO CAPITAL GAINS

Asset prices have a measurable effect not only on consumption expenditures and private capital investment but also on government outlays as well. Municipalities that depend heavily on property taxes do ratchet spending up and down as the market values of assessable properties fluctuate. As federal budget receipts rise from taxed capital gains and stock option grants, the fiscal status of the government improves, creating leeway for Congress to spend more. The dot-com boom, for example, produced the budget surpluses of 1998 to 2001 for the federal government and many states. No elected officials in modern times seem to resist being enticed by unexpected surplus cash sitting around, uncommitted. But outside of the extremes of boom and bust, the effect of more workaday fluctuations of asset prices on ups and downs in federal spending is surely minimal.

In summary: In Exhibit 4.6, I trace the overall effect of year-over-year changes in equity values (with a one-quarter lead) on year-over-year changes in real GDP.[10] I find that between 1970 and 2012, a 10 percent increase in the market value of holdings of U.S. residents of stocks, bonds, homeowners' equity, and other assets is associated with an annual change in real GDP of 1.3 percentage points.

EQUITY STIMULUS

Since 1952, the combination of equity from stocks and homes has averaged a net annual gain of 7.5 percent.[11] The American economy thus has been "stimulated" by equity in a manner similar to the way fiscal stimulus affects GDP. Both, of course, require debt to convert the programs into spendable funds. Government deficits are funded by government debt. Private realized capital gains cannot be monetized and spent without incurring private debt or issuing stock. But there are, of course, important differences. Fiscal stimulus is initiated by deliberate action of government. Equity stimulus is a result of private sector decision making, the economic consequences of which can be affected by government actions for good or ill. In Chapter 7, I compare the contribution of fiscal stimulus to the economic recovery of 2009 with that of equity stimulus.

CAPITAL EXPENDITURES

I was a director of fifteen listed corporations at various times in the quarter century before I joined the Federal Reserve. I cannot remember a single instance when a chairman[12] presented a new capital project to his board and cited the corporation's rising stock price as a determining factor for authorizing a capital expenditure. Yet the data unambiguously indicate that the market value of corporate equities (stock prices) is an important determinant of capital spending (see Box 4.1).

BOX 4.1: STOCK PRICES AND CAPITAL SPENDING

In a paper I published in 1959,[13] I related the ratio of the market value of existing U.S. corporate net assets (stock prices) to the replacement cost of those assets (the price of newly produced private plant and equipment).[14] In the simplest example of this process, a new office building will tend to be funded if the market value of contiguous office buildings significantly exceeds the expected construction cost of the new investment. (See "Asset Prices," page 80.)

The ratio of stock price to cost of construction of capital assets correlated quite well with machinery orders (capital investment) going back into the 1920s. I recently updated the 1959 analysis and was amazed at how well this simple relationship still works, even tracing the recent years' sharp fluctuations in real private capital investment (Exhibit 4.7). Since 1993, for example, a 10 percent change in stock prices relative to the cost of replacing plant and equipment from scratch has been associated with a 4 percent change in real capital expenditures relative to the stock of fixed assets.

I know of no corporate executives who explicitly determine a corporation's total capital budget based on such calculations, but implicitly they all do.

HOW IT'S DONE

In theory, to optimize the long-term market value of a firm, the ultimate goal of corporate investment, corporate executives need to simultaneously consider the entire universe of potential investments: their prospective rates of return and whether they should be funded wholly by equity, wholly by debt, or some combination of the two. This implies, for example, that all capital projects be identified and evaluated for any year on January 1, and then management continually reevaluate throughout the year all the assumptions that went into the initial conclusions as new evidence inevitably emerges. But no corporate executive committee has the ability to go through that exercise.

In practice, as a rough approximation of the theoretically optimal procedure, most corporations constrain capital spending to the level of cash flow, adjusted for the preferred degree of leverage (or de-leverage) of their balance sheet. These choices reflect management's general level of confidence about the future over the time frame of prospective capital investments. Of course, all capital budgets are made up of myriad individual investment projects that must be evaluated.

FROM GUT TO REASON

The cap-ex ratio (capital expenditures as a share of cash flow) captures the essence of business investment decision making. But how do corporate managers make such judgments? In years past, it was too often the "gut feel" of the CEO (not to be probed further). In more recent decades, the process has become more formal, though gut feel (intuition) has never been fully discarded (see Chapter 1).

The investment process obviously differs from company to company, but all, especially larger corporations, follow more or less the same approach. For example, the executives of an oil company contemplating whether to expand capacity may instruct the company's technical and marketing people to create a best estimate of the potential future market and profitability of a newly introduced petrochemical feedstock over the expected life of the proposed production facility.

If that rate of return exceeds the corporation's cost of raising new equity capital and is within the bounds of any overall corporate leverage constraint,[15] the analysis then proceeds to stage two. What is the expected *range,* or variance, of best estimate outcomes? This judgment, as I have observed over the years, largely determines whether the investment is implemented. An investment with a respectable 20 percent average annual expected rate of return could nonetheless be rejected if the long-term outlook is so cloudy that the range of that estimate is, for example, between negative 20 percent and positive 60 percent.

The fewer the variables that need to be evaluated in making a forecast, the narrower the range of possibilities and the lower the variance. A clouded business climate owing to an uncertain outlook of future tax regimes, for example, obviously increases investment outcome variance by adding new uncertainties to the decision-making process. That can, and usually does, exact a toll on the level of a company's capital investments. Some uncertainties can be ameliorated by slightly altering the nature and terms of a project. While the calculation of the expected rate of return is straightforward, the determination of the level of variance that is acceptable is not. In my experience, the relative skills in making variance judgments determine to a large extent which companies are most successful.

The ratio of capital investment to cash flow is thus not only an important measure of the level of corporate confidence, but it is also a useful indicator of corporation leverage. The acceptable degree of overall corporate leverage is revealed in the choice of total capital expenditures' share of cash flow (the cap-ex ratio).[16] A corporation that finances capital expenditures wholly with cash flow, that is, with no *net* borrowing, has a ratio of 1.0.[17] A ratio exceeding 1.0 defines the degree of increase in leverage. A ratio less than 1.0 indicates the degree of de-leveraging. For nonfinancial corporate business between 1952 and 2007, for example, the (unweighted) average of that ratio was 1.05, with all of the annual observations falling between 0.82 and 1.29 (excluding 1974). Thus, some net borrowing, on average, is associated with corporate investment. Corporate managers are always aware of the value of the equity buffers that stand between debt and bankruptcy as they set the appropriate amount of leverage that their corporation will take on.

CORPORATE CULTURE

During my tenure as a director of JPMorgan (just prior to joining the Federal Reserve), I was impressed by the value the bank accorded to its AAA rating. They recognized that in the short run, they could achieve a higher return on equity through increased leverage. But they feared that that could lower the bank's AAA rating, an important factor in their long-term ability to attract low-cost liabilities. Most important, the rating was required to sustain a reputation for prudence, an essential characteristic of their historic franchise that dated back to the time of John Pierpont Morgan himself. Similar considerations led to constrained leverage on the part of many non-financial corporations for which I have worked over the years.

Most firms will borrow only so much, even though they recognize they may be forgoing profitable opportunities by failing to more fully leverage certain investments (a reluctance far greater than is evident among financial firms). This business reluctance to borrow beyond a determined limit relative to cash flow is evident in Exhibit 7.2. Because investment less cash flow is necessarily equal to net borrowing, the data indicate a relatively narrow range of leverage. This is true for business in general. If at any interest rate or level of cultural restraint business borrows less, governments are free to borrow more.

Regression analysis indicates that higher mortgage rates suppress home prices (Exhibit 3.3), and home prices are critically tied to home investment (Exhibit 7.4). That accounts for about a fourth of crowding out of private investment. I suspect that interest rate suppression of less than investment grade companies accounts for a significant additional amount. But in general it appears that roughly half of the displacement of gross private savings by budget deficits can be attributed to interest rate crowding out, and the residual other half to corporate culture restraints.

Both crowding out owing to elevated interest rates and crowding out owing to corporate culture restraints in the end come out in the same place. Elevated costs of funding will often render a relevant prospective investment unprofitable. But that is also what occurs when an individual company self-limits its degree of leverage. Even triple-A firms restrict their debt issuance, and that implies that certain contemplated investments are stillborn.

A company with very little debt has considerable leeway to leverage and maximize the rate of return on equity. It can thus accept a relatively low potential operating rate of return[18] and, through leverage, bring the return on equity up to a satisfactory level. A firm with an already high degree of leverage does not have that opportunity. Since it cannot borrow, it needs a higher operating rate of return. Therefore, other things equal, an already highly leveraged firm will invest and borrow less than a firm not so debt encumbered. In the end, it behaves like an unleveraged firm inhibited by a rise in interest rates.

To be sure, that's not the way investment judgments are made in the textbooks on optimum capital allocation. Human propensities too often warp objective decision making. But most large firms do adhere to a rigorous paradigm. In my experience, most medium- and, especially, smaller-sized companies do not. When they reach a certain debt level, they behave as though they were crowded out by higher rates. A model that fails to embody such economic forces (and most do not) misses an important constraint on the forecast results.

FIVE

FINANCE AND REGULATION[1]

I n recent years, the ongoing debate on the merits of capitalism has homed in on a crucial pillar: Adam Smith's fundamental premise of free markets, the idea that people acting in their own self-interest spur competition that advances society as a whole.[2] In the purest form of that paradigm is the idea that markets are essentially self-regulating.

Although I always have been, and remain, a strong supporter of free market capitalism, my support is not based on the belief that all market participants behave solely in their own rational self-interest at all times. As someone brought up in the canyons of Wall Street, I saw too much of what we now describe as the influence of animal spirits to entertain such a view.[3] I nonetheless found the broad success of free markets, with all their shortcomings, intellectually and empirically too compelling to ignore and the arguments for alternative economic systems flawed and unpersuasive.

I believed in years past that the aberrations from rationality and efficiency—often reflecting the effects of animal spirits—were sufficiently infrequent and random to evoke little more than economic noise. I was thus especially shaken by the breakdown in 2008, which could scarcely be characterized as economic noise. Moreover, it had an eerie historical familiarity about it—1929 and 1907 for example. Did these breakdowns reflect "noise" or some systematic propensity of human nature? The crack in my view of the economic world manifested itself in a widespread failure of one of the most important pillars of a stable market economy, whose roots lay deep in postwar academia: rational financial risk management.

I noted in an op-ed piece early in the crisis, "those of us who look to the self-interest of lending institutions to protect shareholder equity have to be in a state of shocked disbelief."[4] That episode led me to rethink my view of the importance of animal spirits. And in the aftermath of the failure of financial risk management, I was led to conclude that a tightening of regulatory capital standards was long overdue.

The events of the crisis demonstrated that financial managers could not be counted on to maintain an equity buffer adequate to withstand a broad range of economic outcomes. The willingness of many financial firms to allow their tangible capital, at the height of the boom, to become razor thin was a folly largely explained by herd behavior and an underestimation of the ephemeral nature of market liquidity. The financial and economic instability that followed in its wake induced a sharp political response toward increased regulation, most notably in the form of the Dodd-Frank Act. In political terms, that response was understandable. The problem is that substituting government regulations is rarely an improvement and, indeed, as I note later, if overdone, turns out to be counterproductive.

As poorly as certain private financial managers performed leading up to the crisis of 2008, government regulators fared no better (see Chapter 2).

FINANCIAL INTERMEDIATION AND REGULATION

The Purpose of Finance

The role of regulation in a market economy is determined by the nature of what is being regulated. The ultimate goal of a financial system in a market economy, for example, is to direct the nation's savings (including depreciation[5]), plus any savings borrowed from abroad (the current account deficit), toward investments in plant, equipment, and human capital that offer the largest risk-adjusted returns on capital and presumably the greatest increases in the nation's output per worker hour. Nonfinancial output per hour, on average, rises when obsolescent facilities (with low output per hour) are replaced with facilities that embody cutting-edge technologies (with high output per hour). This process improves average standards of living for a nation as a whole. There is no alternative to what Joseph Schumpeter aptly called "creative destruction." In the United States, the success of finance through the last decades of the twentieth century in directing our scarce savings into real productive capital investments may explain the generous compensation that nonfinancial market participants had been willing to pay to the domestic producers of financial services (see Box 5.1).

BOX 5.1: COMPENSATION

Prior to my Federal Reserve tenure I spent a good deal of my time as a director of a number of American corporations, large and small, including two banks and a savings and loan holding company. In *The Age of Turbulence* (page 426), I complained about the consultants hired by corporations to advise boards of directors on corporate compensation packages. I was distressed that all seemed to be arguing that boards of directors needed to offer above-average compensation. It is a neat trick to get everyone doing better than the average of all. At the same time, it has been my experience serving as a consultant and, at times, as a director of many large financial corporations that small differences in the skill level of senior bankers tend to translate into large differences in the bank's bottom line. Competition for even the slightly more skilled is accordingly fierce. Senior bankers operate as largely independent entities whose "clients" are often more theirs than the banks'; they leave with the "star" when he or she changes organization. It is doubtful that legislation can work in such an arena. My experiences in such issues have made me skeptical, and data do indirectly support such skepticism. If directors, in seeking bank executives, believe that senior officers of the bank contribute to the bank's bottom line, you would expect the bank's executive compensation to mirror the market value of the bank. The larger the bank, the greater the dollar gains and losses from management decisions. I have not tried to match the figures bank by bank, but the aggregate CEO compensation of the S&P 500 corporations, a good proxy, does exhibit a surprising stability over time with the market value of the firms (Exhibit 5.1).

The share of U.S. gross domestic product accruing as income to the private finance and insurance sectors rose fairly steadily from 2.4 percent in 1947 to 7.9 percent in 2012 (Exhibit 5.2).[6] Many other global financial centers exhibit similar trends.[7] Only a small part of the rise of U.S. finance and insurance represented an increase in net foreign demand for U.S. financial and insurance services.[8] Income accruing to finance and insurance results from their services being purchased by nonfinancial firms and foreign businesses. These are consolidated figures. Banks cannot generate income by trading with themselves.

A Misread?

Given the historic breakdown of 2008, did nonfinancial market participants over the decades misread the efficiency of finance and inappropriately compensate this segment of our economy? The prevalence of so many financial product failures during the crisis certainly suggests so. The share of finance and insurance in GDP, at 8.2 percent in 2006, fell back to 7.3 percent in 2008, the lowest level since 1999. But it bounced back sharply in the following years, moving to 8.0 percent in 2010 and 7.9 percent in 2012. The demand for financial services prior to 2008 was apparently not a misread of the efficiency of finance.

The proportion of nonfarm employment accounted for by finance and insurance since 1947 has risen far less than the share of gross income originating in that sector. This implies a significant upgrading of the salaries paid by financial institutions. There is little doubt that highly skilled mathematicians, model builders, and number crunchers have flocked to finance.[9] By 2007, a quarter of all graduates of the venerable California Institute of Technology were entering finance, according to the *Economist*.[10]

What are we to make of these extraordinarily persistent and stable uptrends? Is it wholly accidental? (After all, there is no evidence of such a trend in the prewar years.) The rising value of assets to be managed accounts for part, but only part, of the increase.[11] The answer to this question matters because in the context of financial reform, we must address whether the growing share was evidence that a rise in financial services was *required* to intermediate an ever more complex American division of labor. Alternatively, the growing share of finance in the economy could reflect problems with the structure of, and incentives surrounding, those people working in the financial industry.

I raise the issue because many policy recommendations in the Dodd-Frank Act seem likely to result in a diminished share of financial services income in GDP. Would such policies affect the growth of U.S. nonfinancial productivity and, with it, our standards of living? More important, given the recent failures of risk management and regulation, could increased financial regulation at this time thwart or, through increased stability, enhance economic growth? We need a far deeper understanding of the role of financial intermediation in promoting growth to answer that question. The Dodd-Frank Act does not, in my judgment, address those issues. I explained my general concern with the act in March 2011, worrying that "it fails to capture the degree of global interconnectedness of recent decades which has not been substantially altered by the crisis of 2008. The act may create the largest regulatory-induced market distortion since America's ill-fated imposition of wage and price controls in 1971."[12] More than two years later I have seen nothing to alter that appraisal.

How finance evolves in the postcrisis years should bring clarity to many of today's uncertainties. We have to assume that the greater the level of capital that financial institutions are required to hold, the less the degree of financial intermediation. That, in turn, is likely to result in slower growth, but presumably more financial stability and less risk of a breakdown in the financial structure of the magnitude of 2008.

Risky Financial Intermediation

As I noted earlier, prior to the crisis, the size of the modeled extreme negative tail of the distribution of risks failed to reflect the reality that emerged with the default of Lehman. So long as there are bank *debt* obligations, there will always be *some* risk that bank capital cannot cover, and if that risk materializes, some, perhaps even many, banks will fail.

But that need not become a systemic problem if equity capital and liquidity requirements are raised sufficiently and/or a significant part of an intermediary's debt takes the form of mandated contingent convertible (CoCo) bonds—that is, debt that is automatically converted to equity when equity capital falls below a certain threshold. Still, we must consider the possibility that private financial intermediaries will falter, with systemic consequences of a magnitude that requires sovereign credit to keep vital intermediation functioning. Short of the elimination of all debt, risk of default can never fall to zero so long as financial intermediaries require leverage (debt) to obtain an adequate return on equity capital.

Central bankers are always aware of the potential for a breakdown in private financial markets. Indeed, in the United States as recently as 1991, in contemplation of the unthinkable and at the urging of the Federal Reserve Board, section 13 (3) of the Federal Reserve Act was reconsidered and amended by Congress. The section, as revised, granted virtually unlimited authority to the board to lend in "unusual and exigent circumstances," the statutory basis of much postcrisis economic intervention.[13] More than a decade ago, addressing that issue, I noted:

> There is a . . . difficult problem of risk management that central bankers confront every day, whether we explicitly acknowledge it or not: How much of the underlying risk in a financial system should be shouldered [solely] by banks and other financial institutions? . . . [Central banks] have all chosen implicitly, if not in a more overt fashion, to set our capital and other reserve standards for banks to guard against outcomes that exclude those once or twice in a century crises that threaten the stability of our domestic and international financial systems.
>
> I do not believe any central bank explicitly makes this calculation. But we have chosen capital standards that by any stretch of the imagination cannot protect against all potential adverse loss outcomes. There is implicit in this exercise the admission that, in certain episodes, problems at commercial banks and other financial institutions, when their risk-management systems prove inadequate, will be handled by central banks [sovereign credit]. At the same time, society

on the whole should require that we set this bar very high. Hundred-year floods come only once every hundred years. Financial institutions should expect to look to the central bank only in extremely rare situations.[14]

At issue is whether the crisis that arrived a few years later is that hundred-year flood. At best, once-in-a-century observations yield results from which it is difficult to draw robust conclusions. But recent evidence suggests that what happened in the wake of the Lehman collapse, as I noted earlier, is among the most severe global *financial* crises ever, if not the most. In the Great Depression, of course, the collapse in economic output and the rise in unemployment and destitution far exceeded that in the 2008 crisis. And, of course, the widespread bank failures of the Great Depression era markedly reduced short-term credit availability. But short-term financial markets continued to function.

Financial crises are characterized by a progressive inability to float first long-term debt, then eventually short-term debt, and finally overnight debt. Long-term uncertainty, and therefore risks, are always greater than near-term risks, and hence risk spreads almost always increase with the maturity of the financial instrument in question.[15] While widespread economic havoc can be spread by a collapse in asset prices, I find that the depth of a financial crisis is best characterized by the degree of collapse in the availability of short-term credit.

One has to dig very deep into peacetime financial history to uncover episodes similar to 2008. The market for call money, the key short-term financing vehicle of a century ago, shut down at the peak of the 1907 panic "when no call money was offered at all for one day and the [bid] rate rose from 1 to 125%."[16] Even at the height of the

1929 stock market crisis, the call money market functioned, although annual interest rates did soar to 20 percent. In lesser financial crises, availability of funds in the longer-term markets disappeared, but overnight and other short-term markets continued to function.

The withdrawal of overnight money represents financial stringency at its maximum. Investors must be willing to lend overnight before they feel sufficiently protected by adequate capital to reach out for more distant, and hence riskier, maturities.

The evaporation of short-term credits, especially trade credits, in September 2008 was global and all encompassing. But it was, on a much grander scale, the same process that I had previously observed at a more micro level. As the credit of New York City became suspect in the mid-1970s, the first failure of issuance was evident in long-term municipal bonds, followed by failures in progressively shorter maturities, until even overnight markets started to crumble. A similar progression led up to the Mexican financial crisis of 1994–95.

REGULATORY REFORM

Principles of Reform

Given the recent unprecedented period of turmoil, by what standard should proposals for reform of official supervision and regulation be judged? I know of no form of economic organization, from unfettered laissez-faire to oppressive central planning, that has succeeded in achieving both maximum sustainable economic growth and permanent stability. Central planning certainly failed, and I strongly doubt, given the foibles of human nature, that complete stability is achievable in capitalist economies. The latter are governed by an always-turbulent competition driven by fear, euphoria, and herd behavior. In capitalist economies, however, markets do tend to be drawn toward, but never quite achieve, an equilibrium that is continually shifting.

Although there are often multiple objectives of regulation, when it can identify and inhibit irrational behavior, under certain conditions, regulation can be stabilizing. But there is an insidious cost of regulation in terms of economic growth and standards of living when it reaches beyond containing unproductive behavior. Parenthetically, I do not consider addressing fraud to be regulation. Rampant fraud can significantly diminish the effectiveness of market competition, but fraud is theft and an issue of law enforcement.

Growth Versus Stability

Regulation by definition imposes restraints on competitive markets. The elusive point of balance between growth and stability has often been a point of contention, especially when it comes to financial regulation.

During the postwar years prior to the crisis, with the exception of a limited number of bank bailouts (Continental Illinois in 1984, for example), private capital proved adequate to cover virtually all provisions for commercial bank lending losses.[17] As a consequence, there was never a definitive test of the precrisis conventional wisdom that an equity capital-to-assets ratio of 6 to 10 percent on average (the range that prevailed between 1946 and 2003) was adequate to support the U.S. banking system. Risk managers' assumption of the size and configuration of the negative tails of the distributions of credit and interest rate risk were, as I noted earlier, of necessity conjectural, and we had not had a test of those conjectures for many decades.

Most of the shape of the perceived distribution of risk of outcomes was developed from data gathered in the precrisis years, which included only "moderate" financial turbulence and mild euphorias. But since compilation of modern financial data began, we never had experienced a "hundred-year flood" that revealed the severe consequences of a shock in the negative tail of the probability distribution.

Risk managers, of course, knew in earlier decades that an assumption of "normality" in the distribution of risk was unrealistic,[18] but because this approximation greatly facilitated calculation, it prevailed. Even as the mathematics implied by fat tails began to be better understood, our number-crunching capabilities fell far short of making the required calculations to guide practical actions, except at prohibitive cost. That is no longer the case.

Clearly what we observed in the weeks following the Lehman default is exactly the type of market seizure that conjecture about so-called fat tails was supposed to capture, and in practice did not. Having experienced Lehman, risk managers will be far more cautious in evaluating future risk—at least for a while.[19]

Indeed, the Lehman default and its aftermath strongly suggest that the negative tails of the risk distribution were considerably larger than almost anybody had earlier imagined. The failure of risk managers to fully understand the effect of the emergence of shadow banking may have been partly responsible for the underestimation of systemic financial risk. Shadow banking was a form of financial innovation that may well have increased rather than moderated the overall level of risk. The creditors of these shadow banks were not being adequately compensated by higher capital buffers for the added risk posed by these entities.

The Illusion of Market Liquidity

When risk premiums are low over a protracted period, as they were, for example, from 1993 to 1998 and from 2003 to 2007, investors' willingness to actively bid for all types of financial assets, such as the high-risk tranches of collateralized debt obligations, creates an illusion of permanent market liquidity. In the latest episode, this turned out to be especially intoxicating. It led several major investment banks to sail into the financial storm with financing that depended on a level of liquidity that was about to vanish.

The Needed Reforms

Thus, the most pressing needed reforms in the aftermath of the crisis, in my judgment, are fixes to the levels of regulatory risk-adjusted capital, liquidity, and collateral standards required by counterparties.[20] Private market participants are now requiring economic capital and balance sheet liquidity well in excess of Basel requirements. The shadow banks that survived the crisis now are having to meet significantly tighter market standards set by their counterparties, with respect to capital, liquidity, and collateral, than existed before the crisis. Likewise, global regulators will need to assess required changes to capital and liquidity standards to better protect against systemic breakdowns.

All risk-adjusted capital adequacy measures need to be raised and due consideration needs to be given to the proportion of liabilities funded with overnight or other short-term debt. Regulatory capital requirements prior to the crisis, although based on decades of experience, were clearly too lax. Home mortgages were perceived as far safer than they, in retrospect, turned out to be. And, unfortunately, a large proportion of investment portfolio decisions was, by law, accorded "safe harbor" status if those decisions adhered to the credit risk judgments (or rather, misjudgments) of the credit-rating agencies.

To ensure that financial intermediaries have adequate cash to meet ongoing commitments in the event of a shutdown in external funding, international regulation of bank liquidity should match the tightening already evident in private risk management paradigms. Collateral (customer assets) has shown itself particularly subject to rapid recapture. Bear Stearns had nearly $20 billion in pledgeable liquid funds a week before it collapsed. Morgan Stanley lost more than a half trillion dollars of pledgeable collateral during the height of the crisis. In the United States, to lower the risk of a "run on the broker," the amount of customer assets held by broker-dealers that cannot be commingled with their own assets needs to be increased. That would decrease the amount of funds that can "run." However, such action must be measured and coordinated with other global regulators to avoid regulatory arbitrage.

Hedge Funds

Unaffiliated hedge funds have weathered the crisis—as extreme a real-life stress test as one can construct—without taxpayer assistance or, as I noted earlier, default. Although hedge funds are only lightly regulated, much of their leveraged funding comes from more heavily regulated banks. Moreover, as Sebastian Mallaby wrote, "Most hedge funds make money by driving prices *away* from extremes and toward their rational level."[21] In so doing, they supply much-needed liquidity to financial markets when other competitors have withdrawn. Regulations that inhibit the ability of hedge funds to supply such services have the potential to be counterproductive.

Capital, liquidity, and collateral, in my experience, address almost all of the financial regulatory structure shortcomings exposed by the onset and aftermath of the crisis. In retrospect, there has to have been a level of capital that would have prevented the failure of, for example, Bear Stearns and Lehman Brothers. (If not 10 percent capital, think of partnerships with 40 percent capital.) Moreover, generic loan loss reserves have the regulatory advantage of not having to forecast which particular financial products are about to turn toxic.[22] Certainly, very few investors foresaw the future of subprime securities or the myriad other broken products. Adequate generic capital eliminates the need for an unachievable specificity in regulatory standards.

The jerry-built regulatory structure that has evolved over the decades in the United States has become much too complex. During the debates that led to legislation resulting in a badly needed opening up of financial competition (the Gramm-Leach-Bliley Act of 1999), policy makers and lawmakers nonetheless failed to recognize that increased competition—especially through shadow banking—also increased negative tail risk.[23] And increased negative tail risk necessitates higher capital requirements.

Much, though not all, of what advocates of broadened oversight of consumer finance are combating falls under the scope of fraud. Again, this is not the province of regulation but of enhanced law enforcement. Misrepresentation, the major source of consumer complaints, is fraud and should be readily addressed in more widespread enforcement of existing law.

Upward Revisions of Bank Economic Capital

How much capital counterparties require of financial institutions should influence *regulatory* capital requirements. It is probably too soon to have definitive long-term answers. But very rough approximations for U.S. commercial banks can be inferred from the response of bank credit default swaps (CDS), a market measure of bank insolvency risk, to postcrisis events.[24] (See Box 5.2.)

BOX 5.2: BANK CAPITAL

Movements in the CDS market should also give us some direct insight into when the banking system is perceived to have overcome the market's still prevalent fear of widespread insolvency—and beyond that, to when markets perceive that banks will feel sufficiently secure to return to the free lending of the precrisis years.

Starting late in 2008 and accelerating into the first quarter of 2009, the U.S. Treasury, through its Troubled Asset Relief Program (TARP), added $250 billion to bank equity, the equivalent of adding approximately 2 percentage points to the equity capital-to-assets ratio. The effect of this added capital was consequential and immediate.

As the financial crisis took hold and deepened, the unweighted average spread of five-year CDSs of six major U.S. banks—Bank of America, JPMorgan, Citigroup, Goldman Sachs, Wells Fargo, and Morgan Stanley—rose from 14 basis points in early 2007[25] to 170 basis points just before the Lehman default on September 15, 2008. In response to the Lehman default, the five-year CDS average price rose to more than 430 basis points by October 10. On the *day* the TARP was announced (October 14), the price fell to 211 basis points, or essentially by half (Exhibit 5.3). In other words, a 2-percentage-point addition to the banks' book equity capital-to-assets ratio reversed roughly half the crisis surge in the price of five-year CDSs. We shouldn't make too much of this, but we shouldn't make too little of it either; it's a real data point in an argument that has precious few of them. If we assume a linear extrapolation, which is admittedly a big assumption, this implies an overall additional 4-percentage-point rise (from nearly 10 percent at the end of the third quarter of 2008 to 14 percent ultimately) in the equity capital cushion required by market participants to fund the liabilities of banks. (This also presumes, of course, that the probability of a TARP before the Lehman default was de minimis. The abruptness of the market reaction to the TARP announcement appears to confirm such a presumption.)

Current book equity-to-assets ratios are still far from 14 percent. The average ratio for commercial banks (as reported by the FDIC) was 11.4 percent on March 31, 2013, compared with 9.4 percent in late 2008. That banks still have more equity capital to add in order to return the market's perception of risk to precrisis levels is also indicated by the fact that the five-year CDS price remained around 100 basis points in the spring of 2013, which was still significantly elevated relative to the 14 basis points that prevailed in early 2007, when 10 percent capital prevailed.[26]

There is little doubt that the TARP's cash injection mark-edly reduced the fear of bank default through early 2009. More difficult to judge is the effect on bank CDSs of the dramatic increase in bank equity at *market* value relative to bank assets at market value. That ratio rose from 7.3 percent at the end of March 2009 to 11.6 percent at the end of December 2009 (Ex-hibit 5.4). (Bank capital-to-asset ratios are typically quoted in book value terms, which is to say the value based on established accounting conventions. Market value is simply the stock price [per share] times the number of shares outstanding.)

Higher market values of bank equity have materially increased the solvency of banks, though far less effectively, dollar for dollar, than a more permanent change in book value equity. CDS prices, which reflect the probability of default, can be used as a basic arbiter of whether book or market value of bank equity is the more relevant measure of buffer against default. CDS prices and bank stock prices are highly correlated, of course. But statistically significant regres-sion analysis indicates that only one fourth of a change in the ratio of bank equity to bank assets at market value translates to the book value equivalent of that ratio. This is wholly understandable given that market values are more ephemeral than book values. Presum-ably only a fourth of market change is assumed to be a permanent increase in the buffer to default, measured by book value.

Much of the repayment of the 2008 TARP investments to the U.S. Treasury was doubtless financed by new equity issuance. That new equity issuance was, in turn, made possible by a more than half-trillion-dollar increase in the market value of U.S. commercial bank equity and by borrowings made much easier (and cheaper) by the increased equity buffer engendered by gains in market-valued bank equity. The parceling of relative contributions of the TARP and of capital gains to bank solvency and willingness to lend may not be fully clear even in retrospect.

The TARP not only inserted capital but also induced market participants to infer that the U.S. Treasury would, at least for a while, stand behind the liabilities of the banking system. This may explain the divergence since mid-September 2009 between short-term (one- and three-month) London Interbank Offered Rate less overnight indexed swap rates (LIBOR-OIS) spreads (an alternative to CDS spreads as a short-term measure of the likelihood of bank default) and five- and ten-year CDS spreads. Short-term LIBOR-OIS spreads had returned to their precrisis level by the end of September 2009. Long-maturity CDS prices are, as yet, only partway back (Exhibit 5.5). The one-year LIBOR-OIS spread falls in between. Clearly, markets are discounting some of the rise in the bank capital cushion at market value five and ten years hence. That discounting likely reflects the perceived increased volatility of stock prices and the uncertainty surrounding the political willingness, or ability, of the U.S. government, after markets return to normal, to initiate another bank bailout.[27]

Given the foregoing set of fragile assumptions and conclusions (they are all we have), I would judge that regulatory equity capital requirements in the end will be seen to have risen from the 10 percent precrisis level (in terms of book value) to 13 percent or 14 percent by 2015, and liquidity and collateral requirements will toughen commensurately.

What Supervision and Regulation Can Do

What, in my experience, supervision and examination *can* do as backup to capital requirements and counterparty surveillance is promulgate rules that are preventative and *are not predicated on regulators being able to accurately predict an uncertain future.*

SUPERVISION
- can audit and enforce capital and liquidity requirements,
- can require that financial institutions issue some contingent convertible debt that will become equity should equity capital become impaired,
- can put limits or prohibitions on certain types of concentrated bank lending,
- can inhibit the reconsolidation of affiliates previously sold to investors, especially structured investment vehicles (SIVs),[28] and
- can require "living wills" in which financial intermediaries indicate, on an ongoing basis, how they can be liquidated expeditiously with minimum effect on counterparties and markets.

Some Lessons of Equity Capital History

In the late nineteenth century, U.S. banks needed to carry equity capital of 30 percent of assets to attract sufficient deposits and other forms of borrowing to fund their assets. In the pre–Civil War period, that figure topped 50 percent (Exhibit 2.1). Given the rudimentary nature of payment systems and the poor geographical distribution of bank reserves in what was then an agricultural economy, competition for bank credit was largely local. It enabled national banks, on average, to obtain returns (net income) on their assets of well over 200 basis points in the late 1880s, and probably more than 300 basis points in the 1870s (compared with 70 basis points a century later).

The increasing efficiency of financial intermediation, owing to the consolidation of reserves and improvements in payment systems that allowed capital-to-assets ratios to decline, exerted competitive pressure on profit spreads to narrow. Accordingly, the annual average net income rate of return on *equity* was amazingly stable, rarely falling outside a range of 5 to 10 percent, measured annually, during the near century from 1869 to 1966 (Exhibit 5.6). That stability meant that net income as a percentage of assets and the degree of leverage were roughly inversely proportional during that century.

The rates of return enjoyed by financial intermediaries on assets and equity (despite the decline in leverage) moved modestly higher during the period from 1966 to 1982, owing to a rapid expansion in noninterest income, for example, from fiduciary activities, service charges and fees, and securitizations. Then, as a consequence of a marked increase in the scope of bank powers, noninterest income again rose significantly between 1982 and 2006, boosting net income to nearly 15 percent of equity. That increase reflected in part the emergence in April 1987 of court-sanctioned and Federal Reserve–regulated "section 20" investment banking affiliates of bank holding companies.[29] The transfer of such business is clearly visible in the acceleration of gross income originating in commercial banking relative to that in investment banking starting in 2000.[30]

I tentatively conclude that the relative stability of average net income-to-equity ratios dating back to the post–Civil War years reflects an underlying competitive market-determined rate of return on intermediation, a result consistent with stable time preference and real long-term interest rates.

In summary, the crisis of 2008 has left in its wake a significantly higher capital-to-assets ratio requirement, both economic and regulatory, that must be reached if intermediation is to be restored to the point where banks and other financial institutions are confident they have a sufficiently secure capital cushion to lend freely. An open question is whether, in line with history, a rise in the ratio of capital to assets in banks will also nudge up the ratio of net income to assets in the process. This is obviously an implication of higher capital-to-asset ratios.

Too Big to Fail

Beyond the need to increase capital requirements, we still face the necessity of addressing the problems of some financial firms being "too big to fail" (TBTF) or, more appropriately, "too interconnected to be liquidated quickly." The productive employment of the nation's savings is threatened when financial firms at the edge of failure are supported with taxpayer funds (savings) and designated as systemically important institutions.

I agree with Gary Stern, the former president of the Federal Reserve Bank of Minneapolis, who has long held that "creditors will continue to underprice the risk-taking of these financial institutions, overfund them, and fail to provide effective market discipline. Facing prices that are too low, systemically important firms will take on too much risk."[31]

After remaining in the backwaters of economic analysis for years, "too big to fail" has finally gained the prominence it deserves.

Firms that are perceived as too big to fail have arisen as major visible threats to economic growth. It finally became an urgent problem when Fannie Mae and Freddie Mac were placed into conservatorship on September 7, 2008. Before then, U.S. policy makers (with fingers crossed) could point to the fact that Fannie and Freddie, by statute, were *not* backed by the "full faith and credit of the U.S. government." Market participants, however, did not believe the denial, and they consistently afforded Fannie and Freddie a special credit subsidy. It ranged between 13 basis points for short-term debt to 42 basis points for longer-term debentures, with a weighted average of about 40 basis points.[32] On September 7, 2008, market participants were finally vindicated.

Fannie Mae and Freddie Mac need to be split up into smaller companies, none of them too big to fail, and then reconstituted as stand-alone securitizers. Alternatively, they could be phased out by gradually lowering the size of the loans they can guarantee and securitize.

Seventeen systemically important U.S. banks have been designated by at least one major regulator as effectively too big to fail, rendering them guaranteed by the federal government. As has occurred with Fannie Mae and Freddie Mac, the market has already accorded these TBTF institutions subsidized funding. This is evident in the cost of funding of large banking institutions relative to competing smaller institutions not favored with subsidized borrowings. IMF researchers in a recent working paper estimated "the overall funding cost advantage of global SIFIs as approximately 60 basis points (bp) in 2007 and 80 bp in 2009."[33] The top forty-five U.S. banks in this study exhibited about the same degree of support as the global average. In competitive financial markets, 40 to 80 bp is a very large advantage.

Such a market-based subsidy will enable a bank or other financial intermediary to attract part of the nation's savings to fund its operations, even if its policies and portfolio, unsubsidized, would fail. Banks that become inefficient because they chronically fund inefficient firms should be allowed to fail. The viability of our economic system requires it. Even more worrisome, the market players are beginning to conjecture that in the event of the next crisis, most of the American financial system effectively would be guaranteed by the U.S. government.

As I noted earlier, sovereign credit should be employed as a backstop only during periods of extreme financial breakdown. Sovereign credit is not without cost. It creates institutions that are too big to fail, a short step from crony capitalism (see Chapter 11). More important, it becomes addictive, offering a seemingly politically cost-free avenue to a solution for every conceivable adverse aberration in economic activity.

ADDRESSING THE DIFFICULT

How to deal with systemically important institutions is among the major regulatory problems for which there are no easy solutions. Early resolution of bank problems under the Federal Deposit Insurance Corporation Improvement Act of 1991 (FDICIA) appeared to have worked with smaller banks during periods of general prosperity. But the notion that risks can be identified in a sufficiently timely manner to enable the liquidation of a large failing bank with minimum loss proved untenable during a crisis in which many large banks were at risk of failing at once. And as I noted in Chapter 2, I suspect solving the problem of large failing banks by "prompt corrective action" will prove untenable in future crises as well.[34]

The solution, in my judgment, that has at least a reasonable chance of reversing the extraordinarily large moral hazard that has arisen in the wake of the crisis is, as I noted, to require banks and possibly all financial intermediaries to issue CoCo bonds, as I mentioned earlier. Such debt will, of course, be more costly on issuance than simple debentures.

However, should contingent convertible bonds prove insufficient, we should allow large institutions to fail. If regulators determine that an institution is too interconnected to liquidate quickly, that institution should be taken into a special bankruptcy facility when normal debtor-in-possession financing is available. When debtor-in-posession financing is not available, the regulator should be granted access to very limited taxpayer funds to facilitate the gradual liquidation of a failed institution. Its creditors (when equity is wholly wiped out) would be subject to statutorily defined principles of discounts from par ("haircuts"), and the institution would then be required to split up into separate units, none of which should be of a size that is too big to fail. The whole process could be administered by a panel of judges who are expert in finance.

I assume that some of the newly created firms would survive, while others will fail. If, after a fixed short period of time, no viable exit from the bankruptcy appears available, the financial intermediary should be liquidated as expeditiously as feasible.

An interesting speculation is whether the crisis that emerged in August 2007 from the extraordinary leverage (as much as twenty-five to thirty times tangible capital)[35] taken on by U.S. investment banks would have occurred had these firms remained the partnerships that they were nearly four decades earlier. The 1970 New York Stock Exchange ruling that allowed broker-dealers to incorporate and gain permanent capital seemed sensible at the time.[36] Nonetheless, as partnerships, Lehman Brothers and Bear Stearns almost surely would not have departed from their historically low leverage. Before incorporation, fearful of the joint and several liabilities to which general partnerships are subject, those entities shied away from virtually any risk they could avoid. Their core underwriting of new issues rarely exposed them for more than a few days.

To be sure, the senior officers of Bear Stearns and Lehman Brothers lost hundreds of millions of dollars from the collapse of their stocks. But none, to my knowledge, has filed for personal bankruptcy.

A Whiff of the Past

The prototype for any restoration of partnership finance in today's environment may well be my very first employer as an economist (in 1947), Brown Brothers Harriman, the oldest and largest privately owned bank in the United States. Because of its partnership structure, it refrained from engaging in much of the risk-laden investment strategies of recent years, and emerged unscathed from the crisis. Its credit ratings are high, its balance sheet highly liquid, and in recent years it has reported no nonperforming loans. This, if my memory serves me, sounds a good deal like the balance sheets that investment banks generally exhibited through most of their existence as partnerships.

To be sure, since partnerships are limited in size, to do the nation's business the economy would require a far larger set of financial institutions than exists today. While replicating the incentive structure of partnerships should be a goal whenever feasible in future reform, that goal will doubtless be compromised given that the corporate structure is seen as being required to raise capital on a scale perceived as necessary in today's global market. To eliminate moral hazard, it should not be necessary to follow Hugh McCulloch, our first comptroller of the currency, in 1863, who went somewhat over the edge in proposing that the National Bank Act "be so amended that the failure of a national bank be declared prima facie fraudulent, and that the officers and directors, under whose administration such insolvency shall occur, be made personally liable for the debts of the bank, and be punished criminally, unless it shall appear, upon investigation, that its affairs were honestly administered." Under such a regime, moral hazard surely would not exist.

Regulations Embodying a Forecast Fail with Regularity

The crisis has demonstrated that neither bank regulators nor anyone else can consistently and accurately forecast whether, for example, subprime mortgages will turn toxic or to what degree, or whether a particular tranche of a collateralized debt obligation will default, much less whether the financial system as a whole will seize up. A large fraction of such difficult forecasts will invariably be proved wrong. Regulators can sometimes identify heightened probabilities of underpriced risk and the existence of bubbles. But they almost certainly cannot, except by chance, effectively time the onset of crisis.[37] This should not come as a surprise.

A financial crisis is almost always accompanied by an abrupt and sharp decline in the price of income-producing assets. That decline is usually induced by a dramatic spike in the discount rate on expected income flows as market participants swing from euphoria to fear. Implicit in any sharp price change is that it is unanticipated by the mass of market participants, for were it otherwise, the price imbalances would have been arbitraged away.

Indeed, for years leading up to the increase in foreclosure starts that began in the summer of 2006, it was widely expected that the precipitating event of the "next" crisis would be a sharp fall in the dollar in response to the dramatic increase in the U.S. current account deficit that began in 2002. The dollar accordingly came under heavy selling pressure. The rise in the euro-dollar exchange rate from around 1.10 in the spring of 2003 to 1.30 at the end of 2004 appears to have *gradually* arbitraged away the presumed dollar trigger of the "next" crisis. The U.S. current account deficit did not play a prominent direct role in the timing of the 2008 crisis, although because of that, it may in the next.

Many analysts argue that forecasting is not required for regulation. A systemic regulator, they hold, could effectively adjust capital and liquidity requirements to match the stage of the business cycle. Properly calibrated, such requirements presumably could be effective in assuaging imbalances. But cycles are not uniform, and it is difficult to judge at any point in time exactly where we are in the cycle. For example, the low of the unemployment rate at cyclical peaks (as identified by the National Bureau of Economic Research) since 1948 has ranged between 2.6 and 7.2 percent. Would policy makers have judged a turn in the business cycle when, for example, the unemployment rate rose to 5.8 percent in April 1995, up from 5.4 percent in March of that year? In the event, the unemployment rate soon reversed itself and continued to fall for five more years.

The Federal Reserve has been concerned for years about the ability of regulatory supervisors and examiners to foresee emerging problems that have eluded internal bank auditing systems and independent auditors. I remarked in 2000 before the American Bankers Association that "in recent years rapidly changing technology has begun to render obsolete much of the bank examination regime established in earlier decades. Bank regulators are perforce being pressed to depend increasingly on greater and more sophisticated private market discipline, the still most effective form of regulation. Indeed, these developments reinforce the truth of a key lesson from our banking history—that private counterparty supervision remains the first line of regulatory defense."[38] Regrettably, that first line of defense also failed in 2008.

A century ago, examiners could appraise individual loans and judge their soundness.[39] But in today's global lending environment, how does a U.S. bank examiner judge the credit quality of, say, a loan to a Russian bank, and hence of the loan portfolio of that bank? That, in turn, would require vetting the Russian bank's counterparties and those counterparties' counterparties, all to judge the soundness of a single loan. In short, a bank examiner cannot make a judgment and neither can a credit-rating agency. How deep into the myriad layers of examination is enough for certification?

The complexity of our financial system in operation spawns, in any given week, many alleged pending crises that, in the event, never happen, and innumerable allegations of financial misconduct. To examine each such possibility at the level of detail necessary to reach meaningful conclusions would require an examination force many multiples larger than those now in place in any of our banking regulatory agencies. Arguably, at such levels of examination, sound bank lending and its necessary risk taking would be impeded.

The Federal Reserve and other regulators were, and are, therefore required to guess which of the assertions of pending problems or allegations of misconduct should be subject to full scrutiny by a regulatory workforce with necessarily limited examination capacity. But this dilemma means that in the aftermath of an actual crisis, we will find highly competent examiners failing to have spotted a Bernie Madoff. Federal Reserve supervision and evaluation is as good as it gets, even considering the failures of past years. Banks still have little choice but to rely upon counterparty surveillance as their first line of crisis defense.[40]

SIX

SCHOONER INTELLIGENCE AND THEN SOME

F̲ew Americans in the nineteenth century probably thought much about broader economywide developments, but those who did more likely than not embraced the conventional wisdom of Adam Smith and his followers: Markets were always self-adjusting and bouts of unemployment were temporary. All economic forces were inevitably pressing for full utilization of the nation's resources. If supply was excessive, prices would fall, and lower prices would galvanize suppressed demand. To be sure, much attention was given to booms and busts, but business discussions of the state of the economy overall were phrased in general, qualitative terms: "Business is depressed" or "money is very tight." Indeed, a century later researchers produced such "annals" going back to 1790.[1] We did have some hard data: The decennial census of population, which increasingly included economic data, gave analysts a general idea for census years of the size and makeup of the overall economy. But timely numbers for the American economy as a whole were scarce prior to the twentieth century.

Government was seen by almost all as having little role in the economy, other than providing security against crime and war and fostering a rule of law with particular emphasis on the protection of property rights. Prior to the Civil War, revenues to sustain these functions came almost exclusively from customs fees and some sales of public lands. The introduction of income taxes had to await the Sixteenth Amendment to the U.S. Constitution, which did not arrive until 1913.

There were no official fiscal and monetary policies in today's meaning of the terms. The government was not seen as having a role in directing macroeconomic developments. There were, of course, isolated instances in which the U.S. Treasury, and especially the Second Bank of the United States, appeared to have engaged in what we today term fiscal or monetary policy. But these actions were not systematic, and they were a very pale comparison to today's policy response to every pending shortfall of economic performance from its perceived optimum.

ECONOMIC FORECASTING AS PRIVATE ENTERPRISE

Through nearly the first century and a half of American history, such economic forecasting as occurred was chiefly a matter for private enterprise and prior to the Civil War was largely related to agriculture and shipping. What businessmen sought above all was information on the competitive forces that affected them directly. In recent decades, we have grown so accustomed to receiving news in real time that we take it largely for granted. But timely information in the first half of the nineteenth century was precious and costly to acquire in a way no one thinks about today. The thirst for information, especially from financial markets, was unquenchable in those early days of the republic. The flow of imports into the populous U.S. East Coast during that century was much less predictable, altering supply and prices, often in unexpected directions. To address that pressing issue, the *Journal of Commerce*,[2] a primary source of breaking shipping news, cleverly deployed two deepwater schooners to intercept incoming ships to get trade stories ahead of the markets. Schooner intelligence was the information high technology of its day. The wasted effort created by lack of timely information was widespread. When, for example, prior to 1850, similar commodities were traded in separate markets, with participants in each market unaware of what was concurrently happening in the others, the price-making process was decidedly suboptimal.

The major information breakthrough in the United States occurred when Samuel F. B. Morse demonstrated a commercially viable telegraph in 1844.[3] Within a decade, Morse's telegraph blanketed much of the country east of the Mississippi River and, shortly thereafter, much of populated California. But that left a large void in the center of the country. In the late 1850s, it still took more than three weeks, by a combination of telegraph and stagecoach, to convey a message from one coast to the other. Starting in 1860, the foreshortened route of the legendary Pony Express brought the transmission time to under ten days.[4] But the information innovation of the Pony Express came to an abrupt end on November 15, 1861, when the transcontinental telegraph was joined and business could communicate across the continent in a matter of minutes.

There can be little doubt that in the seventeen years between 1844 and 1861 the contribution of information transfer to national productivity was enormous. From the point of view of financial markets, however, the poor state of transatlantic communications still remained a problem. The front page of the *New York Times* of September 18, 1850, well before the laying of the transatlantic telegraph cable, was typical of that period. The *Times* announced that "the Royal Mail Steamer Europa arrived at Boston yesterday [and] her mails of September 8th reached this city at an early hour last evening. . . . The news has considerable interest."

The U.S.-European information merger finally took place (after several false starts) on July 28, 1866, when the transatlantic cable went into operation. On that day, market participants in New York, San Francisco, and London could communicate with one another nearly in real time. Those flows of information greatly facilitated more efficient pricing throughout these geographically diverse locations and undoubtedly improved the allocation of global resources.[5]

As a consequence of these remarkable new technologies, financial information dissemination finally turned national and global after the Civil War. The *Wall Street Journal* emerged in 1889, eventually becoming the icon of business news and, of course, the creator of the Dow Jones Industrial Average.

LOCATION MATTERS

Signaling to participants in financial markets in real time profitable ways to invest a society's savings enhances productivity and standards of living. But if enhanced information can add value to economic output, so too can reduced costs of transportation. Location matters. In the mid-twentieth century, steel sheets coming off a rolling mill near Pittsburgh had less economic value than the same steel entering an automotive assembly line in Detroit. Minimizing the resources necessary to move goods to final users increases net value added.

Railroad expansion and the Homestead Act,[6] during and after the Civil War, opened up the Great Plains to a massive migration that led to the more than doubling of national wheat production. Steel production, the backbone of American industrial advance in the last quarter of the nineteenth century, was propelled forward by the invention of the Bessemer furnace (1856) and the discovery in 1866 of iron ore in Minnesota's Mesabi Range. By 1890, U.S. iron ore production had quadrupled. Northern Michigan's canal locks, at Sault Ste. Marie, which opened in 1855 and linked Lake Superior and Lake Huron, enabled Mesabi ore to be shipped to the burgeoning steel industry of the Midwest, and channeled a substantial part of national grain output through the Erie Canal and on to the populous East Coast.

A century earlier, aside from coastal and river shipping, transportation was largely horse driven. Horses in those days were a major part of our economy's capital stock. They, along with oxen and mules, were the key to travel and transport until they were displaced by the railroad and motor vehicles. During the closing years of the nineteenth century, real-time economic information and efficient transportation expanded dramatically, materially reducing the costs of producing the nation's output. The building of the transcontinental railroad (completed in 1869) reduced the travel time across the continent from six months to six days. And the emergence earlier of the telegraph was to communication what the railroads became to the transportation of goods and people.

In today's world of global real-time communications and jet travel, we tend to lose sight of what was all too evident to our forebears: that the value of production depends on timely location of goods and the speed at which information on prices, interest rates, and exchange rates becomes available to producers. These seminal relationships are covered further in Chapter 8.

THE BIRTH OF THE AGE OF DATA

By the twentieth century, enough data existed to develop estimates of the size and changes in national economic output. Railcar loadings became a popular means of judging production. (I still use those data to help track industrial activity on a weekly basis.) By the 1920s, economic analysts were soon citing weekly bank clearings (excluding data from heavily financial New York City) to gauge nonfinancial economic trends nationwide. Regular "bank letters" emerged as a major source for interpretations of ongoing business activity, the forerunner of today's vast commentary on economic trends. The National City Bank letter, originated by George Roberts in 1914, and the Chase National Bank letter, originated in 1920 under the direction of Benjamin Anderson, became prominent. The *Economist*, published in London, increasingly included articles on U.S. business. The Federal Reserve started producing measures of economic activity in 1919. Successive improvements led to something close to current practice in 1927.

In the 1930s, Simon Kuznets, an economics professor at the University of Pennsylvania, filled the need for more comprehensive measures of national economic developments. Funded by the National Bureau of Economic Research (NBER), Kuznets assembled time series data on national income back to 1869, broken down by industry, final product, and use—a method significantly more detailed than any previous study had produced. His work set the standard for gross national product (GNP) measurement that was later

adopted by the Department of Commerce. Eventually ongoing estimates of national income and GNP became available. Efforts to measure the national economy got a major push from the desire to better
understand the depth and nature of the contraction of economic activity during the Great Depression, and then received another impetus from the need for planning during the Second World War.

Until the efforts by Kuznets to develop the national accounts,
most macroeconomic measurement was directed toward producing
a coherent qualitative narrative of the business cycle. That work is
most closely associated with Wesley Clair Mitchell, the first director
of research of the NBER, which was founded in 1920. Later, Mitchell
coauthored with Arthur Burns the 1946 tome *Measuring Business
Cycles,* in which they identified a large number of statistical indicators of economic expansion and contraction that enabled them to
identify the turning points of past business cycles. This was the cul-
mination of Mitchell's thirty-six-year examination of business cycles
that dated back to his highly acclaimed 1913 treatise on the subject.

Arthur Burns, under whom I studied at Columbia University in
1950, was also one of my predecessors as Federal Reserve chairman
(1970 to 1978) and as chairman of the Council of Economic Advisers (1953 to 1956). We forged a close relationship that continued for
nearly four decades. Coincidentally, in 1946, I took an undergradu-
ate course in statistics from Geoffrey Moore, a colleague of Burns's
at the NBER. Moore in later years formalized the work of Burns and
Mitchell into a series of "Leading Business Cycle Indicators," still
published by the Conference Board.[7] Business cycle turning points,
to this day, are "official" dates announced (often well after the fact)
by a committee chosen by the NBER. Those turning points have
been virtually universally accepted by both private and government
economists.

As late as 1947, 18 percent of the U.S. population still lived on farms. (Today the figure is 2 percent.) Economic forecasting was thus still heavily focused on the outlook for crops and livestock; expected crop production was dependent on the then-poorly forecastable weather, and livestock forecasts were dependent on the price of feed grains. Farm output continued to loom large even as industrial production began to take an ever increasing share of GNP in the latter part of the nineteenth century as the United States gradually wrested global economic hegemony from the United Kingdom. Day-to-day economics for a large part of the country, however, was still tied to crops, cattle, and weather that remained decidedly local.

The massive addition of railroad mileage (which peaked in 1930) helped in expanding the division of labor in the U.S. economy beyond its heavily local character during most of the nineteenth century. The development of the motor vehicle industry provided yet another large impetus to industrial activity. The motor vehicle, supported by a rapidly growing petroleum industry, carried us into post-World War II America. Of course, the value offered by ever faster travel and transport must always be balanced against the monetary and nonmonetary costs of achieving those gains. Our short-lived dalliance with supersonic aircraft demonstrated that what is technologically feasible is not always economically or politically viable.

POSTWAR YEARS

The huge statistical bureaucracy that was spawned during the New Deal, and especially during World War II, morphed into innumerable government statistical agencies after the war. Data collection systems by private research organizations such as the National Industrial Conference Board and the National Bureau of Economic Research (both dominant in the 1920s) covering trends in American business were gradually displaced by government statistical collection that previously had largely been restricted to data collected as part of the decennial census. And the census, originally limited to the population estimates required by the Constitution, gradually over the decades began to ask economically related questions. The advent of the computer and later the Internet vastly expanded the detailed statistical chronicling of America.

FIRST EXPERIENCES

My career in forecasting over the past six decades has roughly coincided with its increasing prominence in both the private and public spheres. I was one of the founding members of the National Association for Business Economics in 1959, and I became its president in 1970. I also became chairman of the Conference of Business Economists in 1974 and was scheduled to be chairman of the Economic Club of New York in 1987 had I not joined the Federal Reserve. While business economists in those early years dabbled in macroforecasting, most of us were much more heavily focused on microforecasting—for firms and for industries. Macroforecasting remained largely in the hands of academia and the government.

MACROFORECASTING

My first experience with macroforecasting was more confusing than edifying. As World War II was winding down, Keynesian macroforecasters predicted that with the end of military spending, a "mature" America, as the eminent Keynesian Harvard economist Alvin Hansen put it, would slump back into the "secular stagnation" that prevailed in the prewar world of the Great Depression.[8] Hansen's thesis was widely supported and I, as a college student, found his arguments persuasive. My first tutorial in contrary opinion, however, arose when I read an equally convincing tome by a nonacademic microeconomic practitioner, George Terborgh of the Machinery and Allied Products Institute. His book *The Bogey of Economic Maturity* was published just after the war. In the event, the U.S. economy boomed in the postwar period. The origins of that boom were probably more nuanced than Terborgh had argued and less damning to Hansen's view of the economy than might appear on the surface. But the lesson that I drew was that when it came to macroeconomic forecasts, intelligent people could make big mistakes.

TO WORK

My first job out of college in 1948 was with the highly respected business research organization known today as the Conference Board. I left the Conference Board in 1953 and joined William W. Townsend, a veteran Wall Streeter forty-one years my senior, to form a small consulting firm, Townsend-Greenspan & Company. We had a wonderful relationship for five years until he passed away in 1958. I carried on, little knowing what lay ahead. I was finally in the forecasting business, though not yet as a macroforecaster. However, my forecasting experience was widening at the industry level.

I look back fondly to the 1950s and 1960s, when I specialized in individual industry (micro) forecasting with a bit of finance thrown in. I immensely enjoyed delving into how individual markets worked at a level of detail not feasible in macromodels. In my early years, when steel was a specialty, I read all eight hundred pages of the industry bible, *The Making, Shaping and Treating of Steel*. Years later, in 1997, when appearing before a meeting of the American Iron and Steel Institute, I asserted with no small amount of nostalgia that I was the only Federal Reserve chairman who had read that book from cover to cover. Nobody challenged my assertion.

As the years rolled on, Townsend-Greenspan became quite diverse, employing micromodels to help analyze a wide variety of markets—some global—in oil, natural gas, coal, pharmaceuticals, and motor vehicles, though not yet high tech, whose prominence was still in the future. We were increasingly successful through the 1960s dispensing our brand of microeconomics, and we prospered.

The broad scope of industries we eventually covered inevitably brought us close to forecasting macrodevelopments. But using the same techniques we devised to evaluate individual industries did not always go well when expanded to the global stage. We had, for example, assumed that with global demand for petroleum products being demonstrably historically price inelastic (that is, unresponsive to price change), the rapid escalation of oil prices that emerged from the OPEC oil embargo of 1973-74 could continue for years. But oil demand, to my surprise, fell off sharply as prices rose, indicating that the demand for oil was more elastic with respect to price than I and many others had previously appreciated. The rate of oil consumption per dollar of real GDP unexpectedly turned downward, lessening pressures on inflation. I was well wide of the mark on that forecast.

COMPETITORS

Our forecasting competitors also made some massive errors from time to time. In retrospect, some of our more important collective errors reflected an incomplete understanding of the growing complexity of finance. Even the economists for banks and financial institutions did not distinguish themselves as great forecasters of either the economy or financial markets. The two presumably more sophisticated computer-based macroeconomic forecasting firms—Data Resources Inc. (commonly known as DRI) and Wharton Econometric Forecasting Associates (both founded in 1969)— had their share of forecast misses but nonetheless built formidable successful and econometric-driven firms.

DRI and Wharton Econometrics remained at the forefront of the macroeconomic forecasting business for decades. DRI was headed by Otto Eckstein, a noted Harvard professor and member of President Johnson's Council of Economic Advisers. Wharton Econometrics' roots were more academic than those of its competitor. Founded by Lawrence Klein[9] of the Wharton School, the firm grew out of the school's economics research unit. That unit had received so much sponsorship from U.S. corporations in the preceding few years that it needed a more defined structure to manage the burgeoning volume of projects coming through its doors. DRI grew until eventually merging with Wharton Econometrics in 2001.[10]

As DRI and Wharton continued to grow, so did Townsend-Greenspan and our microforecasting work.

THE FORD YEARS[11]

I carried my statistical experiences with me as I took a leave of absence from Townsend-Greenspan to become, in September 1974, chairman of President Gerald R. Ford's Council of Economic Advisers. Shortly thereafter, the economy was in trouble. New orders received by businesses for their products were declining, production began to fall rapidly, and unemployment started to increase in discontinuous jumps. That the economy was heading into a recession (if it were not in fact already in one) didn't require much debate.

As 1974 drew to a close, retail sales and home building were soft, and much of what we consider final demand was slipping. By Christmas 1974, the key question for economic policy was whether we were experiencing an inventory recession, which meant a sharp but temporary erosion in production and employment as businesses worked off excess inventories, or a far more dangerous softening in the economy brought about by a more persistent weakness in final demand. This was the burning issue for President Ford. An answer had to be formulated as quickly as feasible because the types of economic policy initiatives that one should employ depended on the answer.

For a short-term inventory recession, the optimum policy, as we saw it, was to do as little as politically possible and let the natural forces of the economy bring the recession to a halt. If it looked as though the bottom were falling out of final demand, much more drastic policy options would have to be considered. The problem was that I felt our existing economic intelligence was inadequate to monitor the rapidly weakening economy.

The political advice being offered to the administration was unequivocal. George Meany, the president of the AFL-CIO, was typical. "America is in the worst economic emergency since the Great Depression," he testified in March 1975. "The situation is frightening now and it is growing more ominous by the day. This is not just another recession, for it has no parallel in the five recessions in the post–World War II period. America is far beyond the point where the situation can correct itself. Massive government action is needed."

The Council of Economic Advisers initially didn't have even a monthly GNP series to guide policy, but starting in December 1974, we developed what amounted to a weekly GNP. It may not have passed the rigid statistical standards of the Bureau of Economic

Analysis (BEA) of the Department of Commerce, but it was more than adequate—in fact quite instrumental—in answering the question of whether we had an inventory recession, a final demand recession, or both.

While the Department of Commerce has since abandoned its weekly retail sales series, it nonetheless did yeomanlike service during that period in indicating that personal consumption expenditures were not undergoing a downward plunge. The other sectors of the economy had to be estimated more indirectly. Industry trade sources, coupled with the latest data on building permits and housing starts, outlined the residential sector for us on a weekly basis. Survey forecasts of plant and equipment, monthly new orders and shipments for machinery, data on nonresidential construction, and, with a delay, imports of capital equipment were a crude proxy for capital investment. From the unemployment insurance system we were able to get a rough indicator of aggregate hours worked, which, combined with an estimate of output per work hour (which were little more than educated guesses), yielded a rough estimate of total real GNP, which was then reconciled with its component parts.

Putting all of these statistics together indicated, with some degree of robustness, something that we knew for a fact only much later: that the rate of inventory liquidation—the gap between GNP and final demand—was exceptionally large by historic standards. That gap reflected the fact that production had been cut well below the level of final demand in order to work off the excess inventories that had accumulated. Therefore, if final demand continued to stabilize, as apparently it was doing in the early weeks of 1975, the recession's low point was close at hand and a marked rebound from the downturn was highly likely. Inventory liquidation cannot go on indefinitely. It must eventually slow, and that process closes the gap between final demand and production. It soon became clear from

the weekly insured unemployment data and several qualitative indicators that the worst was over.

At that point we could conclude that further expansionary measures would be unnecessary and in the long run could turn out to
be counterproductive.[12] Short-term emergency GNP monitoring
was no longer necessary, and the short history of the weekly GNP
came to a very creditable end.[13]

POLITICS

Looking back on that period, President Ford exhibited unusual political courage in 1975 by acquiescing in only a very small stimulus
when "conventional wisdom" at the time was for a policy response
that was far more aggressive. Ford nonetheless persevered. In much
the same way, so did Ronald Reagan by his unwavering support of
Paul Volcker and the Federal Reserve's tight money policy of 1980–82,
when political opposition to the Fed's efforts was most intense.

In any democratic society, it is very difficult for presidents, con-
gressmen, central bankers, or any other economic policy makers to
move ahead of conventional wisdom, which is often reinforced by
the pressures of herd behavior. To lead markets requires a conviction
that is rare among public officials because running ahead of markets, of necessity, implies holding a view contrary to the participants
in markets themselves, who invest real money. And in my experience, if policy makers are in a minority and wrong, they are politically pilloried. If they are in a majority, and wrong, they are tolerated
and the political consequences are far less dire. Presidents Ford and
Reagan were more politically courageous than I had realized at the
time.

When in public office myself, I became acutely aware of the pull of political bias. Politicians are driven to take a stance that (1) the outlook is unequivocally good (the result of their policies) and no change in policy stance is required (an upbeat assumption that is always acceptable, even if proved wrong), or that (2) things are not good and nothing short of *maximum* response is acceptable, for if events do in fact turn dire, half measures appear as (politically) ineffectual as no action at all.

Most nonelected public policy makers, in my experience, are able to fight this political bias but probably never fully successfully. I tried to insulate myself when I became chairman of the Council of Economic Advisers in 1974. I told Ford's chief of staff, Donald Rumsfeld, that I could not continue the practice of the CEA chairman's being the administration's chief economic spokesman, because I was certain that I would differ with, and hence could not support, some of the president's economic initiatives—the WIN (Whip Inflation Now) buttons, for example. As I requested, the task was given back to the secretary of the treasury. But much to my surprise and delight, there were very few economic initiatives pursued by President Ford with which I strongly differed.

BACK TO PRIVATE ENTERPRISE

Ford's term as president ended at noon on January 20, 1977, and I was on the noon shuttle to New York that day and by 2 p.m. was back in my old office at Townsend-Greenspan overlooking New York Bay. I immediately fell into my pregovernment routine of following and forecasting the American—and later the world—economy. In fact, my daily activities were not that much different from what I had pursued in Washington for two and a half years. The sole innovation was that I was devoting time to construct a macroeconometric model and created a computer-based forecasting system for the first time. While Townsend-Greenspan remained active in industry-based microforecasting, my efforts to develop a macroeconometric model grew out of my growing interest in understanding the workings of the economy as a whole and the complementary benefits that would flow to our industry-based work.

I joined the boards of Mobil, JPMorgan, Alcoa, General Foods, Capital Cities-ABC, and ADP. Most were, or became, clients of Townsend-Greenspan. After President Reagan was elected, I was appointed a member of his Foreign Intelligence Advisory Board, much of the time advising on the accuracy of foreign statistics, especially those of the Soviet Union. In addition, during the Reagan administration years I served on numerous presidential commissions, most important, the Social Security Reform Commission (1983).

AT THE FED

I joined the Federal Reserve in August 1987, two months before the bottom fell out of the stock market. The stock market decline of more than one fifth on October 19, 1987, created a massive contraction in market wealth. Accordingly, the Fed opened up the money spigots to full throttle. I was deeply puzzled as the weeks went on by the small effect the capital losses had on economic activity. It was not until I experienced the demise of the dot-com and housing bubbles that I finally concluded that the reason for the economy's unresponsiveness to the shock of October 19, 1987, was that the stock market investors who absorbed the huge losses at that time were wholly unleveraged.[14]

On becoming chairman of the Federal Reserve Board, I soon realized that it had as an integral part of its organization something like 250 of the most skilled PhDs in economics, certainly in the United States and very probably in the world. That group was led through my eighteen-year tenure by Mike Prell and David Stockton as the heads of the Division of Research and Statistics, and Ted Truman and Karen Johnson as heads of the board's International Division. There wasn't a question I could imagine to which I couldn't find some expert to respond somewhere in the organization. Domestic forecasting was directly or indirectly processed through the Federal Reserve's macroeconomic model of the U.S. economy, though there was extensive tweaking of the model's output to capture economic forces not captured by the model.

Despite the fact that the model missed the collapse of 2008 along with virtually all other models, its historical record has been better than most.

While decisions of the Federal Reserve's Federal Open Market Committee (FOMC) are not legally subject to alteration by any other agency of government, it has always been clear that lurking in the background is the possibility that a Congress and/or a president, irate at monetary policy, could, through legislation, alter the Fed's degree of independence, thereby crippling its effectiveness. In my eighteen and a half years as Fed chairman, I received a figurative truckload of requests from Congress urging an easier monetary policy. I don't recall ever receiving a single request urging the Fed to tighten.[15]

The Fed grew concerned in August 1991 when Senator Paul Sarbanes introduced a bill to restrict FOMC votes to governors only. This would be an irreversible step toward chronically easier monetary policy because, in my experience, the evidence *does* support the view that presidents of the Federal Reserve banks have been more "hawkish" than the presidentially appointed (and Senate confirmed) governors. The bill did not muster the support needed to become law. With the economy expanding, at times briskly, threats to the Fed's independence from mid-1991 to 2008 were minimal.

But, as I noted in the Introduction, the Fed came under increasing pressure for greater congressional oversight when, in response to the financial breakdown of 2008, it invoked the rarely used provision of the Federal Reserve Act that enables it to lend virtually without limit to virtually anyone, in the United States or abroad. The Fed lent $29 billion to JPMorgan to facilitate the bailout of Bear Stearns in March 2008. I viewed it as the Fed's acting in its long-honored role as fiscal agent of the U.S. Treasury, and would have preferred the U.S. Treasury to immediately swap Treasury securities with the Fed for its claims against JPMorgan.

When I raised the issue of the Treasury's quickly taking over the central bank's commitments, I was told by a senior Treasury official that that would have required the administration to request appropriated funds from the Congress (true)—a political nonstarter. That was a most regrettable failure, especially because it was not a matter of substance but a quirk in fiscal bookkeeping. Whether claims are held as an asset of the central bank or by a subsidiary of the U.S. Treasury makes no difference to markets or taxpayers. The liabilities of the Treasury and the Federal Reserve are both interchangeable sovereign liabilities of the U.S. government.

In the aftermath of the financial crisis, much of the Federal Reserve's independence appeared for a time to be at risk of being severely weakened. In the event, however, the response of the Congress with respect to the Federal Reserve has been fairly muted to date. The basic structure and functioning of the system has remained intact, including the voting power of the bank presidents.

SEVEN

UNCERTAINTY UNDERMINES INVESTMENT

T he first recovery out of recession I ever tracked, as a neophyte economist, was in 1949. I had recently joined the National Industrial Conference Board and every researcher in the shop was focused on an economic phenomenon no one had experienced for years. The American economy had, of course, faltered in 1945 as military spending fell sharply. But output of consumer goods surged from late 1945 through 1946 in a drive to fill inventories of such goods after years of shortages and rationing. The associated acceleration in inventory accumulation could not be sustained and production decelerated in late 1948 and 1949. The inventory recession, however, was short-lived. Marriages had hit a high of 2.3 million in 1946, sparking the beginning of the baby-boom generation a year later. Newly formed households extended the wartime boom in home ownership. In 1950, single-family housing starts rose to a then-unprecedented level of 1.2 million units. The sharp resurgence in building construction in general was a major force for re-covery. Although I couldn't know it at the time, that cyclical pattern of construction was to dominate the American business cycle for more than a half century thereafter.

In fact, private construction has been a major contributor to every recovery out of recession since 1949—except that of 2009. Both nonresidential and, especially, residential construction had impor-tant roles in the previous ten recoveries of postwar America. But construction as a share of GDP, after falling sharply in the wake of the economic collapse of 2008, has failed to fully recover since the recession officially ended in the second quarter of 2009 (Exhibit 7.1).[1] A deep-seated reluctance of business and households to invest in projects with a life expectancy, or durability, of more than twenty years (predominantly buildings) explains virtually all of the weak-ness in business activity and rise in the unemployment rate follow-ing the Lehman Brothers default in September 2008 (see Box 7.1).

BOX 7.1: THE MATURITY OF GDP

To measure the degree of aversion to investing in long-lived as-sets, I constructed a series of the average maturity or durability of personal consumption expenditures and private fixed in-vestment (combined, they compose almost nine tenths of total GDP). Software, according to the Bureau of Economic Analysis, lasts 3.5 years, nonresidential structures 38 years, and homes approximately 75 years. Where there are no official estimates, I fill in the missing numbers—mainly for short-lived services— haircuts one month, for example. Not unexpectedly, the resulting series parallels the share of construction in GDP closely. Other than construction, most components of GDP have recovered more or less as would have been expected in a "normal" recovery.

The business community's willingness to invest in fixed assets, as I noted in Chapter 4, is best captured by the proportion of liquid cash flow that nonfinancial corporate businesses *choose* to commit to difficult-to-liquidate equipment and structures—the "cap-ex ratio."[2] It is a useful measure of the degree of business confidence about the future. It doesn't rely on what people say but on what they do. In 2009, that ratio had fallen to the lowest peacetime annual level since 1938 (Exhibit 7.2).[3] More economically relevant is what market-driven forces "explain" the cap-ex ratio. As can be seen from Exhibit 7.3, the operating rate of nonfarm business is, not surprisingly, an important explanatory variable of the measured variance. Less obvious is the very significant impact of the federal deficit, adjusted for business cycle variation, on capital investment. This displacement (crowding out) by federal deficits is covered more generally in Chapter 9. Similarly, the cyclically adjusted interest rate spread between the U.S. Treasury's thirty-year and five-year obligations, currently the widest in history, reflects the degree of heightened uncertainty beyond five years and explains why long-lived assets have been so heavily discounted and scaled back in recent years.

Individuals displayed the same aversion to investing in long-term assets. Their disengagement was reflected in the sharp fall in the value of their purchases of illiquid homes[4] as a ratio of household gross savings[5] (the equivalent of business cash flow). In 2010, that ratio fell to a quarter-century low (and barely above the postwar low), reflecting the diversion of gross savings from household illiquid fixed investments to the paying down of mortgage and consumer debt and the accumulation of liquid assets. Fearful of their future finances, households curtailed committing a large part of their gross savings to an asset which might be difficult to sell, except at a loss. Signs of a recovery have been mounting as the overhang of vacant homes has been drawn down. Homes prices have recovered a third of their losses. But homeownership as share of total occupied dwelling units through the second quarter of 2013 failed to show signs of recovery.

In short, the sharp increase in the aversion to long-term asset investment risk had induced an equivalent withdrawal from long-term commitments by both households and businesses. As the global economy imploded, both groups turned on a dime and retrenched, abruptly switching from long-lived to short-term asset investment with an emphasis on cash accumulation and debt repayment.

In the boom years that preceded the crash of 2008, business executives were drawn to the higher, though riskier, rates of return on long-term investments, and households (prior to 2006) to the prospect of capital gains through homeownership.[6, 7] Price bids *above* the latest public offered price on a home were common, as anxious buyers, goaded by herd instinct, wanted to make sure they obtained the home of their choice. Homeownership rose by more than 1.3 million units annually between 2001 and 2004,[8] becoming the principal driver of the boom.

Cash flow and capital gains are the dominant factors in determining overall business capital investment. The use of cash flow is not costless, because it can be employed either to fund capital investment, to build up cash balances, or to pay down debt. The cap-ex ratio is thus significantly affected by business confidence overall, in addition to the intrinsic value of individual projects. It is high in periods of prosperity (indeed it is a major cause), and low as business slumps. The cap-ex ratio in peacetime has not exceeded 1.29 (excluding 1974) or fallen below 0.67 since 1938 (Exhibit 7.2). These data suggest that the degree of leveraging and deleveraging of investment is relatively tightly constrained, an issue I addressed in Chapter 4.

COST SAVING OUT FRONT

The significant rise in nonfinancial corporate domestic profitability from the spring of 2009 through the end of 2010 appears to have resulted almost wholly from gains in output per hour, most likely resulting from investments in cost-saving facilities.[9] Throughout the prolonged expansion in economic activity between 1983 and 2006,[10] capital investment was predominantly for risky, high leverage capacity expansion, and was expected to yield quite high rates of return—and it did. Cost-saving investments during those years, though moderately profitable, were markedly less risk laden than capacity-expanding outlays. In discussing the issue with business executives during those years of euphoria, I sensed that many were reluctant to engage in cost-saving investments in part because they viewed such investments as diverting cash flow from more profitable capacity-expanding investments. Furthermore, cost-saving investments that entailed discharging people, an unsavory activity, are largely avoided in times of boom and euphoria.

Following the crash of 2008, capacity-expanding capital investments declined sharply. But the backlog of potential cost-saving investments, forgone during the protracted economic expansion, offered significant opportunities for investment. Reluctance to shed workers vanished. The payoff was a major increase in profit margins and profits through the fourth quarter of 2010. (See Box 7.2.)

BOX 7.2: COST-SAVING INVESTMENTS ARE LESS RISKY

In contrast to an illiquid investment made to foster expansion, a cost-saving replacement of an existing facility is almost always a safer, more predictable wager, and thus requires a much lower rate of return to be authorized. The reason is that the potential increase in demand from a new market, a source of considerable uncertainty, does not enter the replacement facility calculation as it does for capacity-expanding investments. For cost-saving investments, analysts can take the level of future expected demand as a given, and evaluate only the alternatives to the existing facilities for achieving that output. The variance of returns to cost-saving investments therefore tends to be considerably less than the variance of returns to riskier expansion projects. Acceptable rates of return on cost-saving projects thus tend to be far lower than those required to greenlight an expansion.

FULL RECOVERY THWARTED

Investment in longer-lived assets (structures) was shunned. They are far more sensitive to uncertainty than investment in shorter-lived assets (equipment and software).[11] Thus, the greater the life expectancy of the investment, the higher the rate of return required to justify the outlay. That propensity has never been more pronounced, in my experience, than in the period of stunted recovery in the immediate aftermath of the crisis of 2008.

I have found the yield spread between the U.S. Treasury's thirty-year bond and five-year note to be the most useful measure of uncertainty beyond five years, and hence beyond most effects of the business cycle. It captures the degree of uncertainty associated with expectations of inflation, taxation, climate change, future technologies, and the innumerable only partially identified events that could alter investment plans over the very long run.[12]

The shunning of homeownership, long-term commercial lease rental commitments, and new factories resulted in the dramatic greater than 40 percent decline in new construction, in real terms, from its cyclical peak reached in 2006 to its trough in the first quarter of 2011. Home price increases over the past year are encouraging signs that the depressing overhang of vacant single-family homes is largely behind us. Nonetheless, single-family housing starts in June 2013 were still only a third of their 2006 peak.

THE WEDGE

The collapse in construction during the years 2008 to 2011 opened up a wide chasm in growth rates between total real GDP and real GDP, excluding private structures. The share of private fixed investment going to structures declined by more than a third from 1955 to 2011. The huge shortfall in real GDP caused by this decline (Exhibit 7.6) accounted for the equivalent of a more than 2-percentage-point rise in the unemployment rate[13] by the first quarter of 2011.[14] It has since receded in part. The implied gap represented by the ratio of employment to the civilian noninstitutional population is far more worrisome.

The effect has been to create a two-tier economy: one comprising more than 90 percent of the economy, producing goods and services with a duration of less than twenty years, and since 2009 operating at a modestly respectable rate of potential; and another comprising the remainder of economic activity—that encompassing components with a duration of more than twenty years (almost all construction)—operating at barely more than half of potential. The distortion, as I noted earlier, resulted in sharply lower expected profit returns on business structures and imputed returns on homeownership (mostly expected home price inflation) because they were discounted at the ever increasing rates associated with longer-lived assets. Those elevated discount rates sharply suppressed the level of such investment. A significant part of real GDP, in effect, has been put on the shelf and removed from prospective output. The CBO's real output gap, a measure of economic slack, is 6 percent (Exhibit 7.7). The shortfall in effective demand is also suppressing credit demand (see Chapter 12). Presumably, so long as the current degree of uncertainty persists, the disproportionate loss of long-lived asset investment is likely to frustrate full recovery.[15]

AVERSION TO INVESTMENT

That business had become markedly averse to investment in fixed long-term assets appears indisputable. The critical question is why? Although most in the business community attribute the massive rise in their fear and uncertainty to the collapse of economic activity,[16] many judge its continuance since the recovery took hold in early 2009 largely to be the result of widespread government activism in its all-embracing attempt to accelerate the path of economic recovery and regulate finance. The evidence tends to largely support the latter judgments.

POLICY DISAGREEMENTS

In these extraordinarily turbulent times, it is not surprising that important disagreements among policy makers and economists have emerged on the issue of the size of government and the extent of policy activism. Almost all agree that activist government policy was necessary in the immediate aftermath of the Lehman bankruptcy, when many critical overnight markets ceased to function, arguably a once-in-a-century event. This necessitated special policy treatment because it was a unique market breakdown that did not occur in pre-2008 financial crises where prices crashed but market structures remained intact.[17] The tendency for market prices to seek equilibrium cannot occur if market structure is dysfunctional. The powerful forces of free market adjustments fail. Under such circumstances, the substitution of sovereign credit for private credit is essential to quickly restore market structure. The U.S. Treasury's equity support of banks through the Troubled Asset Relief Program (TARP) and the Federal Reserve's support of the commercial paper market and money market mutual funds, for example, were critical in arresting the free fall. All financial markets, however, were functioning again by early 2009.

But the government activism as represented by the massive 2009 $831 billion federal program of fiscal stimulus[18] (the American Recovery and Reinvestment Act, or ARRA),[19] in addition to housing and motor vehicle subsidies, and innumerable regulatory interventions, continues to be the subject of wide debate. The evidence of this once-in-a-lifetime event is such that policy makers and economists can harbor different, seemingly reasonable expositions of the forces that govern modern economies. At root these differences reach down to the fundamentals of how economies—free market based or otherwise—operate. If common agreement on how capitalist markets function existed, I presume the differences among economic policy makers would have long since been resolved. Regrettably, that is not the case.

THE DEEP DIVIDE

Most difficult to bridge are the differences among forecasters, or economists more generally, with respect to the broad conceptual framework of models of how all the elements of a market economy interact and how the economic world works. But many, if not most, of the key interrelationships are not directly observable—such as in a simple case of the shape of supply and demand curves that create prices and interest rates. We never observe the internal market process directly because it exists only as abstract mathematical constructs of economists. Perhaps the most important divergence between "liberal" and "conservative" economic policy makers is the extent to which each view market-driven economies as competitive, flexible, and hence self-correcting. Programmed government expenditures and taxes (fiscal policy) or central bank interest rates (monetary policy) exhibit unobservable channels of causation through which these policies affect economic outcomes. In short, all forecasts of economic developments ultimately rest on how each analyst fits the *ex post* facts he or she observes in the marketplace into an all-encompassing, unobservable *ex ante* construct of the way an economy works toward its observable *ex post* data.[20]

A rare partial insight into how financial markets under extreme stress work behind the scenes became accessible as the 2008 financial crisis unfolded. A half century ago, economists had envisioned a risk distribution of market outcomes represented by a bell curve (that is, a normal distribution) whose outcomes were determined wholly by chance, such as coin tossing. Later in the postwar years, it became apparent that there were more fat-tail events—that is, extreme outcomes previously perceived as low probability—than would be expected from a normal distribution of expected outcomes. On the morning of October 19, 1987, for example, prior to the opening of the New York Stock Exchange, the probability of a more than 20 percent decline in stock prices that day, eclipsing any previous one-day collapse, was at least ten thousand to one, and more likely a million to one. It happened. And during the lead up to the crisis of 2008, many events occurred that could not easily be explained by any stretch of conventional wisdom.

Economists, chastened by many such back-to-back highly improbable economic outcomes, tilted toward assuming more fat-tail distributions. But as the years 2007 to 2009 traced out the outcomes of the crisis, we came to understand that the "extreme" tails of probability outcomes such as 2008 were downright obese—"highly improbable" catastrophic market breakdowns had begun to happen too often. Examination of the data has altered previous views of the way financial risk operates—mine in particular.

It is dismaying when the real world runs counter to a cherished paradigm or, in the words of Thomas Huxley, the famous nineteenth-century biologist, commits "the slaying of a beautiful hypothesis by an ugly fact."[21] Physical scientists go through the same routine as economists and other social scientists, but the world with which they deal is far more stable and predictable than the economic world.[22] The vagaries of human nature do not affect the physical world. The laws of physics, for example, once identified, rarely have to be revised. Yet there are still famous differences among physicists. Albert Einstein never felt comfortable with the probabilistic nature of quantum mechanics. As he famously said, "God doesn't play dice with the universe." He sought certainty in the world, not probability.

ENTER POLITICS

As I've noted, at the very center of the postcrisis political confrontations is the debate over whether free markets are ultimately self-correcting, or as a large number, perhaps a majority, of economists and policy makers currently believe, the shortfalls of faulty human nature–driven markets require significant regulatory direction, periodic fiscal stimulus, and a vast safety net for those who fall through the cracks of a largely self-regulated market system.

Stock prices were largely left free to seek their own level as the 2008 crisis unfolded.* To be sure, the Federal Reserve's more than doubling of its balance sheet in the fall of 2008 (QE1) appears to have lowered real long-term interest rates that, other things equal, would tend to lower the earnings yield and raise the price of common stocks. However, given the already nearly unprecedented heights of economic angst following the Lehman default, no further explanation of this classic selling climax and subsequent price rebound seems necessary. Nonetheless, having observed the impact during the years 2000 to 2005 of falling long-term interest rates on the subsequent global asset price boom (see Chapter 3), there is always doubt in such matters.

The month-long stock selling climax that ended on March 9, 2009, absorbed the market disequilibria and defined the price bottom.[23] Unencumbered, the price level has since doubled and re-

---

*In late 2008 the SEC published a list of stocks that could not be shorted. Its effect was minimal.

couped all of its losses from its historic peak of October 2007. The extent to which markets, if allowed to adjust, will self-correct is at the core of the political debate. Free market imbalances are addressed either by allowing markets to correct themselves through a selling climax or through government intervention that delays the adjustment and, from my perspective, makes the ultimate adjustment even more problematic. In my experience, extensively regulated markets and those rife with crony capitalism have eviscerated, or at a minimum, significantly impaired, the automatic stabilizers of the market process.

SELLING CLIMAX LIMITS

Government policies that endeavor to prevent market liquidation are based on the implicit premise that market declines not countered by intervention would feed on themselves virtually without limit. That would be true if fear could rise indefinitely in a self-reinforcing cycle. But it does not. Accordingly, markets do not fall indefinitely, as the stock market selling climax of March 2009 and the experience of the Resolution Trust Corporation two decades earlier demonstrate. At the height of a fear-driven selling climax, asset prices invariably fall to levels consistent with a level of extreme fear that our psyches rebel against and to which they eventually adjust. As I note in Chapter 4, fear inevitably lessens and stock prices rebound. Were it otherwise, markets would not recover as rapidly as they do from "oversold" bear market lows.

Today, the political pressure on government officials to respond to every perceived shortcoming in economic performance has become overwhelming. I observed it build over my more than two-decade stretch in public office. Even if policy makers acknowledge that allowing market declines to exhaust themselves may indeed return markets to balance, there always exists *some* uncertainty of how long an unimpeded market decline will persist or how deep it will go.[24] Accordingly, in recent years policy always has seemed biased toward activism when, more often than not, allowing markets to rebalance and heal is the most prudent policy.

It has been my regrettable experience that the political response to policy makers' actions heavily biases the policy makers toward catering to short-term benefits, largely disregarding long-term costs. As I note in Chapter 6, policy makers who intervene to support market prices but do not succeed are nonetheless praised for trying. But the policy maker who allows markets to liquidate and prices to fall is less fondly treated, even if, as Paul Volcker, my predecessor as chairman of the Federal Reserve Board, experienced in 1981, he is vindicated in the end. And as I also note in Chapter 6, President Gerald Ford, who took a principled stand against more-than-token intervention to counter the sharp recession of 1975, was accused by AFL-CIO head George Meany, just as the American economy was finally stabilizing, of reckless policies. So was the Resolution Trust Corporation when it allowed the real estate properties of defaulted savings and loans (S&Ls) to be sold at auction in 1989 at "bargain" prices far below their price at mortgage origination. While that act was instrumental in saving American taxpayers tens of billions of dollars, it was quickly forgotten.[25]

THE CONSEQUENCES

Preventing overbought markets (bubbles) from liquidating will create an overhang of market offers of undesired inventories in both product and financial markets that frustrates a normal rebound out of recession, or worse. Until, for example, the 2006 glut of single-family vacant homes for sale began to shrink substantially, U.S. home prices had difficulty recovering from their suppressed levels. It is hard to visualize a housing recovery in which higher home prices do not play a, if not *the*, key role. I suspect that had the government stood by and allowed foreclosures to proceed without mediation, the housing crisis more than likely would have been deeper but far shorter. I have always thought that giving cash assistance or a voucher to financially troubled homeowners is a far more efficient policy than distorting the foreclosure process. It is revealing that more than 60 percent of mortgages modified in the third quarter of 2008 re-defaulted within a year of modification. Despite the rise in prices, however, the re-default rate, after declining, has apparently remained above 20 percent (Exhibit 7.8).

But while bailouts of financial institutions and even intervention into mortgage markets could, with a stretch, be nonprecedential, the bailout of General Motors and Chrysler was clearly new ground.[26] There are now no areas of the economy that are beyond the responsibility of the federal government. Had General Motors and Chrysler been forced into bankruptcy court, union contracts would almost surely have been revised, and the companies financially restructured and doubtless scaled down. The number of dealerships would have been reduced, and I have no doubt that non-American car brands would have gained market shares. That would have meant a larger share of foreign nameplate vehicles assembled in nonunionized American plants. But aggregate purchases by American buyers probably would have changed only marginally, if at all, and domestic automakers' balance sheets would have emerged unencumbered by toxic debt.

There is, regrettably, an understandable considerable difficulty in allowing icons that have historically been the symbols of America's rise to global economic hegemony to fall by the wayside. We cannot emotionally easily countenance the demise of so symbolic an American icon any more than we would contemplate the obsolescent grandeur of the U.S. Capitol being replaced with a modern building. But American Woolen and Kodak, icons in their day, scaled back without economic disruption. Of the original names that made up the Dow Jones Industrial Average more than a century ago, only General Electric is still on the list.

As I discussed in Chapter 5, because firms designated as "systemically important" are accorded an implicit government guarantee of their liabilities, investors perceive those firms as near riskless and grant them interest rate subsidies. That accords them a competitive advantage not achieved through enhanced productivity. Savings are being directed to the politically powerful, not the economically efficient. Future productivity gains and standards of living are being put at risk.

HISTORY

Between the end of the Civil War and World War I, America was plagued with financial crises that at the time seemed everlasting. To this day there is a dispute as to whether the waves of crisis were fostered by the inelastic currency that arose from provisions of the National Bank Act of 1863. But in all cases, we liquidated the toxic assets and returned to full employment, often quickly.[27] These crises are the regrettable result of our natural propensity to swing between euphoria and fear. And short of going to a rigid collectivized (and stagnant) economy, we have never been able to keep animal spirits from swinging between extremes.

I do not doubt that in the post-2008 climate of severe uncertainty, demand for longer-lived assets—homes—was always doomed to be depressed. But if policy activism had not been so unremitting, I strongly suspect that the pall of uncertainty would have lifted sooner and the severe discounting of long-term investments would have been far less—and it would have long since been over.

The major political problem in allowing markets to liquidate is that this was precisely the remedy for recessions supported by Andrew W. Mellon, President Herbert Hoover's long-serving secretary of the Treasury. Because he is so associated with the boom and bust of the 1920s, such advice is promptly rejected.

POLICY ACTIVISM

Policy activism is the propensity of government, by fiscal, monetary, or regulatory policies, to alter the path of market outcomes from what would otherwise emerge from the unrestrained interplay of competition. To those policy makers who extol competition, activism threatens to widen the variance of expected outcomes of the projections of rate of return on prospective new private investments for both business and households. But perhaps just as inhibiting is the threat of arbitrary intervention perpetually overhanging a market.

To those policy makers who view competitive markets less benignly, governments must be on alert to address "market failures." The massive stimulus program initiated in early 2009 (the American Recovery and Reinvestment Act), the bailout of General Motors and Chrysler, the extensive and largely futile effort to prevent the home mortgage foreclosure process from running its course, and the vast and troubled financial regulations mandated by the Dodd-Frank Act are prime examples. The Dodd-Frank Act restructures the financial system presumably based on how legislators believe markets should work. And indeed it largely provides goals of regulation to be implemented. But in the three years since the act was signed into law in 2010, it has become apparent that its remedies to the undisputed overreach of financial institutions have been based on an uninformed view of the role of finance and how it actually works. What is most disturbing about the current period is that it echoes the policy disputes of the 1930s.

NEW DEAL ACTIVISM

While the degree of activism brought on by the New Deal was far more intense than any of the interventions of the last five years, there are distinct parallels in initiatives to jump-start the private economy. The Great Depression's National Industrial Recovery Act (NIRA) viewed excessive competition as the cause of falling prices, and the Roosevelt administration did everything it could think of in response, from raising the price of gold to propping up crop prices (the Commodity Credit Corporation). As Harold Cole and Lee Ohanian point out,[28] the NIRA attempted to cartelize firms composing four fifths of private nonagricultural employment. It led to huge economic distortions until it was declared unconstitutional by the Supreme Court in May 1935. But the level of economic rigidity remaining until wartime subjected virtually the whole U.S. economy to government controls. From 1932 to 1940, the monthly unemployment rate averaged 19 percent and never fell below 11 percent. Nonfinancial business capital investment as a percent of cash flows fell to 48.2 percent in 1934 and 59.8 percent in 1938 but rallied in 1937 and 1941. (For 2012, the percentage, by comparison, was 79.6 percent.) The business cycle had ups and downs in the 1930s, but the level of activity for the decade, on average, was suppressed, a state consistent with today's persistently high degree of risk aversion to illiquid long-term asset investment. The enemy of economic recovery, now as then, is uncertainty.

EIGHT

PRODUCTIVITY:
THE ULTIMATE MEASURE
OF ECONOMIC SUCCESS

The early stages of what became known as the dot-com boom were evident in late 1993. By February 1994, we at the Federal Reserve had become sufficiently concerned about the pace of the expansion and the associated risks of inflation that we decided to press down on the monetary brakes. We continued to tighten for a year with some success. Our cumulative increase of 3 percentage points in the federal funds rate brought a nascent stock market boom to a halt (temporarily, as it would turn out), and we were preparing ourselves for the first soft landing in our collective monetary policy memory. "Soft landing" is a term that economists have borrowed from aviation to describe the aftermath of a period of monetary tightening that would ease an economy onto a glide path of noninflationary growth. The Federal Reserve's previous experiences with aggressive tightening had often led to recession or, even worse, to a recession that did not succeed in restraining inflation.

In July 1995, we lowered the Fed funds rate by 25 basis points, and did so again in both December 1995 and January 1996 when we read the data as suggesting that a soft landing was taking hold. But no sooner had we stopped patting ourselves on the back for adroit monetary policy than we were confronted with a seeming reeemergence of the boom. By the spring of 1996, there was clear evidence that cyclically sensitive manufacturing activity was picking up, and the pressing question of whether renewed policy restraint was warranted was again on the table. The unemployment rate had been falling since mid-1992. Wage rates and prices, however, remained remarkably subdued—a condition that ran contrary to prevailing policy wisdom that as labor markets tightened and unemployment fell below the presumed "natural rate" of 5.5 percent, inflationary pressures would mount. They didn't.

By late 1997, wage rates finally did begin to accelerate but price inflation remained contained despite stable corporate profit margins.[1] The only way that could happen was for output per hour to rise at least in tandem with wage costs. Rising productivity and profit margins would also explain why new orders for capital equipment and software had risen persistently from 1993 forward. It had been my experience in the private sector that such a prolonged upswing in orders and capital spending would not have continued unless corporate management had judged the rate of return on newly installed equipment to be attractive and the improvements in productivity as real and sustainable.

Given stable prices, rising wage rates, and expanding profit margins, output-per-hour growth, by my arithmetic, almost surely had to be accelerating.[2] The problem was that the published statistics gave no hint of an acceleration in productivity. The most reliable independent measure of output per hour, our conventional proxy for productivity, was that produced by the Bureau of Labor Statistics (BLS). Between the fourth quarter of 1993 and the fourth quarter of 1995, nonfarm productivity exhibited a tepid annual growth rate of only 0.75 percent.[3]

My optimistic productivity message was thus not universally cheered at the Federal Open Market Committee (FOMC). As Governor Larry Meyer years later described the atmosphere in the meetings, "the staff were skeptical, and they didn't mind saying so. For example, at the August 1996 meeting, Mike Prell[4] bluntly told the Committee: 'There simply isn't any statistical evidence to suggest that productivity is taking off.' I wouldn't say the staff abandoned the Chairman in this matter, but they came close."[5] The FOMC remained split on this issue for quite some time. Our monetary policy, of course, had to consider whether inflation was under control. If inflation was viewed as a looming threat, the FOMC would need to contemplate tightening policy, perhaps aggressively. This was especially true given that a number of members of the FOMC noted that the Fed had made considerable progress on the maximum employment component of its dual mandate.

Finally, our path became unambiguous in early 1997 when the BEA's nonfarm business productivity measure finally accelerated, reflecting the realities of a burgeoning technological boom. The federal funds rate reached 6 percent in February 1995, and for the next five years it fluctuated between 4.75 percent (November 1998) and 6.5 percent (May 2000). Inflation remained subdued over this period and the unemployment rate continued to decline. It finally dipped below 4 percent in April 2000, without inflation visibly gaining traction.

The acceleration of productivity was obviously a welcome development after its lackluster performance in the 1970s and 1980s. As financial markets digested the accompanying implications for the expected path of earnings, stock prices provided a further boost to the economic expansion. However, as so often occurs, animal spirits transformed a rational capitalization of improving fundamentals into an "irrational exuberance" that ultimately manifested itself in the so-called dot-com bubble. Even the substantial acceleration of productivity could not fulfill the unrealistic expectations for earnings growth that had become embedded in equity valuations.

So eventually, the dot-com bubble burst, resulting in a substantial decline in equity markets and household net worth. Nonetheless, the macroeconomic consequences of that destruction of perceived wealth were, by late 2000 and into 2001, surprisingly muted.[6] Indeed, the accompanying recession, at that point, was rated as the mildest in postwar history.

THE LONGER VIEW

Productivity is arguably the most central measure of the material success of an economy. The level of productivity ultimately determines the average standard of living, and is a defining characteristic that separates the so-called developed world from the developing world. Innovation, a critical determinant of productivity's rate of growth, reflects how quickly new ideas are effectively implemented and absorbed into the production process.

Economists' main problem with productivity is that it has been devilishly difficult to forecast. Conventional forecasting wisdom with respect to productivity growth is probably best epitomized by the five-year forecasts of the Congressional Budget Office. Exhibit 8.1 shows clearly that these five-year projections of output per hour are more accurately characterized as moving averages of the *recent past*.[7] Merely projecting that the future will replicate the recent past may not be very edifying. But there are nevertheless some important stabilities in long-term trends in productivity, as I note later, apparently largely rooted in human nature and culture,[8] that afford us some confidence in using the past to predict the future.

Between 1870 and 1970, America's annual rate of increase in nonfarm output per worker hour, the key measure of the productivity of our nonfarm workforce,[9] averaged 2.2 percent.[10] Given that the accumulation of knowledge is largely irreversible, we would expect a persistently rising level of productivity.[11] And, indeed, over any fifteen-year period since 1889 (the first year of annual data), average yearly output-per-hour growth has never exceeded 3.2 percent or fallen below 1.1 percent (Exhibit 8.3). But why does the long-term growth ceiling in the United States seem limited to a 3 percent rate, and why was long-term productivity growth relatively stable for more than a century?

THE MAGIC 3 PERCENT?

With the exception of the immediate postwar years,[12] output-per-hour growth in most advanced economies appears to have been subject to the 3 percent growth ceiling.[13] But why couldn't the current level of technology and productivity have been achieved in, say, 1960, rather than a half century later? The answer appears to be that we human beings are apparently not smart enough to have produced such a leap.

I suspect that the relatively stable rate of growth of productivity that we observe from 1870 to 1970, despite the persistent degree of market churning, reflected a combination of the long-term unchanging inbred rate of time preference, which sets the time horizon for our innovative initiatives, and our inbred propensity toward optimism and competitiveness. They, I assume, are capped by the upside limit of human capability to create and apply knowledge over the long run. Certainly there is nothing to demonstrate a major difference during the past two millennia in the degree of intelligence of, for example, Euclid, Newton, and Einstein, the icons of outer-edge human intelligence of their respective eras.[14] Technology may accumulate, but given the apparent ceiling to intelligence, the pace of knowledge accumulation, of necessity, is limited.

MULTIFACTOR PRODUCTIVITY

The widely accepted paradigm for evaluating and projecting productivity is called multifactor productivity (MFP).[15] Simply put, MFP is a change in output that cannot be accounted for by changes in the combined inputs of labor and capital. It is presumed that an increase in MFP is owed mainly to improvements in technical efficiency and to the new ideas that lie behind those improvements. We use the term "technology," or, broadly speaking, applied "innovation." MFP will also reflect increased timeliness in the transportation of people and goods; advances in communication capabilities; improved efficiencies in the use of energy, materials, and services; economies of scale; better ways to organize production; and finally, the increasingly important use of robots that sustain the level of production but significantly decrease the number of *human* hours required to produce the output. It would be useful if we could quantify these cost reductions in the official estimates of MFP. (Not to be readily dismissed as a factor is measurement error. It can sometimes be disturbingly large.) Applied innovation is a major component of output per hour, as can be seen in the equation in endnote 19 of this chapter.

My former colleagues at the Federal Reserve, in one of their many related analyses, documented the prominent role of both the production of information technologies and their increasing use in the acceleration of labor productivity between 1995 and 2006.[16, 17]

THE METRICS

Multifactor analysis can be employed to forecast business output and output per hour given projections of hours, an adjustment to labor quality (the educational attainment of the workforce, for example), capital services,[18] and finally the extent of applied innovation (MFP).[19] Capital expenditures, their level and mix, and applied innovation statistically prove to be the most important determinants of labor productivity growth.

The share of GDP devoted to capital investment peaked in the late 1970s at around 25 percent and has since trended steadily downward to a low of 18 percent in 2009. The major reason, as I note in Chapter 9, is the dramatic decline in the rate of domestic savings, the prime source of funding of domestic capital expenditures (along with borrowed savings from abroad). The trade-off between social benefits (mainly Social Security, Medicare, and Medicaid) and savings, as I demonstrate in Chapter 9, is almost a dollar-for-dollar substitution of consumption[20] for gross domestic savings. That detracts from the funding of capital investments, and hence from output per hour.

The diversion of the flow of savings of households from capital investment to consumption depressed the rate of growth of the stock of productive capital, a key component of productivity growth. As I note in Chapter 9, the pace of growth of output per hour has slowed since the mid-70s, but remained at a still respectable 2 percent per year until 2010, when it dipped to a less than 1 percent annual rate.

MFP grew at an annual rate of 2.1 percent between 1947 and 1965. That pace almost surely reflected the buildup of a large backlog of applications of technological insights that could not be applied during the suppressed environment of the 1930s, and, of course, during World War II. Apparently having run through the significant backlog of new ideas, the process significantly slowed its pace of rise from 1965 to 1995. But for the next decade it regained momentum as the Internet's role in information technologies during the dot-com boom broadened, and the pace of new insights and applications accelerated at close to the early post–World War II level. The crisis of 2008, of course, put a hold on many (but by no means all) innovative applications.

FORECASTING INNOVATION

Forecasting innovation is particularly challenging largely because innovation (an idea or application of an idea), by definition, is something which nobody has previously discovered. In that sense, innovation is presumably unforecastable. It is very easy in retrospect to identify the emergence of telegraphy as a major innovation in the nineteenth century. But would it even have been imaginable to anticipate it before the identification of electricity? Certainly before the electrical properties of silicon were discovered, no one would have imagined its monumental implications for the future.[21]

I suspect that the only forecasting assistance historical data can offer is to spell out the ranges of growth in innovation, say, over the past half century. We can generalize that the necessary environmental conditions for the blossoming of innovation are the enforcement of property rights and other political and economic conditions that have proved conducive to innovation. Propensities to innovate can be thwarted by culture, religion, or state repression.

EBBS AND FLOWS OF PRODUCTIVITY AT HOME AND ABROAD

For much of the near century and a half that U.S. output per hour has been more or less reliably measured, shortfalls in productivity growth have been followed by catch-ups that brought its level back to its long-term trend. But the unprecedented slowdown in savings starting in 1965 eventually funded a persistent below-average growth of capital investment and hence of nonfarm output per hour between 1973 and 1995, with estimates of growth closer to a 1.4 percent annual rate than to the average annual rate between 1870 and 1970 of 2.2 percent.

Throughout much of the 1970s and 1980s, Japan was heralded as the economy that would soon displace the United States as the world's productive powerhouse. Herman Kahn's highly influential 1971 treatise *The Emerging Japanese Superstate: Challenge and Response*[22] was close to subsequent conventional wisdom. That perception was reinforced by the relatively lackluster performance of productivity in the U.S. economy and the apparent dynamism and productiveness of Japan. Lying ahead was the dot-com dynamism of the United States and the prolonged post–1989 stagnation of Japan.

Now there is an emerging belief that China will soon be displacing the United States not only in the level of GDP but eventually even in per capita GDP as well. That conclusion is by no means self-evident. China's spectacular growth in recent years rests on technology largely borrowed from the rest of the world. Little to date, apparently, has been homegrown. China's businesses have yet to demonstrate a capacity for innovation on a par with those in many advanced economies, most notably those of the United States. In a November 2011 study, Thomson Reuters identified what it saw as the one hundred most innovative global companies. No Chinese company was on the list; America had forty.[23] As I note in Chapter 10, it is not surprising that an authoritarian state that discourages political and other nonconformity will not sanction a climate that fosters ideas wholly out of the mainstream. Yet such ideas are the defining characteristic of innovation. It is precisely those who tread beyond the bounds of conventional behavior who innovate. Yes, growth in Chinese output per employee is reported at a stunning 9.5 percent annual rate between 1990 and 2011. But much, if not most, of Chinese innovative technology originated in developed-country firms. China is already running into rising real wage costs that have significantly narrowed their competitive advantage in global manufacturing. Lurking in the background is a rapidly growing robotics industry that substitutes low-"wage" robots[24] for people. Even China will have trouble competing with them. As Japan found out, forecasting innovation is precarious.

IT TAKES TIME

Most productivity increases are incremental. It takes time for new ideas to filter through the process of trial and error and meet the test of the marketplace before adding to the level of a nation's capacity to produce.[25]

Forecasting productivity from the pace of new inventions and the level of patents has always proved challenging (see Box 8.1). Only if an economic infrastructure is ready to capitalize on an innovation can that innovation percolate up through the economy to add to productivity. According to economic historian Paul David of Stanford University, writing in 1989, it often takes a number of decades for major innovations to be applied in a manner that increases output per hour. As I noted in *The Age of Turbulence*, following Thomas Edison's spectacular illumination of lower Manhattan in 1882, it took some four decades for even half of the nation's factories to be electrified. Electric power did not fully exhibit its superiority over steam power until a whole generation of multistory factories was displaced after World War I. David explains vividly what caused the delay. The best factory buildings of the day were poorly designed to take advantage of the new technology. They ran on so-called group drives, elaborate arrangements of pulleys and shafts that transferred power from a central source—a steam engine or water turbine—to machines throughout the plant. To avoid power losses and breakdowns, the lengths of the shared drive shafts had to be limited. This was best achieved when factories rose vertically, with one or more shafts per floor, each driving a group of machines.[26]

Simply substituting large electric motors to power the existing drive shafts, even when feasible, did not improve productivity very much. Factory owners realized that electricity's revolutionary potential would require far more dramatic change: Power delivered by wire made central power sources, group drives, and the very buildings that housed them obsolete. Because electricity opened the way to equipping each production machine with its own small, efficient motor, sprawling single-story plants came into vogue. In them, machinery could readily be arranged and rearranged for greatest efficiency and materials could be moved about with greater ease. But abandoning city factories and moving to the wider spaces of the countryside was a slow, capital-intensive process. That was why, David explains, electrifying America's factories took dozens of years. But eventually millions of acres of one-story plants embedding electric, motor-driven power dotted America's midwestern industrial belt, and growth in output per hour finally began to accelerate.

In more microexamples of absorption delay, color fashions in everyday clothing did not become widespread until vat dying became commonplace in the 1930s, and, of course, truck transportation did not take on its full potential until a highway system was created to facilitate its commerce after World War II. Moreover, highways fostered the development of suburbs that, in turn, improved the productivity of land use. The value of land almost always rises as its use shifts from sparsely settled rural environments to today's population concentrations in urban areas. Denser populations tend to further refine the division of labor and, accordingly, boost incomes and increase the value of the land on which people live.

Thus, much of today's level of productivity rests on insights that were spawned decades ago but could not be capitalized upon until other insights facilitated their integration. A vivid example of back-logged innovation emerging as increased output per hour occurred following the sharp contraction in economic activity that resulted from the debacle of 2008, as I explain in Chapter 7. The surge in output per hour from the first quarter of 2009 through the first quarter of 2010 reflected the dramatic crisis-driven efforts to cut costs and concentrate on cost-saving capital investment, a backlog of which had been built up during the boom years when capital investment was primarily dedicated to expanding markets rather than reducing costs (see Chapter 7).

BOX 8.1: PATENTS

What I find puzzling is that we gain so little insight into productivity forecasting from data on patents that the federal government has tabulated since 1790. Patents unquestionably cover much of the innovation that in the end is reflected in gains in productivity. Accordingly, I would have expected that they would be a useful indicator of forthcoming productivity gains. The result of the analysis that I exhibit in Statistical Appendix 8.1 is disappointing: Patent issuance parallels but does not, as might have been expected, statistically lead new additions to the level of productivity.

ENTER FINANCE

The speed of absorption of innovations often depends importantly on the efficiency of financial markets in signaling which of a whole array of prospective investments will add to productivity and hence profitability.

As I noted in Chapter 5, the purpose of finance is to direct the scarce savings of a society, including depreciation plus borrowed savings from abroad,[27] if any, to our most potentially productive intellectual and physical investments. (In Chapter 10 I address the determinants of savings and the culture that breeds it.) When competition is pervasive and allowed to function,[28] those investments with the highest rates of prospective return and least variance of expected profit also promise to contribute the most to growth in output per hour. It is the gap between the level of output per hour embodied in new capital investment, presumably employing up-to-date technologies, and that of obsolescent, low-productivity facilities (that are gradually being retired) that over time engenders net gains in average output per hour, and hence increases in real per capita income and standards of living.

HOW IS IT DONE?

But how do profit-seeking savers or their surrogates, such as hedge funds or banks, know where to place new savings? They are guided by the signals of the marketplace: stock prices, asset prices more generally, interest rates, exchange rates, and the whole panoply of information that pours out of research departments of financial firms, governments, and academia. The market signals, in turn, are driven by the chronic imbalances endemic to financial markets. These imbalances arise because some prospective investments are being inadequately financed relative to competing investments with similar risk profiles, and hence the latter yield abnormally (uncompetitive) high profits in the marketplace. Rising stock prices, reflecting a shortage of invested capital relative to profitable performance, attract new capital inputs until demand to acquire the stock of a company is sated as the company becomes adequately funded. "Overvalued" and hence overcapitalized companies, on the other hand, will yield low prospective rates of profit until the excess capital is withdrawn and presumably reinvested in more promising ventures.[29]

These investments address the initial capital misallocation and, because of the associated expanding or diminishing returns, continually adjust the investment's prospective rate of return on equity to competitive levels. This complex process is constantly churning as new information on supply, demand, and price emerges out of the ongoing competitive trading of markets and the arbitraging of all prospective rates of return (adjusted for risk) toward equality. That equality, however, is never fully achieved because new forces invariably intercede before the adjustment is complete.

The equilibria that markets are seeking and generally closely approximate are those governed by human propensities best described as an admixture of neoclassical and behavioral economics. While over the long run, market prices do seem to converge on values defined by humans' rational long-term self-interests, as described by the neoclassical school, it is decidedly not necessarily so in the short run.[30]

Indeed, as the episode of the dot-com bubble made clear, on occasion, euphoria combined with herd behavior can result in financial markets that for a time become divorced from realistic evaluations of future corporate earnings prospects. During this period of dot-com euphoria, funds flowed to virtually any activity with a "dot-com" affixed to its name, whether or not the firm had a reasonable and realistic business plan and any significant prospect for making a profit in the foreseeable future.

The dot-com productivity acceleration, as my colleagues at the Federal Reserve Board demonstrated,[31] was primarily driven by major advances in information-processing equipment and software. First, the industry itself exhibited outsized gains in output per hour. But of even greater importance, the rapid application and absorption of such technologies had a major effect on virtually every niche and corner of American business and on households as well. Fed economists Stacey Tevlin and Karl Whelan[32] have demonstrated the implications for productivity measurement of the rapid declines in prices of information-processing equipment and software, especially computers. After a long period of relative price stability, prices fell at a 1.5 percent annual rate between 1980 and 1985, accelerating to a 3.9 percent rate decrease between 1985 and 2010, then slowing to a less than 1 percent annual rate of decline during the last two years (Exhibit 8.4). If profit margins in the production of information-processing equipment and software were essentially stable, as they apparently were, unit costs would, of necessity, be falling pari passu. Adjusting for wage rate changes, that implies an extraordinary rise in productivity. The dot-com boom was very largely pure innovation and would be expected to enhance MFP, as it did. Price declines for information-processing equipment and software have correlated remarkably well with MFP over the last three decades (Exhibit 8.4).

Innovation, as a driver of productivity, has always been a key component of rising output per hour, though not always as dramatically as was evident in the few years of the dot-com boom. Manufacturing technologies that reduce the rate of scrappage and rejects and hence reduce materials input, for example, are an insufficiently heralded source of lowered unit cost and rising output per hour. Prior to the 1950s, for example, steel mill products' yield from ingot averaged less than 75 percent. Ingots had to be cropped before entering the rolling mills. But with the advent of continuous casting, "home scrap" (that is, internally generated scrap) has fallen dramatically.

Advances in the speed and efficiency of the transportation of goods increase GDP. Aluminum plate is more valuable at an aerospace assembly plant than at the plate mill. The spread in the 1870s between the prices of cattle at ranches in Texas and those at the railheads in western Kansas narrowed sharply with the substitution of rail transport for expensive, legendarily long cattle drives. With the onset of transcontinental railroads, the time it took to move goods from the East Coast to the West Coast fell from six months to six days.[33] The number of workers required to move a ton of freight one mile fell materially, a development that added significantly to lower costs and hence higher national value added.

Aside from the production and transportation of goods, remarkable innovative advances in business services also added importantly to output. Quickened communication of information that facilitates the arbitraging of markets improves the accuracy of the vast system of relative prices, which, in turn, assists in directing our scarce savings into the most efficient technologies. As noted in Chapter 6, with the introduction of effective telegraphy (1844) and especially the transatlantic cable (1866), the cost and timeliness of acquiring information that determined key decisions in producing and moving a good to its final place of consumption fell sharply, and standards of living rose commensurately.

Perhaps most important, information significantly lessens the amount of real resources required to produce any level of output because it reduces short-term uncertainties. Before this generation's revolution in information availability, most twentieth-century short-term business decision making had been hampered by uncertainty created by inherent delays in the transfer of information. In college I worked part time at a department store to make ends meet. I was astonished by how many people and how much time the store employed trying to keep track of inventories. By the time the inventory count was completed, it was already out of date. Owing to such paucity of timely knowledge of customers' needs and of the real-time size and location of inventories, businesses generally required substantial programmed redundancies in the use of energy, materials, and people to function effectively. Because decisions were made from information that was days or even weeks old, production planning required costly inventory safety stocks to respond to the inevitable unanticipated and misjudged levels of demand. Through most of the twentieth century, determination of the amount of inventories on hand often required laborious and time-consuming counting of individual items. Inventories often built up for weeks before management had become sufficiently informed to curtail production.

Today, executives have real-time accounting for inventories, receivables, and payables, and can act promptly to address emerging imbalances.[34] Clearly, the remarkable surge in the availability of real-time information in recent years has enabled business management to remove large swaths of inventory safety stocks (thanks to just-in-time inventorying) and programmed redundancies of labor. That means fewer goods and worker hours are absorbed by activities that, while perceived one or two generations earlier as necessary insurance to sustain valued output, in the end, most often produce nothing of enduring value themselves.[35]

These developments emphasize the essence of information technology: the expansion of knowledge and its obverse, the reduction of short-term uncertainty. As a consequence, risk premiums that were associated with many forms of business activities have permanently declined, reducing the amount of capital required to back up the information systems. In short, information technology raises output per hour for the total economy, in part by reducing hours worked on activities needed to guard productive processes against the unknown and the unanticipated.

It's worth singling out one innovation that both increases the effectiveness of labor hours and at the same time enhances the climate-related quality control of output: air-conditioning. Willis Carrier introduced the first modern form of air-conditioning in 1902, and it quickly widened location options for plants and revolutionized manufacturing and commerce in America's South.

THE PHYSICAL DOWNSIZING OF OUTPUT

For generations Americans had reveled in acres upon acres of massive motor vehicle assembly plants, ever taller skyscrapers, enormous dams, and longer bridge spans. I never ceased being in awe of America's industrial might in the 1950s as I drove along the south shore of Lake Michigan toward Chicago, passing one huge steel mill complex after another. But running parallel, starting in the early postwar years, was a growing view that ever larger and more resource intensive production had an upside limit. I recall walking the streets of downtown Pittsburgh in the late 1950s with coke oven ash crunching under my feet. Pollution and the environment were terms that rarely captured public attention, but that was about to change.

In the years immediately following the war, belching smoke stacks were symbols of industrial progress. I remember pondering in my youth where all the waste from the coal emitted from our chimneys ended up. I assumed, as did most of my acquaintances, that big blue skies and deep blue seas had an unlimited ability to absorb and cleanse. It was never true of course; industrial production imposed unpriced externalities on society. Industrial polluters were getting the services of waste disposal for "free." But industrial progress was very high on the nation's agenda, and pollution was inexorably tied to progress, hence tolerated. The same view appears to be held widely in modern-day China, although it may be changing.

In 1962, biologist Rachel Carson's *Silent Spring* detailed the effect of the widely used pesticide DDT and other chemicals on the environment. Largely as a result, the Environmental Protection Agency (EPA) was born in 1970. A couple of years later, the Club of Rome commissioned a book, *The Limits of Growth,* evaluating the ever larger consumption of the world's raw materials and speculating about possible future chronic shortages and inflationary imbalances. That forecast did not materialize, but the notion of ever greater waste creation from economic growth fueled by ever more humungous structures and physical goods remained.

No doubt, the emergence of the environmental movement led to some shift in tastes away from ever greater material consumption and especially away from consumption most likely to result in a degradation of the natural environment. This likely provided some spur to the downsizing of real output. But by far the more important factor driving down the physical component of output and driving up the conceptual content of output was the discovery of the electrical properties of silicon chips and the development of the integrated circuit. This technological development and all the innovations that followed in its wake revolutionized the structure of advanced economies. The fabrication of integrated circuits required negligible quantities of physical materials such as silicon, a natural resource in widespread abundance.

DOWNSIZING AND PRODUCTIVITY

The discovery of the electrical properties of silicon and transistors created a world in which the creation of economic value has shifted dramatically toward conceptual and impalpable values, with decidedly less reliance on physical heft.

Three quarters of a century ago, our radios were bulky and activated by large vacuum tubes. Years later, owing to the insights that followed from modern electronics, the same function was served by pocket-sized transistor packs. Today we have iPhones that also serve as cameras, flashlights, GPS, portable media players, and docks for a seemingly endless (and growing) list of applications, all in a small handheld device. Moreover, there were other significant technological downsizing developments well beyond the silicon chip. Metal beverage cans are now rolled to thinner tolerances than was conceivable decades ago. Lightweight fiber optics replaced vast tonnages of copper. Space-heating technology enabled reduction in the fabric weight of apparel because people didn't need to wear warm clothes indoors. Advances in architecture and engineering, and the development and use of lighter but stronger materials, now give us the same working space in newer buildings with far less concrete and steel tonnage than was required decades ago.

Even the physical quantity of goods consumed in creating economic services has been affected. Financial transactions that historically were buttressed with reams of paper are now memorialized electronically. The transportation services industry now moves more goods with greater convenience, while consuming substantially less fuel per ton mile of transportation.

The considerable increase in the economic well-being of most advanced nations in recent decades has come about without much change in the bulk or weight of their gross domestic products. The weight of nonfuel raw materials that are consumed in the United States has not been growing measurably since the late 1970s (Exhibit 8.5), with raw tonnages no greater today than they were three or four decades ago. This means that increases in the conceptual components of GDP—that is, those components reflecting advances in knowledge and ideas—explain almost all of the rise in real GDP in the United States, and presumably elsewhere in the industrial world. Services, at constant prices, however, with no physical weight, are roughly the same share of *real* GDP as they were in 1949, and hence have contributed only modestly to downsizing. The brunt of the change has been in the downsizing of goods.

So the economy has gotten lighter without question. Quantifying this, however, is not all that straightforward. Similarly, measuring the weight of GDP is difficult. We cannot put the total GDP on a scale and read off the number of tons. We do have estimates of the total (nonfuel) tonnages of raw materials that enter into goods production, and if we assume that the physical weight of input is proportional to the tons of output, we would have an unambiguous measure of GDP output tonnage. In practice, however, technological advances have probably improved the ratio of output to input.[36]

But the key measure of output—real GDP—raises a series of questions. Real GDP is supposed to measure nominal GDP in dollars of constant purchasing power. That requires a measure of price that reflects and incorporates the ever-changing quality of goods. A new car purchased in 2013 almost certainly has many features undreamed of by the purchaser of a new car in 1998. I am astounded at how close we are to being able to vocally direct our cars while sitting back and enjoying the ride. There is a vast economic literature on how to convert nominal dollars into constant (real) dollars, and unending changes over the years in the statistical techniques employed. What the Bureau of Economic Analysis seeks is a quality-adjusted price for goods and services, most recently a measure of the quality-adjusted real output in 2005 dollars.[37]

To estimate the weight in tons of U.S. GDP goods, I employed the data compiled by the U.S. Census Bureau on both the value and weight of imports and exports transported by water and air back to 1953. Those data enable us to calculate the weight of both imports into the U.S. production process and exports ultimately destined to contribute to production abroad, relative to the constant 2005 dollar value of imports and exports.

For U.S. imports since 1955, the ratio of weight to real (constant 2005 dollar) value has fallen by a relatively stable 3.1 percent annual rate. Since 1977, the ratio has declined by an average of 4.6 percent per year (Exhibit 8.6). Assuming that this ratio can be applied more broadly to all private real goods output in the United States creates a tonnage estimate for aggregate output that is broadly consistent with an independent compilation of raw commodity inputs into the production process, such as iron and copper ore, cement, and steel scrap (Exhibit 8.7).[38] Both estimates indicate that the weight of private GDP output has leveled off since the 1970s. Of course, the composition of imports is not the same as the composition of the economy-wide goods GDP. But there is little evidence that this ratio is significantly biased by the shifting composition of imports, at least relative to tonnage estimates.

THE TURNING POINT

The correlation between growing economic activity and growing weight of real GDP apparently peaked in the late 1970s. In recent years, the conceptual contribution to economic activity has reflected importantly the explosive growth in information gathering and processing techniques, which have greatly extended our capability to substitute ideas for physical volume.

In the years ahead, telecommunications and advanced computing will doubtless take on an even greater role. By expediting the transfer of ideas, information technology creates value by facilitating the substitution of intellectual for physical labor in the production process, much as the American railroads in an earlier time created value by transferring physical goods to geographic locations where relative shortages made those goods more valuable. At the turn of the last century, for example, we created economic value in the United States by moving iron ore from Minnesota's Mesabi Range down to furnaces in Pittsburgh, where it was joined with West Virginia coal to produce steel. In today's environment, economic value is increasingly created by fitting ever smaller silicon chips ever closer together with still larger data capacity than earlier, much bulkier units. At least to date, Moore's law still prevails. (Though as Gordon Moore himself recognized, miniaturization has physical limits that some see approaching in the near term.[39])

THE BENEFITS

Two clear benefits of the economy's "weight loss" are the reduced depletion of the world's finite natural resources in the context of growing populations and the expansion of international trade. Obviously, the smaller the bulk and the lower the weight, the easier it is to move goods across national boundaries. High-value computer products are a major and increasing factor in global trade.[40]

Also implicit in the downsizing of products is the increased integration of many of the world's production facilities. Inflationary bottlenecks tend to emerge when domestic productive facilities are pressed to capacity by burgeoning domestic demand. But if additional supplies from other world producers can be made readily and quickly available, such pressures can be significantly eased, effectively reducing the level of domestic capacity required for any given global demand for a commodity. The cost of moving gravel across continents makes it difficult to envisage foreign gravel pits as backup for excess domestic demand. But the ease with which downsized electronic components can be moved essentially integrates much of the world's electronic component capacity. Misplaced or displaced production facilities become a much smaller problem.

Thus, as we move beyond the current crisis and the general downsizing of economic output continues, worldwide production and inventory controls become far more feasible and price pressures associated with production dislocations less likely. One can only imagine the downsizing that will emerge with maturing nanotechnology and 3-D printing. Goods or their electronic versions may eventually be moved in a manner that brings to mind *Star Trek*'s instantaneous teleportation devices.

MILLENNIA OF STAGNATION

Many, if not most, innovations fail and are quickly forgotten. But innovators keep trying. We are continually pressing forward. Life and our competitive propensity seemingly require it. However, if innovation and productivity growth is a human propensity, why was it essentially stagnant for nearly two millennia prior to the eighteenth century's Age of Enlightenment?[41] Clearly, the propensity to enhance our material state of living is a necessary but not a sufficient condition for the actual achievement of such growth.

Economic growth requires that the interactions between market participants are governed by a rule of law in which the rights of ownership are effectively enforced; it implies a legal framework (for example, contract law) that facilitates the free interchange of goods and services in a society. Economic growth also requires a degree of abstinence from consumption to provide the savings required to fund a sufficiently large addition to our capital stock that, in turn, is needed to leverage human inventiveness on the path to rising levels of productivity. The insights of the eighteenth century's John Locke, David Hume, and Adam Smith, among others, developed such a framework that spread rapidly throughout the then-developed world, accelerating standards of material well-being twentyfold in the subsequent more than two centuries. Real per capita GDP of the Western world, according to economic historian Angus Maddison[42], which had been virtually stagnant during the millennium preceding the eighteenth century, has accelerated at a 1.7 percent annual rate since 1820. Productivity trends will have more to do with material standards of living in, say, 2030 than any other single economic statistic.

STATISTICAL APPENDIX 8.1

To place both productivity and patent issuance on a comparable basis, I treat the annual series of output per hour (a flow) from the perspective that it is the stock of cumulative embedded technology. In essence, the level of productivity is best thought of as being a measure of the previously accumulated level of knowledge.[43]

I then assume that the rate of depreciation of the real capital stock, as estimated by the BEA, can be substituted (not implausibly) for the annual rate of depreciation of the "stock" of accumulated technology (output per hour). The *gross* additions to the stock of technology are then estimated by adding the net change in the technology stock during the year to the amount of depreciation estimated from the BEA rate of depreciation of the related real capital stock. That series is shown in Exhibit 8.8 along with annual patent issuance. Both series are measures of gross new additions to the infrastructure that produces productivity. Patent issuance, as I concluded, does parallel gross additions to the stock of productivity but does not lead it.

NINE

PRODUCTIVITY AND THE AGE OF ENTITLEMENTS

On August 14, 1935, President Franklin Delano Roosevelt signed into law a statute that was destined to have an enormous effect on America's economy and the nation's politics for the next three quarters of a century. It was the Social Security Act. From its beginnings, Social Security tried to project the aura of private fully funded insurance; beneficiaries perceived Social Security not as charity or welfare but as a return, with interest, on the contributions they and their employers paid into a fund during their working years.

I remember well the first meeting of the 1983 National Commission on Social Security Reform (NCSSR). We were tasked to solve a problem, namely, that the Social Security trust funds were about to run out of money. During our first meeting, I, as the commission's chairman, had assumed that when confronted with the distasteful choice of raising Social Security taxes or decreasing benefits, the commission might opt instead for the easy political solution: replenish the depleted trust funds from the Treasury's general revenues. It would require no more than a bookkeeping entry.

So I reluctantly concluded that if we, as a commission, were headed in that direction, we might as well do it quickly and save time and effort, and I said so. I was surprised, however, when Claude Pepper, a Democratic congressman from Florida and a longtime idol to supporters of Social Security, arose in indignation and denounced such an action. He argued that it would brand Social Security as "welfare." The rest of the commission quietly acquiesced, including such formidable political heavyweights as senators Bob Dole, John Heinz, Daniel Patrick Moynihan, and AFL-CIO president Lane Kirkland. Pepper's successful intervention effectively required the commission to address the politically difficult choices of raising taxes, reducing benefits, or, as was finally the case, both.

The issue was still sufficiently politically sensitive three decades later that during the heat of the 2012 presidential campaign President Barack Obama felt the need to assert that "Medicare and Social Security are not handouts."[1] In a similar vein, an advertisement for the American Association of Retired Persons (AARP) had a retiree (or an actor) reiterate the belief that "I earned my Medicare and Social Security."[2]

WORDS MATTER

In social and political discourse, how ideas are characterized matters a great deal. Whether a payment from one person to another, or from government to citizen, is characterized as "charity" or an earned "entitlement" has profound implications on politically influenced economic behavior. Charity has always been considered a highly moral act from the giver's perspective, but to almost all who perceive themselves with pride as solidly self-reliant, to fall into a state of charitable dependence is a very debilitating blow to their self-esteem. It is particularly apparent when middle-class families, proud of achieving self-sufficiency, are forced by circumstances to become recipients of charity—in the wake, for example, of natural disasters.[3] Moreover, as the *Economist* noted, "Plenty of poor people in America are wary of programmes like the Earned Income Tax Credit (EITC) because the idea of getting a handout from the government reinforces a sense of helplessness."[4]

But the perception that Social Security trust funds replicate private pension trust funds has long diverged from the reality. The contributions by employees and their employers, plus interest, set aside to fund promised future benefits, have fallen far short of what fully funded private defined benefit pension funds would have required.[5,6] The trust funds have struggled and failed even to keep payments on a pay-as-you-go basis without transfers from Treasury general revenues. The Social Security trust funds have done better than the Medicare Fund, but under current projections of their actuaries, they will run out of funds in 2033. The Medicare fund will become insolvent by 2026.[7]

The size of the full funding shortfall was documented by the actuaries of the Social Security trust fund in early 2013. To achieve "sustainable solvency" over the long run, they concluded, would require a permanent tax increase on payrolls of 4.0 percentage points (an increase of almost a third), or a permanent cut in benefits of almost one fourth, or some combination of the two. Every year of delay in implementing a fix would increase the required size of subsequent policy action. The actuaries argued in 2013 that Social Security's official arbitrary convention for budget "solvency" of only a seventy-five-year funding horizon "can lead to incorrect perceptions and . . .

policy prescriptions. . . ."[8, 9] I might add that the Medicare Board of Trustees was also skeptical of the estimates on Medicare funding they were required to make under current law. They noted in the 2012 report that projected Medicare spending will require "unprec- edented improvements in health care provider productivity. . . . Given these uncertainties, future Medicare costs could be substan- tially larger than shown in the Trustees' current-law projection."[10, 11]

EARLY PERCEPTIONS

I recall that when I was a freshman in college, President Harry S. Truman took pains, in describing his broad national health-care ini- tiative (a precursor to Medicare), to emphasize that his proposal was "not socialized medicine" when addressing the Congress in 1945.[12] That pejorative term resonated in early postwar America, and it was used successfully for years to fend off such legislation.

Medicare finally became law in 1965, and took on the same ac- tuarial trappings as Social Security. But it was only partly financed with a hospital trust fund, which also has long since failed to meet any notion of full funding. Individual and employer contributions to the fund fall far short of what would be necessary to ensure long- term solvency. Beneficiaries get social insurance at a substantial dis- count under its true cost.

THE BARGAIN

Given these subsidized bargain prices for retirement and health benefits, and the government-guaranteed certainty of payment, it is no surprise that they have become overwhelmingly politically popular. The electoral power of entitlement programs has been painfully evident to those who, in running for political office, suggest even a modest paring of future benefits. There is a bipartisan view that Social Security is the "third rail" for politicians: "Touch it and you lose." Political constituencies vigorously defending each social benefit have organized around every new entitlement program; such entitlements, once bestowed, have proved extremely difficult to rescind or even reduce. In this political atmosphere, social insurance inexorably expanded to broader and broader coverage. It soon became a political grab bag for buying votes—by *both* Democrats and Republicans. Fiscal probity was nowhere in sight.

After decades of moderate growth, social benefit programs gained unexpected momentum. As Exhibit 9.1 demonstrates, between 1965 and 2012, the average annual rate of increase of social benefits exceeded 9.4 percent, as benefits' share of GDP rose from 4.7 percent to 14.9 percent. Particularly surprising has been the fact that it was not the political descendants of FDR but "fiscally prudent" Republican administrations who led the charge. Since 1969, during the Republican administrations, social benefit spending rose by 10.4 percent annually (Reagan's mark was 7.3 percent). Meanwhile, "spendthrift" Democrats since 1965 oversaw a "mere" 8.1 percent annual increase (Clinton's was 4.5 percent). Of the overall rise, 40 percent occurred during the twenty years of Democratic administrations and 60 percent during the twenty-eight years of Republican administrations.

This seeming political anomaly was explained to me by President Richard Nixon (who introduced automatic indexing of Social Security benefits in 1972): "If we (Republicans) don't preempt the Democrats and get the political credit, they (the Democrats) will."

Much to my retrospective distress, neither presidents Ford nor Reagan, for whom I worked, could or would effectively constrain the benefits juggernaut.

THE TECTONIC POLICY SHIFT

What was it about the early 1960s that set the stage for the remarkable surge in what later became known as "government social benefit payments to persons"?[13] Certainly in the eight years of the Eisenhower presidency, the shift to expansive economic and fiscal policy was nowhere on the political horizon. In his 1956 State of the Union address, President Dwight D. Eisenhower captured the ethos of his time: "A public office is, indeed, a public trust. None of its aspects is more demanding than the proper management of the public finances. I refer . . . to the prudent, effective and conscientious use of tax money. . . . Over the long term, a balanced budget is a sure index to thrifty management—in a home, in a business or in the Federal Government."[14] In the political world, budget deficits were then considered as worrisome to the nation's economic health as they are to the financial health of a household unable to make ends meet.

This broadly held notion was quietly shelved by the breakout of Keynesian economics from the heady but cloistered atmosphere of academia to the "practical world" of everyday American politics. That breakout was facilitated by the first American president born in the twentieth century, John F. Kennedy, who, on coming to office in January 1961, brought with him a coterie of academic economists thoroughly schooled in the early versions of what we now call Keynesian macroeconomic policy. I trace the beginnings of the social benefits boom in part, at least, to what President Kennedy's

Council of Economic Advisers in the 1960s called "fiscal drag," a persistent propensity toward budget restraint. As President Kennedy himself put it later, "Only when we have removed the heavy drag our fiscal system now exerts on personal and business purchasing power and on the financial incentives for greater risk-taking and personal effort can we expect to restore the high levels of employment and high rate of growth that we took for granted in the first decade after the war."[15]

FISCAL DRAG

The economy was expanding rapidly in the early 1960s with impressive productivity growth. Tax revenues were flowing into the U.S. Treasury at a pace that, to the Council of Economic Advisers, conjured up the specter of large deflationary federal surpluses. And indeed, from 1959 to 1966, the federal government's net savings was in rare surplus.[16] But there was no shortage of recommended remedies. The tax cut of 1964 and the riveting (and expensive) venture to send an American to the moon were in the forefront of initiatives to counter the feared drag of budget surpluses. But none matched the expansion of social benefit programs. With both Democrats and Republicans vying to outpromise each other, the seeds of the historic entitlement boom were being sown.

As social benefit spending accelerated, government savings as a percent of GDP began, with little fanfare, to decline, turning negative in the 1970s (Exhibit 9.2).[17] Since 2009, annual government *dissavings* (deficits) have exceeded 5 percent of GDP.

Between 1965 and 2012, as a consequence of falling government savings, total gross domestic savings (as a percent of GDP) declined from 22.0 percent to 12.9 percent, or 9.1 percentage points. The erosion of U.S. gross domestic savings as a percent of GDP, in peacetime, is historically unprecedented. (See Box 9.1.)

As can be seen from Exhibit 9.2, the 9.3-percentage-point fall in government savings as a share of GDP since 1965 is more than accounted for by the sharp rise in social benefit spending. No other component of either receipts or outlays of federal, state, and local financing exhibited changing shares of GDP large enough to credibly be seen as a major contributor to the dramatic decline in government savings (Exhibit 9.3).[18, 19] And because private savings as a share of GDP was unchanged between 1965 to 2012, social benefits are also the major contributor to the decline in overall gross domestic savings.[20]

Exhibit 9.2

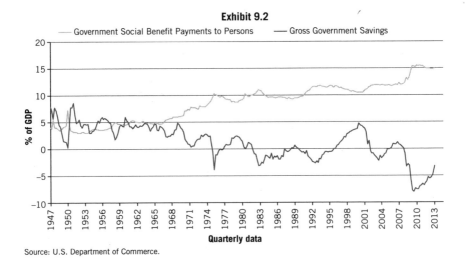

—— Government Social Benefit Payments to Persons   —— Gross Government Savings

Quarterly data

Source: U.S. Department of Commerce.

BOX 9.1: BACK TO BASICS
ON SAVINGS

One of the most fundamental propositions of economics is that advances in standards of living require savings. Part of ancient harvests were set aside as seed grain for future plantings or as insurance against famine owing to crop failure. People soon realized that abstaining from immediate consumption to build tools enhanced future production, consumption, and standards of living. They accordingly chose to divert their physical effort to producing hammers and axes, rather than producing food. Much later came the evolution of finance, an increasingly sophisticated system that enabled savers to hold liquid claims (deposits) with banks and other financial intermediaries. Those claims could be invested by banks in financial instruments that, in turn, represented the net claims against the productivity-enhancing tools of a complex economy. Financial intermediation was born. This system financed the industrial revolution and modern capitalism.

But even in complex modern economies, the buildup of capital assets still requires the forgoing of consumption to allow part of output to be saved and invested in productive capital assets. This principle is no less true in sophisticated modern economies than it was when ancient farmers diverted part of their crops to seed grain for the next year's harvest.

As I've said, for the past century and a half, savings by our economy's private sector—business and households—has exhibited no discernible long-term trend, presumably mirroring the stability of real interest rates. With the exception of two world wars and the Great Depression of the 1930s, annual gross private savings[21] have hovered between 15 percent and 20 percent of GDP since 1886 (Exhibit 9.5). Government savings— federal, state, and local—in peacetime also were stable, ranging between 0 percent and 5 percent of GDP for the century leading up to 1965. Prudence characterized public finance.

Evidence[22] indicates that American savings rates (and investment rates) relative to GDP were climbing during the first half of the nineteenth century. Human nature, of course, did not change, but the new American economy was building up its infrastructure and new political institutions. The data do show persuasively that private savings rates had reached their equilibrium by the 1880s. (See also Box 1.1.)

BOX 9.2: ALTERNATE VIEWS

There are many other views of the cause of decline in the domestic savings rate. Certainly, the mere existence of government-guaranteed retirement and health benefits must have lowered the level of current savings. Before such guarantees, people had to set aside additional savings for their old age. The high savings rates among Chinese households are often attributed to that country's lack of an effective retirement funding regime. It is very difficult to measure the effect of government retirement guarantees on the level of savings of U.S. households. But why has the savings rate continued to fall over the decades? The government guarantee has not changed since the inception of Social Security.

A more compelling alternative to the thesis I have presented in this chapter is the suppression of the level of gross domestic savings, owing to the existence of capital gains on stocks and homes that the data show drive personal consumption expenditures higher (and savings lower). Capital gains and, more generally, the buildup of household net worth, doubtless have a measurable influence on the level of household savings. But most important, it cannot explain the decline in gross domestic savings as a percent of GDP. As can be seen in Exhibit 9.6, the share of personal consumption expenditures attributable to changes in net worth soared for a decade (1997 to 2007), but by 2012, the share had fallen back to where it was in 1965 (12.2 percent). Thus, little if any of the *downtrend* in the household savings rate can be tied to household net worth.

ONE TO ONE

Not only can benefit spending be seen as displacing gross domestic saving, but in recent years it has also been displacing it on almost a dollar-for-dollar basis. Since 1965, much of the *sum* of social benefit spending and gross total domestic savings has remained in the remarkably narrow range of 26 percent to 30 percent of GDP (Exhibit 9.7). Had the ratio of benefits plus savings to GDP been fixed at 28 percent, for example, every dollar of benefit rise would have, of necessity, reduced domestic savings by exactly one dollar. What is important, as I will document, is that a significant part of the surge in benefit spending and consumption was funded by government preemption of private savings (by taxation) that would otherwise have gone to fund domestic capital investment.[23]

CROWDING OUT

Social benefit spending is *not* subject to market forces.[24] It is determined wholly by entitlements and appropriated budget funds that are transferred to beneficiaries irrespective of market conditions. They are, as economists like to put it, an "independent variable." The remainder of the economy has been forced to adjust to the bulge in benefit spending.

Government deficits can, and do, crowd out other borrowers. The federal government will outbid all other potential claimants to the nation's private (and sometimes state and local government) savings to ensure that its *ex post* deficit is equal to its *ex ante* deficit.[25] The federal government, the only issuer of sovereign credit,[26] is the "eight-hundred-pound gorilla" in the marketplace, and every other claimant for private savings is forced to stand in line behind the U.S. Treasury. Private sector participants then jockey for the limited leftover funds available. The allocation of savings is driven indirectly by higher interest rates—especially rates that apply to less than investment grade borrowers—curtailing capital investments that the *ex ante* savings were scheduled to fund. [27]

IT TAKES TWO

Deficit spending thus requires two parties: the government, which is almost always a net borrower of funds, and the private sector and/or foreign investors, who directly or indirectly lend the money. If the federal government cannot induce investors to buy its bonds, deficit spending cannot exist. There are limits to "real" deficit spending.[28] Because it must be financed with private savings, it competes for the consumer dollar with the antisaving propensities of keeping up with the Joneses and herd behavior–driven conspicuous consumption. The pool of private savings from which governments fund their deficits rarely breaches 20 percent of GDP, an apparent upper limit to the amount Americans will voluntarily save out of income (Exhibit 9.5). In World War II, it took official rationing and patriotic fervor to suppress the level of consumption and facilitate a marked rise in household savings to help fund the war.[29] If our government tries to run deficits that exceed *ex ante* available private savings, it would induce either a rise in interest rates and/or force the Federal Reserve to accommodate the increased supply of bonds, as it did in World War II, requiring wage and price controls to suppress inflation.

LENDING AND BORROWING

In the United States, of necessity, all lending *ex post* must be somebody else's borrowing. Hence, the sum of each must be identical.[30] That is true, however, only if we include foreign lending as borrowing by U.S. residents. Because all transactions with foreigners have both an American and a foreign counterpart, it is possible to view the current account balance of payments (deficit or surplus) solely from the American side (which, of course, must be identical to the foreign side, with sign reversed). Thus, having classified our transactions with foreigners as a domestic sector, the borrowing and lending between Americans is always equal, and the difference between the two always zero. Since net borrowing is also equivalent to investment less savings, it follows that, with net borrowing for the United States as a whole always zero, *ex post,* savings must always equal investment. All this necessary balancing derives from the nature of double-entry bookkeeping (see Box 9.3).

BOX 9.3: DOUBLE ENTRY

Because every market transaction has both a buyer and a seller, there are two sets of books—double entry—but only a single set of transaction values. For a market transaction to occur, both sides must agree to the same terms—for example, the price and value of the exchange. Hence, added up separately, the various aggregates from the two sets of books must yield identical results. Gross domestic product, for example, must equal gross domestic income,[31] and when we limit the summations to capitalized transactions[32] only, savings must equal investment. It is those equalities that lock the two sets of matching accounts together.

However, were the widely differing *intentions* of people to invest or save (or their equivalent, to borrow or lend) recorded as they enter the marketplace, they would exhibit no such equalities. In general, *ex post* prices tend to be higher than consumers would prefer and lower than suppliers would prefer. Market negotiations pit "bids" against "asked" until agreement is reached between buyers and sellers. Counterparties come together on the specific terms of their transaction and in the process set prices of products and assets, as well as interest and exchange rates.

Double-entry bookkeeping has the real world role of preventing internal inconsistencies in forecasts. Inconsistencies can exist for *ex ante* demand and supply, but not once market forces set the terms of transactions to a point where agreements are reached and market transactions are completed. Double entry merely recognizes such agreements. It is a requirement that, for transactions to have occurred and economic activity to have taken place, supply equaled demand. That result cannot be altered by outcomes of other equations in the model; it is what economists call an "identity"—that is, definitional equality. Markets reset all prices (for products and assets) and interest and exchange rates until the allocation of lending and borrowing (savings less investment) among sectors sums to zero. Thus, for sectoral balance to be achieved, given a rise in federal deficits, for example, some other sector must have been crowded out.

The end result of double-entry bookkeeping transactions is a set of accounts that are tied together by the terms of agreements already reached. The accounting merely records the same set of transactions from two different perspectives. Gross domestic income is equal to gross domestic product because the former is merely a set of accounts that identify the nature of the income claims to each reported good and service that makes up the GDP. Because what is measured is the same thing but from different perspectives, the sum of each separate account must be identical.

IT MATTERS

These tautological relationships would be of little interest outside of accounting formalities if it weren't for the fact that the federal government, when funding its deficits, preempts part of the supply of private savings; households and/or business, once their transactions in the marketplace are complete, must have borrowed less than they intended and lent more than they intended. For this to happen, one or more private sectors must experience some form of crowding out, either interest rate crowding out or self-imposed corporate culture–induced crowding out.

In the former case, the interest rates borrowers are required to pay render the investments that the savings are supposed to fund unprofitable. Interest rate crowding out is, of course, not uniform across business and households. AAA or even A credits rarely get crowded out. Most of the projects that are put back on the shelf because interest rates are too high are those of less than investment grade businesses or subprime home mortgage borrowers.[33]

PRIVATE SAVINGS

While overall gross private savings as a share of GDP has shown a remarkable stability, the same cannot be said for the proportion of its major components: households and business. Since 1965, and especially since 1984, gross household savings as a share of GDP have declined and gross business savings as a share of GDP have risen as an offset (see Exhibit 9.4). The latter has occurred owing to ever rising depreciation as a share of GDP. The household savings rate declined largely as a consequence of social benefit consumption crowding out household saving.

There is always a great deal of transferring of funds in both directions between government and the private sector: the government—federal, state, and local—takes in tax receipts from households and businesses and makes payouts to households and businesses. When the federal government receives contributions for social insurance from employees who save little of their income, and then turns around and sends checks for comparable amounts to beneficiaries who also save little, the overall effect on the gross domestic savings rate is negligible. But when tax receipts from upper income savers are transferred to lower income beneficiaries, gross domestic savings decline by the amount of the transfer, times the difference between the savings rates of the taxed upper income groups (high) and that of the social insurance beneficiaries (low).

But determining the size of the crowding out of savings by benefit spending is not a simple matter of comparing the *average* savings rates of taxed households and that of beneficiaries. It is their *marginal* rates that matter. For example, a modest cut in income tax rates for a millionaire household is apt to have little to no effect on its level of spending on consumer goods and services. Hence, almost all, if not all, of the tax cut would go to savings. The *marginal* savings rate at that income level is thus close to, if not at, 100 percent.

CALCULATING MARGINAL SAVINGS RATES

The marginal savings rate for upper income quintile households (calculated from the sample BLS Consumer Expenditure Surveys) is shown for 1984 to 2011 in Exhibit 9.9.[34] After adjusting those data to be consistent with BEA savings levels (also shown), the marginal savings rate averages 46 percent over the time frame, but has not trended upwards.*

I then estimate the extent that taxation of upper income households finances social spending (and hence contributes to the decline in both household and total domestic saving).† Between 1979 and 2009, according to the CBO, the upper quintile's share of total individual tax liabilities, driven by our rising degree of income inequality,[35] increased from 65 percent in 1979 to 94 percent by 2009, the latest available data.[36]

Gross domestic savings declined from 22.04 percent of GDP in 1965 to 12.88 percent in 2012 (see Exhibit 9.3). Of the decrease of 9.16 percentage points, 2.51 points (27 percent) was contributed by direct taxation of upper income quintile households, diverting savings from investment to consumption. In addition to estimating federal individual income tax liabilities attributable to upper income quintile households, the CBO also estimates the ultimate tax incidence of corporate, payroll, and excise taxes of upper quintile earners. Those taxes are levied before incomes are paid to households rather than on income already received. I estimate that the reduction of savings of the upper income quintile through this channel accounts for an additional decrease of two percentage points of GDP, or 22 percent of

---

*The high marginal rates reflect the fact that the aggregate (and adjusted) level of savings for the upper income quintile since 1984 has exceeded that of total households every year by between 15 and 25 percent. The four lower quintiles combined exhibit negative savings for both the sample and adjusted surveys.
†For the upper quintile, the marginal savings rate times individual federal income tax liabilities, reduced by a small propensity (of lower income quintiles) to save Social Security benefits, measures the amount of household savings that would have funded capital investment but that has instead been diverted to social benefits that are almost wholly consumed.

Exhibit 9.9
Marginal Savings Rate* of Top Pretax Income Quintile

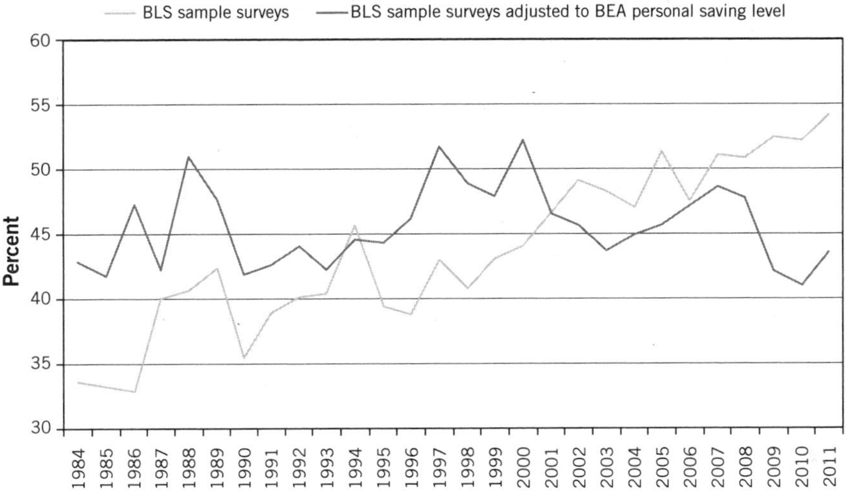

Source: U.S. Department of Labor; U.S. Department of Commerce; author's calculations.
*Marginal Savings Rate = Marginal Savings/Marginal After-tax Income.

the decline in gross domestic savings over the past half century. Taxation directly or indirectly of the upper income quintile thus accounts for almost half of the decline in gross savings since 1965. The remainder of the decline is attributable to increased benefit spending unmatched by tax receipts.

FUNDING CAPITAL INVESTMENT

Only savings can create a claim on productive capital assets. It is only when income exceeds consumption that a household has a surplus and must determine whether it uses the surplus to pay off debt, increase home equity, or accumulate bank deposits and other financial assets. Banks or other financial intermediaries will reinvest their newly acquired inflow of monies to fund some of the economy's fixed capital assets and inventories. Household consumption, on the other hand, by definition, leaves no further imprint on household balance sheets.

Only because we borrowed savings from abroad were we able to limit the decline in domestic capital investment (as a percent of GDP) to 5 percentage points—from 21.4 percent in 1965 to 16.2 percent in 2012—little more than half of the decline in gross domestic savings (Exhibit 9.3). Yet as I detail later in this chapter, even this decline was enough to slow the rate of growth of nonfarm output per hour (productivity) from the relatively stable 2.2 percent per annum that prevailed on average for a century (1870 to 1970) (see Chapter 8), to a 2.0 percent rate between 1965 and 2012—a consequential difference.

THE PRICE OF BENEFITS

Thus, the benefits surge that began in 1965, while clearly a huge political success, appears to have lowered the growth rate of real gross domestic private nonfarm business product by 0.21 percent per annum. That may seem small, but cumulatively, over the past half century, 0.21 percent per annum had created a gap (hypothetical less actual) by 2011 of almost a tenth of real gross private nonfarm business product and somewhat less for real GDP (see Statistical Appendix 9.1). That counterfactual projected GDP gap amounted to approximately $1.1 trillion by 2011, half the rise in social benefits payments of $2.2 trillion that occurred between 1965 and 2011. The evidence suggests that the resources required to augment the benefits of the elderly came largely at the expense of the lower income quintile households, almost wholly through suppressed wage rate gains. Profit margins were not materially affected.[37]

A hypothetical loss of a never-experienced standard of living, of course, is not comparable to a visible and painful setback, such as the evaporation of retirement assets during the stock market collapse of 2008. If the properties of silicon and integrated circuits were never discovered, would we be mourning the loss of a never-existing Internet?

These calculations indicate that if social benefits as a percent of GDP had stayed unchanged after 1965, the resulting gains in GDP would have yielded an annual increase in nonfarm output per hour of 2.2 percent between 1965 and 2011 (compared with the actual 2.0 percent), the same rate of growth that prevailed between 1870 and 1970. That result reinforces the hypothesis that productivity growth would not have slowed down materially from its century-long uptrend had benefits' share of GDP not increased after 1965.[38] Average production worker wage levels would certainly have been higher than those engendered by the tepid increases that have prevailed in recent years. (Productivity growth still would have been significantly slower, however, relative to the initial postwar rise between 1948 and 1965 that averaged an impressive 3.1 percent per year.)

From 1992 to 2008, we borrowed an ever-increasing share of GDP from abroad to help fund our domestic capital investment, ballooning our current account deficit to 6 percent of GDP in 2006. With the collapse of domestic investment during 2008, the need for foreign borrowing has slowed. But as recently as 2011, annual borrowing remained large, mainly from China ($315 billion), Japan ($82 billion), and the Middle East ($45 billion), out of a total current account deficit of $466 billion (3.1 percent of GDP). We are borrowing resources from our children and the rest of the world to be repaid . . . when?

THE NEED FOR CONTAINMENT

Unless the upward momentum of entitlement spending is contained and turned around, the erosion of our gross domestic savings rate will almost surely continue to suppress capital spending, productivity, and growth in standards of living, as it has done incrementally for nearly a half century. *Net* domestic savings are now close to zero. Unless we increase our current rate of borrowing from abroad, additions to our productive capital stock will fall further.

We have pretty much exhausted the low-hanging fruit that has helped fund the rise in benefits as a share of GDP, yet the bulk of baby-boomer retirements still lies ahead. The almost certain further rise in benefits, I presume, will be funded by additional reductions in discretionary spending, as some of our military and financial commitments continue to wind down. That will leave defense spending in 2019, as a share of GDP, at its lowest point since 1940, and nondefense discretionary federal spending (as a share of GDP) at the lowest levels in more than a half century. Social benefit funding from additional reductions in "discretionary" spending, both defense and nondefense, will thus become ever more difficult. Moreover, we are left with little buffer to fund unanticipated new military imperatives or major hurricane-related relief programs, for example, short of printing money—a policy that carries its own problems (see Chapter 13).

OUR GLOBAL REACH

We are the world's reserve currency, which grants us special access to the world's savings. That has given the United States an extraordinary degree of flexibility to act on the world stage. But our heavy borrowing from abroad since 1992 has brought our international investment position from a net credit in 1986 (and for many years earlier) to a net debt of nearly $5 trillion at the end of 2012. Presumably, we can continue to pawn or sell the nation's capital assets to fund growing social benefit consumption, at least for a while. But there is a limit to a reserve currency country's accumulation of foreign borrowings. Should the United States ever reach that limit and sources of new foreign funding dry up, social benefit spending will either be wrenched lower or, more likely, funded by printed money. Our status as the world's leading financial power will be profoundly shaken.[39]

Short of major entitlement reform, it is difficult to find a benevolent outcome to this clash between social spending and savings in this country. The answer, whenever it comes, will surely be political. The Great Depression of the 1930s brought us Franklin Delano Roosevelt. The economic "malaise" of the late 1970s and the financial distress that followed brought us Ronald Reagan and Margaret Thatcher.

BOX 9.4: MONEY ISN'T EVERYTHING

Budget appropriations provide money but not real resources to fund future benefits. There is no limit on the size of appropriations to fund ongoing or new social benefits. The fact that both houses of the Congress vote overwhelmingly for a new benefit, and the president eagerly signs the bill, does nothing to ensure that resources (people and products) will be available to fulfill the obligation. A continued decline in net domestic savings will shortly imply either a halt in the growth in our net fixed assets or increased funding from foreign savings. Net fixed assets, of course, are a major contributor to gains in productivity that, in turn, produce our standard of living, including the ability to meet the real resources requirements of our promises to retirees.

We would do well to heed the caution offered in 1976 by former British prime minister Margaret Thatcher that politicians who are in the forefront of fostering large continual social financial transfers "always run out of other people's money."[40]

Medicare, Social Security, and all other indexed programs are *real* entitlements whose funding burdens cannot be assuaged by general inflation. To implement Medicare and Medicaid in the decade ahead, we will need more physicians,[41] nurses, hospitals, pharmaceutical companies, and other components of the large complex of medical services infrastructure. Making the problem all the more difficult, a significant number of experienced medical practitioners will be part of the wave of baby-boomer retirees in the years ahead. Social Security benefits, indexed to inflation, represent a general claim on the production of consumer goods and services. But in the end, they are just as real as the more specialized resources required to meet medical entitlements.

STATISTICAL APPENDIX 9.1

The relative stability of the sum of social benefits and gross domestic savings implies a near one-to-one tradeoff between benefits and savings. The probability that the relationship is purely accidental or owing to chance is exceptionally small. The R^2 is a robust .75 and the t-statistic is highly significant (Exhibit 9.10). The short-term visual tradeoff depicted in Exhibit 9.7 appears even more persuasive than the formal regression fit.

The hypothetical additional gross domestic savings that would have occurred in 2011 had benefits spending remained at 4.7 percent of GDP (its 1965 share) is nearly $1.6 trillion. Adding those lost savings to the actual amount of gross domestic savings in 2011, and then further adding savings borrowed from abroad ($467 billion in 2011), yields a hypothetical estimate for gross domestic investment $1.6 trillion higher than what actually occurred. Of total gross domestic investment, private domestic business has accounted for a relatively stable three fifths of total gross domestic investment. That yields a hypothetical addition to gross domestic private business investment in 2011 of $975 billion. I then adjust the hypothetical gross private nonfarm business investment into net investment by setting aside a proportion of gross investment to account for depreciation—that is, the wear and tear on the stock of capital assets. Finally, I deflate the hypothetical net investment figures into constant dollars.

That enables me to employ the BLS's multifactor productivity (MFP) paradigm (see Chapter 8) to translate labor input and the hypothetical real net domestic private business investment (converted to "capital services") into hypothetical real gross domestic private nonfarm business product and output per hour.[42]

TEN

CULTURE

I t was the clear but frosty evening of February 8, 1998, outside the tower of the Bank for International Settlements (BIS) in Basel, Switzerland. Inside, the tightly knit, collegial group of governors of eleven[1] of the world's largest central banks was engaged in one of our regular Sunday dinners, hosted by the general manager of the BIS. The meetings were without staff and engagingly uninhibited as we discussed the usual array of pressing international economic issues. Given that eight of the eleven governors were European, the issue of the emergence of what came to be known as the euro was a topic of increasing interest.

The BIS seemed a singularly appropriate place to ponder the awesome complexities of a merging of the seventeen separate currencies that eventually constituted the "Eurozone." There was an explicit recognition among many of the European central bankers that the euro was the next stepping stone toward the political integration of Europe. It was the ultimate goal of some, if not most, of the Europeans sitting around the dinner table that evening. Seared into the European psyche was the devastation of two world wars in less than a third of a century; integration, it was presumed, would go a long way toward fending off future internecine conflict.

The conversations in Basel were generally directed at replicating a currency as effective as the U.S. dollar that served as legal tender across all fifty American states. From the beginning it was recognized that the merging of currencies of the European states could not be directly modeled after U.S. practice. There were more languages, less labor mobility, and less free capital flow throughout the continent than existed across the state boundaries of the United States. But there was an unwavering conviction that economic and cultural barriers would break down under the imperative of a single currency.[2]

Most important, the international financial markets appeared to be buying the hypothesis that the euro could change some deeply embedded cultural behavior. The presumption was that all members of the Eurozone, but especially the Italians, Spaniards, Portuguese, and Greeks, once under the cover of the discipline of the euro, would behave like Germans. In anticipation of the adoption of the new currency, yields on government debt of the prospective members of the Eurozone had been falling sharply in the years prior to our BIS dinner, dramatically closing the yield spread gap against the German bund. In the three years leading up to the introduction of the euro on January 1, 1999, yields on lira-denominated ten-year government bonds declined nearly 500 basis points (5 percentage points) relative to yields on German bunds. Yields on Spanish peso and Portuguese escudo bonds both fell close to 370 basis points against the bunds. Likewise, in the three years preceding Greece's delayed adoption of the euro on January 1, 2001, drachma-denominated ten-year sovereign bonds fell more than 450 basis points relative to bund yields. In stark contrast, in those early years, spread changes against the bund for bonds of France, Austria, Netherlands, and Belgium were all less than 65 basis points.[3]

It was puzzling that the convergence of borrowing rates and corresponding dramatic narrowing of spreads was reflected entirely in the decline of southern European yields toward those of Germany rather than toward an average of all Eurozone legacy currencies, as might have been expected. That underscored the dominant role of the deutschmark (DM) as the shadow anchor of newly minted euros: Markets perceived the euro as a substitute for the DM. In retrospect, the dominance of Germany did not bode well for the working relationship within the presumably collegial group of countries.

EURO: IN WITHOUT A WHIMPER

Much to my surprise, on January 1, 1999, the merging of the currencies came off with remarkable ease. The eleven divergent floating currencies (six others would join later) effortlessly locked together and remained locked with little market tension for almost a decade. The euro seemed to belie the decidedly checkered history of past endeavors to tie exchange rates of culturally diverse countries. Many countries have, for example, succeeded in choosing the U.S. dollar as their legal tender. But these, over the years, have primarily been small Latin American and Caribbean economies. And, of course, many currencies have linked together under the gold standard. But in recent decades, success has been rare. The experience of Argentina is especially noteworthy.

The central lesson of fixed exchange rates is that when they work, they do minimize price fluctuation and render all the benefits of stability and long-term investment that attaches to it. The Bretton Woods Agreement, struck among forty-four countries as World War II was coming to a close, tied all major postwar currencies to the gold-backed[4] U.S. dollar for nearly three decades. The presumption that the euro could easily withstand the internal monetary dynamics of seventeen clashing cultures, however, now seems a decided overreach.

In retrospect, the remarkably benign convergence of Eurozone currencies for nearly a decade can be explained, as best I can judge, by the global boom that funded both the creditworthy and the less so. It enabled even the increasingly uncompetitive Euro-South economies (Greece, Portugal, Spain, and Italy) to thrive as they effortlessly borrowed heavily from their northern neighbors at the low interest rates that the euro accorded them. But hidden beneath the false sense of well-being, the southern members of the Eurozone were becoming increasingly uncompetitive relative to their partners in the north, as indicated by their ever-rising unit labor costs and prices relative to those of Germany (see Exhibit 10.1).

With the collapse of Lehman Brothers in September 2008, followed by the virtual closing down of trade credit on a global scale, recognition of the starkly different international competitive capabilities of Eurozone members emerged with a vengeance after nearly a decade of golden years for the new currency. Fears of sovereign default escalated and southern euro government bond spreads against Germany blew out, after years of Euro-South being able to borrow in international markets at market rates very close to those of Germany. Spreads by late 2008 ballooned back to where they were, in general, before the euro was considered a realistic possibility.

CULTURE REIGNS

There had been a widespread notion that the Italians, once they embraced the euro, would behave like Germans. From day one of the euro, they did not. Nor did the Greek, Portuguese, or Spanish members of the European Monetary Union.[5] Despite the binding restraints of the Maastricht Treaty, the Eurozone has not exhibited the ability to counter the key concern of currency unions: that the value created by a pooling arrangement tends in the end to be distributed disproportionately in favor of the financially less collegial and less prudent members of the pool. We observed this tendency as consumption growth of the south relative to Germany accelerated following the creation of the euro. Unless restrained, the less collegial members of the pool will try, and often succeed, to exploit the advantage available to all members of a pool—that which Greece in particular so brazenly exploited over the past decade.

I believe Kieran Kelly, an Australian financial adviser, captured the Greek ethos best as he noted in October 2011 that "if I lived in a country like this, I would find it hard to stir myself into a Germanic tax-paying life of capital accumulation and arduous labor. The surrounds just aren't conducive."[6]

As can be seen from Exhibit 10.1, the unit labor costs, driven by workers' wage demands, of the countries that make up Euro-South rose persistently from the onset of the euro. In fact, from 1985 to the beginning of 1999, the legacy currencies, calculated in terms of deutschmarks, the hard currency that the creators of the euro seek to replicate, exhibited approximately the same rate of competitive erosion that was evident in unit labor costs in the years immediately following the adoption of the euro. Prior to the launch of the new currency, the Mediterranean nations were able to remain internationally competitive by allowing their currencies to weaken. That had the effect of reducing *real* wages and unit labor costs to internationally competitive levels, at least for a short while. No special cross-border financing was required.

Exhibit 10.1
Legacy Currency and Unit Labor Cost as a Ratio to Germany (*1998=100)

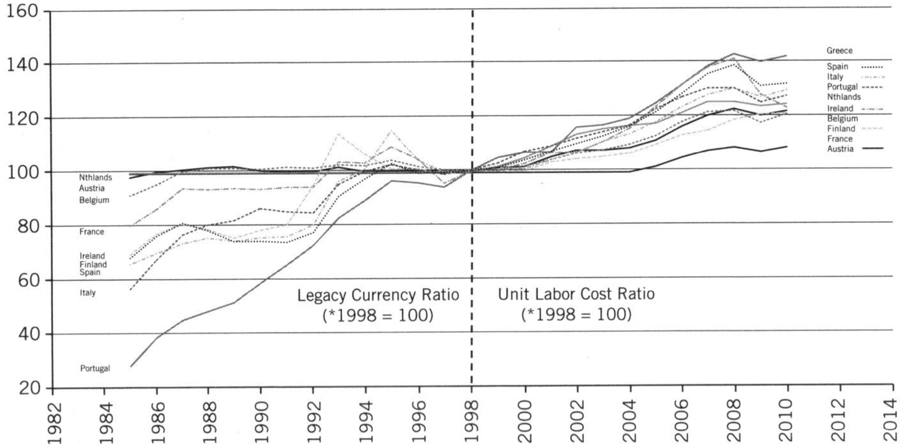

Source: Various official data sources.

*Assumes equality in 1998.

ENTER THE EURO

But with devaluation no longer available after 1998, and the apparently irresistible availability of credit at the low euro interest rates, Euro-South's consumption surged, especially in Greece and Spain. They borrowed heavily from Euro-North. The size of the buildup is best represented by the €750 billion of accumulated credits in the Eurozone central bank clearing system (TARGET2) of the Deutsche Bundesbank by August 2012, and to a lesser extent the credits of the central banks of Netherlands, Finland, and tiny Luxembourg.[7] Southern Europe's sovereign bond spreads widened back to the levels that prevailed during the financially independent pre-euro years. The central banks of Euro-South, especially Italy and Spain, were the major net debtors of TARGET2.[8] Since mid-2012, the TARGET2 spread has narrowed modestly.

There is thus scant evidence that on embracing the euro, Euro-South significantly altered its behavior—behavior which had previously precipitated its chronically depreciating exchange rates against the deutschmark. From 1985 through the end of 1998, Euro-South unit labor costs and prices rose far faster than in the north, and in the years following the onset of a single currency, as I noted, that pace barely slowed. By 2008, according to OECD data, Greece, Spain, Italy, and Portugal had unit labor costs 30 percent to 40 percent higher than that of Germany.[9] The underlying uptrend was stopped only by the financial crisis. Productivity in Germany, after having grown at a steady rate between 1999 and 2008, flattened and has been stagnant since the onset of the crisis. Hourly wages, however, continued their upward, fairly consistent average growth of 2.1 percent per year. The consequence, of course, has been a rise in German unit labor costs since 2008. Moving dramatically in the opposite direction were the unit labor costs of Ireland, Portugal, and Spain, which substantially improved their competitive positions relative to Germany. The unit labor costs of the other major members of the Eurozone relative to Germany since the crisis have largely maintained the ranking they exhibited through the decade prior.

Euro-North has been historically characterized by high savings rates,[10] low inflation, and adherence to the rule of law (the latter can be proxied by the share of illegal activity in GDP). These are some of the metrics of a culture that determine the share of national income that is spent and the share that is saved to finance capital investment. In contrast, negative saving rates—excess consumption—have been a common feature of Greece and Portugal since 2003.

There remains the question, as this book went to press, of whether most, or all, of the south could or would ever voluntarily adopt northern prudence. A breakup of the Eurozone could leave in its wake a number of northern European countries with similar economic cultures—Germany, France,[11] Netherlands, Austria, Luxembourg, and Finland, for example—still devoted to preserving a narrowed but viable Eurozone. In the end, however, a euro breakup may be perceived as too wrenching to the economic structure of Europe.

SECOND THOUGHTS

Many members of Euro-North may be harboring second thoughts about joining the Eurozone, but once there, the process of unscrambling the eggs of finance may be too daunting to contemplate. Pending further structural changes, the European Central Bank (ECB) has effectively thrown off all of the Maastricht Treaty restrictions that bound the bank to the model of the Deutsche Bundesbank. After a whole series of actions gradually loosening its Maastricht reins, the ECB employed its ultimate weapon in the fight to preserve the euro—the innocuous-sounding Outright Monetary Transactions (OMT) facility. The creation of that facility fulfilled the vow of Mario Draghi, the able and credible president of the ECB: "Within our mandate, the ECB is ready to do whatever it takes to preserve the euro. And believe me, it will be enough."[12] It offered virtually unlimited access to central bank credit, a maneuver reminiscent of when banks allegedly stopped runs on their institutions literally by exposing their currency reserves in their windows for all to see. At this writing, no actual lending has been made against the OMT facility. Interest rates on sovereign ten-year notes of Greece, Portugal, Spain, and Italy nevertheless fell dramatically.[13] But the deep-seated tensions of the Eurozone remain.

It may be that nothing short of a politically united Eurozone (or Europe) will be seen as the sole way to embrace the valued single currency. I do not find a *fiscal* union of seventeen welfare states easily sustainable, except as a way station to full political union. A welfare state without control of its budget is a nonstarter.

There is even some question of the viability of a political union with seriously divergent cultures. Germany has not fully economically consolidated East Germany into the Federal Republic. Adjusting from East Germany's communist state to the market competition of the West has not proved as easy as most Germans at the point of consolidation (1990) thought likely. And a meaningful consolidation between Germany and, say, Greece is something else entirely.

ADDRESSING FUNDAMENTALS

Since the onset of the actual crisis in the Eurozone, a particularly distressing issue has been the unwillingness or inability of the nations of Euro-South to address their seemingly intractable budget deficits—the source of the ongoing crisis. A breakup of the Eurozone could create massive deficits and contagion. Moreover, the fear of a euro breakup for those currently heavily subsidized economies is real. No less real is the fear of a breakup to Germany, whose exports are denominated in euros, and whose global exchange rate is far lower than the rate German exporters would confront were they to export under the deutschmark currency regime.[14] Germany would suffer greater unemployment, a sensitive issue for today's narrowly divided German electorate.

Thus, when confronted with the chronic euro crisis, Euro-North has been inclined to continue bailouts, all coming directly or indirectly from central bank (ECB) money. After thirteen months and well over a €1 trillion expansion of lending to euro banks, essentially to indirectly fund the fiscal deficits of Euro-South countries, panic subsided.* This policy has been most apparent since May 2011 as European financial authorities turned to the ECB to print money to fund the persistent fiscal deficits throughout the southern Eurozone (Exhibit 10.2).

Confronted with a choice of ending deficit spending or funding it, Eurozone policy makers invariably chose the latter as the more politically attractive alternative. Such actions did, of course, resolve short-term funding crises but did little to address fundamental deficits. If the ECB—the sole source of sovereign credit in the Eurozone—will do "whatever it takes" to preserve the euro, I must assume that, if necessary, the OMT facility or any future lending vehicle will lend virtually without conditions. Between June 2011 and June 2012, assets of the ECB ballooned by more than half to €3.1 trillion.[15] Such funding is, of course, in addition to the more limited direct taxpayer funding predominantly from Germany. Since mid-2011, confronted with pain-generating budgets cuts, or the ability to ostensibly fund them solely with a stroke of a pen, the choice at every point in the euro crisis has been to temporarily fund the deficit to give policy makers more time to, presumably, address the fiscal imbalances, the ultimate source of the crisis.

The propensity of policy makers to seek the least politically painful solution to a problem is, of course, not the monopoly of Europeans. We see it everywhere. As I note in Chapter 7, when confronted with the choice of solving an economic problem, policy makers most everywhere have clearly been tilting toward "painless" short-term

---

*Since its peak in mid-2012, half of the trillion-euro expansion has been reversed.

actions rather than effective long-term solutions at a cost of short-term pain.

A BROADER PERSPECTIVE

The sorry travail of the euro at the turn of this century is only the latest evidence of the profoundly important role that culture plays in economic affairs. The key lesson of recent history is that while cultures do change over the decades and centuries, at best they do so only gradually. As the short history of the euro appears to demonstrate, culture has been far less susceptible to change than the financial markets had previously assumed. As I have noted, the markets anticipated that Spain and Italy in particular, upon adopting the euro in 1999, would alter their cultures and become more like prudent Germany.[16] After a near decade of seeming validation, however, that presumption failed under the pressure of the 2008 crisis, and the ECB had to scramble to the euro's rescue. However, governments continue to struggle with austerity fatigue. Spending cuts are fomenting strikes and protests, which so far have been contained, but Europe is far from out of the woods.

CULTURE DEFINED

By culture, I mean the shared values of members of a society that are inculcated at an early age and that pervade all aspects of living. Culture is particularly relevant in shaping the type of economic system we choose to construct in the pursuit of material goods and services. It shapes a large body of intuitive and habitual responses to the daily challenges of life. Its embraced rules of behavior enable much of life's complex daily decision-making processes to be carried out on auto-pilot, thereby removing a significant amount of the unwanted tension in our lives. It can be all encompassing, as it is in many religions, and it is rarely merely peripheral.

Aside from the compelling evidence of the history of the euro, examples of the role of economic culture are all around us. I recall a conversation I had in 2000 with Kiichi Miyazawa, the then-finance minister of Japan. I told him I thought Japan could recover more quickly from the sluggish aftermath that beset its economy following the stock market crash of 1990 by liquidating dodgy loans. Their banks had a policy of loan forbearance—that is, their banks were reluctant to call loans (especially on defaulting real estate) and liquidate the collateral, the standard procedure of most Western banks. Miyazawa responded that such provoking actions were not the "Japanese way." Calling a loan, and propelling borrowers into bankruptcy in certain circumstances, would cause them to lose "face." The Japanese just did not behave that way, he informed me. "Face" is a profoundly important aspect of Japanese culture.

The depth of that culture was also on display a decade later in the wake of the tsunami of 2011 that crippled Japan's Fukushima nuclear plant. Kiyoshi Kurokawa, chairman of the Japanese Diet's Nuclear Accident Independent Investigation Commission, asserted that the crisis was the result of "ingrained conventions of Japanese culture . . . our reflexive obedience; our reluctance to question authority; . . . our groupism; and our insularity. . . . Had other Japanese been in the shoes of those who bear responsibility for this accident, the result [might] well have been the same."[17]

A specific brand of culture—populism—has been particularly debilitating to economic progress. In *The Age of Turbulence,* I noted that economic populists are clear about their grievances but are unable to offer credible ways to address them. Capitalism and socialism are specific about the conditions they deem necessary for the creation of wealth and rising standards of living. Populism is not. It is a shout of pain.

Many twenty-first century Latin Americans, in my experience, continue to rail against the United States. Venezuela's Hugo Chavez in particular worked assiduously to his dying day to fan anti-American feelings. But cultures can change, albeit slowly. Brazil, Chile, Mexico, and Peru have had multiple episodes of failed populist policies since the end of World War II, but those formerly populist-driven economies have since successfully adopted more market-sensible policies, and with some backing and filling, have managed to implement significant noninflationary growth in recent years.

The experience of postwar Argentina, on the other hand, has been more sobering. A succession of failed economic programs and periods hobbled by inflation created economic instability. By 1991, the situation had become so desperate that the then-newly elected president, Carlos Menem, turned to Domingo Cavallo, his knowledgeable finance minister, for guidance. With his president's backing, Cavallo linked the Argentine peso one to one to the American dollar. This was an extremely risky strategy and could have blown apart within hours of implementation. But the boldness of the move and the seeming credibility of the commitment impressed world financial markets. Argentine interest rates dropped sharply, and inflation fell from almost 20,000 percent year over year in March 1990 to a single-digit annual inflation rate by late 1991. I was amazed and hopeful.

Gradually but inexorably, however, the buffer of dollar-borrowing capacity was drawn down as deeply rooted populist policies reemerged. The central bank of Argentina, in a losing effort to support the peso-dollar parity, borrowed dollars from abroad to sell for pesos. The bottom of the barrel was reached at the end of

2001. Protecting its remaining reserve of dollars, the central bank withdrew its one-for-one offer of dollars for pesos in international markets. On January 7, 2002, the peso collapsed with mounting disruption to employment and Argentine standards of living. By mid-2002, it took more than three pesos to buy one dollar. A massive default of Argentine debt induced an initial period of soaring inflation and interest rates. But much to my surprise, financial calm was restored relatively quickly. The sharp decline in the peso had spurred export sales and economic activity.

What I found memorable about this episode was not that Argentine leaders in 2001 were unable to marshal the fiscal and monetary restraint required to hold the peso-dollar link, but that they had been able for a while to persuade their population to maintain the degree of restraint that a pegged peso required. It was clearly a policy aimed at inducing a seminal shift in cultural values that would restore the international stature that Argentina had enjoyed in the years immediately preceding World War I. But cultural inertia proved, as it had many times before, too formidable a barrier. The aftermath of that episode plagues Argentinean economic policy to this day.

THE METRICS OF CULTURE

As I note in Chapter 8, for those economies that seek maximum economic growth, it appears that abstinence and prudence are necessary (though not sufficient) virtues for prosperity. Unless part of productive effort is diverted from immediate consumption and directed toward creating capital "tools," continually rising standards of living are not achievable. From an economist's perspective, this may be one of the most important choices of democratic societies.

Exhibit 10.3

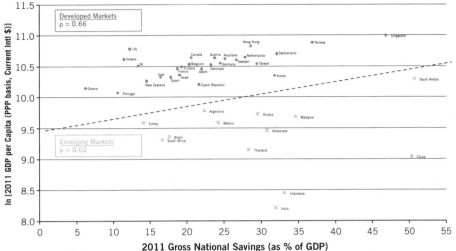

In [2011 GDP per Capita (PPP basis, Current Intl $)]

Developed Markets
ρ = 0.66

Emerging Markets
ρ = 0.02

2011 Gross National Savings (as % of GDP)

× denotes emerging markets.
• denotes developed markets.
Source: International Monetary Fund.

How long and to what extent can a population abstain from immediate consumption?[18] And indeed, the consequences of those choices most recently were reflected in the ranking of the savings rates across the Eurozone. I wasn't surprised to find "spendthrift" Greece at one end of the savings array and "austere" Austria on the other.

The relationship between savings and economic performance, however, is more nuanced. The United States, for example, has by far the highest output per hour and per capita GDP among the world's major developed countries, yet its savings rate over the past forty years has averaged close to that of Portugal. Moreover, China, on the other hand, has a 50 percent savings rate, but much of what is saved is wasted in funding empty high-rise office buildings and pet projects of important provincial leaders that do not foster long-term growth. The complexity of the tie of savings to economic growth is best illustrated by Exhibit 10.3. In the upper section of the scatter diagram lie all of the major "advanced economies" as classified by the International Monetary Fund. The relationship between their gross national savings rates[19] and real per capita GDP (at purchasing power parity) is statistically significant.[20] The lower segment, the emerging economies who are members of the G-20, exhibit no statistically significant relationship between per capita GDP and the country's savings rates.

It is only when we bring finance into the equation that ties between prudence and standards of living become evident. As I noted in Chapter 5, the purpose of financial intermediation is to facilitate the investment of savings, both domestic and borrowed, into high-rate-of-return cutting-edge technologies. The U.S. financial system, despite its periodic breakdowns, has proved historically to be a very efficient economic vehicle to maximize the use of what we put aside to fund our unparalleled productive infrastructure to produce goods and services. Generally, the major developing countries shown in Exhibit 10.3 with a savings rate similar to those in the developed world have per capita GDP only a third to a half as large as developed world nations.[21]

INNOVATION

But beyond prudence and savings, culture also plays a critical role in capital investment. The United States, for example, has historically had a culture of entrepreneurial risk taking that engenders innovation and has maximized the efficient use of our scarce savings to convert innovation into applied technology. The result is highly productive capital assets. China, on the other hand, despite its lurch toward capitalism, has an authoritarian system that in practice discourages ideas not in line with "politically correct" thinking, meaning the views of Chinese political leaders. As I said earlier, innovation is, by definition, outside of conventional thinking and is therefore a potential threat to political control by the Communist Party. As previously noted, according to a 2011 Thomson Reuters survey of the world's one hundred most innovative companies, forty were U.S. based while *none* were Chinese. Saving is thus a necessary, but not a sufficient, condition for high per capita GDP.

Innovative (thinking outside the box) entrepreneurship and prudence are largely, if not wholly, culturally driven traits. Placing hard numbers on such qualitative notions as the protection of property rights and the freedom of labor to organize is difficult terrain for economists. There is inevitably a degree of subjective judgment in such calculations. Nonetheless, the World Bank seems to have credibly surmounted this conceptual barrier and produced a useful para-

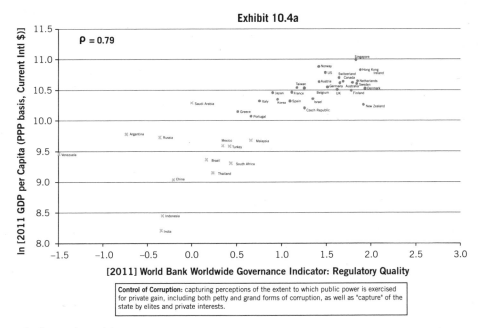

Exhibit 10.4a

$\rho = 0.79$

y-axis: ln [2011 GDP per Capita (PPP basis, Current Int'l $)]

x-axis: [2011] World Bank Worldwide Governance Indicator: Regulatory Quality

Control of Corruption: capturing perceptions of the extent to which public power is exercised for private gain, including both petty and grand forms of corruption, as well as "capture" of the state by elites and private interests.

x denotes emerging markets.

• denotes developed markets.

Source: International Monetary Fund; World Bank.

Exhibit 10.4b

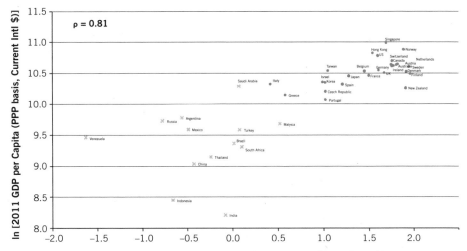

Exhibit 10.4c

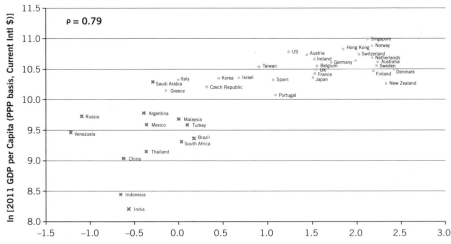

digm to convert the qualitative to the numerical. As can be seen in Exhibit 10.4, various aspects of culture are successfully tied to per capita real GDP. On each scatter plot, I include what the World Bank is trying to capture statistically.[22] In all cases, correlations are between .79 and .81, a remarkably high statistical relationship for qualitative associations such as these. An even tighter correlation exists for the advanced countries, and a very modest one for the emerging countries of the G-20. The World Economic Forum created a Global Competitive Index,[23] which in 2012 was highly correlated with per capita GDP (see Exhibit 10.5). The United States, despite some slippage in recent years, remains first among the large developed countries in competitiveness.

CONSENSUS

While it is rare that a nation has a set of cultural mores embraced without exception by the entire population, there is a visible tendency for much of a society to coalesce around a shared point of view, which can, and often does, differ measurably from the choices of other societies. A functioning society or nation must have some fundamental values held by almost all residents, or it would be in a state of constant internal conflict, if not outright civil warfare. Some organizations have written codes for dress and behavior, such as the military, but many do not.

At a broader national level, we in the United States have the Bill of Rights of our Constitution, which, since our founding, has garnered the virtually unanimous support of our population. Almost every nation has some formal constitution governing the relationship between the state and citizenry, including a set of rules of required behavior. Some nations have no formal written constitution—Great

Britain, for example. And then there are constitutions that have little to do with the way a country is governed—the defunct Soviet Union, for example.

SOCIETAL COMMUNICATION

A society requires a means of facilitating communication among members. A common language is important but not essential (for example, Switzerland and Canada). One rarely discussed aspect of the process of communication in a society is the value not just of a common language but of a similar accent to convey a sense of community and foster a sense of comfort. It enhances the extent that herd behavior hones the conveyance of common values throughout a society, thus facilitating the merging of views on, and the formulation of, public policy.

In my teenage days as a musician, I traveled around the United States extensively. One particular incident from that period tells me a great deal about the extent to which America's culture has changed in the last seven decades. I was on a train from Birmingham to Atlanta, and I happened to find myself seated next to a young southern woman with whom I conversed for the next couple of hours. I can truthfully say that I didn't understand half of what she was saying, and I am sure she had the same difficulty with my New York accent. I knew she was speaking English, but it sounded as if she was speaking in a foreign tongue.

I am fascinated by the extent in this country to which such geographical differences in accents and dialects have diminished. I remember as a youngster listening to a fairly well-known radio program during which a linguist would interview people at random from the audience and identify, not only from which part of the country the individual originated, but also, with a high degree of accuracy, often the county as well. I doubt very much that such a capability exists today. First, the talking movies that emerged in 1927 (*The Jazz Singer*) and the advent of nationwide radio about the same time began to compress the differences in accents, but it was television that greatly accelerated the process. Our tendency to mimic each other has helped merge dialects essentially into an American one in which regional differences are now modest, and still contracting.

POLITICS

Our political institutions mirror our cultural mores. Beyond the shared values implicit in our Constitution, we have always had wide-ranging differences about our political priorities. The size of the differences is readily seen in the political mapping of the Congress. In Exhibit 10.6, I chart the political leanings of the 112th Congress from "very liberal" to "very conservative" (based on their voting records), thanks to data collected by VoteView.com. There are very few "moderates" in this profile. The schism is particularly pronounced in the House of Representatives, where a significant part of the Republican majority reflects the ethos of the Tea Party, which exhibits a faint echo of the predominant culture of the nineteenth century—rugged individualism and self-reliance. The Democrats' roots lie with Roosevelt's New Deal.

The distribution of the four separate caucuses—Democrats and Republicans of both the Senate and the House—have always portrayed patterns similar to those of the current Congress, going back at least to the dawn of the twentieth century. See, for example, the caucus distribution of the 56th Congress (1899 to 1901) (Exhibit 10.7).

Today's political climate, however, seems different from much of American history in that, in earlier generations, members of Congress had major differences (as they do today), but they were willing "to reach across the aisle" to find common solutions. Such collegiality even spilled over into the White House. I well remember when President Ford and Speaker Thomas P. "Tip" O'Neill would argue vehemently with each other from 9 a.m. to 5 p.m., but at 6 p.m., Tip would stop by the West Wing to join his old House buddy Jerry for drinks. The work of government got done.

But while the Senate and House caucuses have always reflected deep differences between Republicans and Democrats, this does not appear to be the profile of the electorate. Surveys indicate a large bunching in the middle.* This seeming anomaly may reflect the severe geographical concentration of Democrats on the heavily populated East and West coasts of the country, with Republicans dominant in the mountain and southern states. I discuss the implication of such trends in Chapter 14.

---

*For example, the monthly NBC News/*Wall Street Journal* Survey shows this unimodal distribution of the electorate going back to 1995.

ELEVEN

THE ONSET OF GLOBALIZATION, INCOME INEQUALITY, AND THE RISE OF THE GINI AND THE CRONY

The generation of Americans who fought and won World War II took the lead in creating our global economic structure tied to the U.S. dollar, and propelled the United States to its unrivaled status among world economic powers. They were famously labeled by Tom Brokaw our "Greatest Generation." "They succeeded on every front . . . [and] saved the world. . . . They gave the world new science, literature, art, industry, and economic strength unparalleled in the long curve of history."[1] They spawned the baby-boomer generation and set out on a path that led the United States to become "the special nation."

America's unprecedented broad postwar assistance[2] to its war-time adversaries—Germany and Japan—as well as to its wartime allies, was instrumental in the recovery from what, for Europeans in particular, had been six years of terror. But starting in the 1960s, America turned its benevolence and wealth to the home front, significantly expanding social benefit programs to assist those who had lagged in participating in America's postwar affluence. The civil rights movement that took hold in the 1950s was instrumental in altering America's domestic priorities.

Despite the onset of rapidly growing government social benefit outlays, income inequality began its inexorable postwar rise by the early 1970s (Exhibit 11.1).[3] Inequality of both income and wealth in recent years has risen to a level that has opened up large crevices in America's political system. Political comity has fallen to its lowest level since before World War II.

INCOME INEQUALITY: THE RISE OF THE GINI

The U.S. economy, which was subject to rigid economic control by government throughout World War II, quickly demobilized and became sufficiently flexible to emerge after the war with a degree of income inequality that remained modest for years. The Gini coefficient—named for Italian statistician and demographer Corrado Gini—a measure of income inequality that ranges between zero and one, that is, from none to total, was about .38 for family incomes shortly after the war and drifted lower until the late 1960s.*

The economy that emerged from the war was heavily industrial-

*As measured by the Census Bureau.

ized. Manufacturing, the high-tech and high-paying industry of its day, accounted for 28 percent of GDP in 1953. Finance and insurance, the source of many of today's high-income recipients, accounted for only 2 percent. By 2011, manufacturing's share of GDP had slipped to 11 percent, while finance and insurance had climbed to 8 percent.

The skills required to operate our capital facilities were readily taught in American high schools and almost a third of our workforce coming out of the war had high school diplomas. In addition, extensive technical training of our military during the war and the educational benefits of the GI Bill[4] following the war augmented the skill mix of our postwar labor force. Those veterans were fully capable of operating complex manufacturing assembly lines and our economic infrastructure in general. The level of output per hour from 1946 to 1973 rose at a vigorous annual pace of 2.7 percent. Real wages rose with it. American business, confronted with a huge hunger for consumer goods immediately after the war, had to produce all out. Strikes that shut down output were very costly and largely avoided by companies meeting most of labor's demands for wages and benefits.[5] Foreign production facilities had been decimated by the war and hence import competition for U.S. manufacturers was rare. Labor unions flourished in such a benign environment for collective bargaining, as companies were able to raise prices and accommodate unions' demands.

THE GOLDEN AGE

Most factory and other skilled workers' income rose to levels that enabled them to buy a home and raise a family.[6] I recall visiting a number of friends back from the war who settled in Levittown on

Long Island, a typical example of the new suburban communities that appeared to rise virtually overnight throughout postwar America. The emergence of the Cold War and threats of nuclear annihilation were real, but they couldn't erase the state of pride and euphoria stemming from America's world hegemony. We had nearly half of the world's GDP and an unlimited future. In these early postwar years (1946 to 1970), income inequality was essentially flat (see Exhibit 11.1). That implied a stable ratio of wages earned in essentially repetitive jobs on an assembly line to those of cognitive occupations. Automation had just begun.

In the years that followed, we experienced the gradual displacement of repetitive jobs by competitive low-labor-cost foreign producers, especially China and East Asia, and increasingly sophisticated robots.[7] The consequent increased inequality was most apparent in hollowed-out middle class incomes. The Gini coefficient turned upward in the 1970s and continued its upward climb for the next thirty-five years. The causes were numerous and interrelated.

GLOBALIZATION

Among the most important was globalization in its many manifestations. As the rest of the world recovered, imports of goods and services into the United States exerted ever-increasing pressure on middle income American jobs, particularly union jobs. The share of our private sector workforce belonging to unions declined, from around 35 percent in the 1950s to 7 percent in 2012. Strikes or threats of strike—labor's most formidable tool of the 1950s—rapidly diminished. In 2012, the number of workers on strike was less than one tenth of the average number that "hit the bricks" throughout the 1950s. Union wage premiums over nonunion wages, as a consequence, have virtually disappeared in recent decades.[8] The Gini coefficient's dramatic rise starting in the 1970s reflected in part the diminishing clout of labor unions.

But while China's gradual displacement of American jobs grabbed the headlines, an increasing number of "superearners" burst onto the international scene, adding upward pressure to the Gini coefficient. This trend was best illustrated by the Beatles' emergence in the 1960s. The four mop-haired youngsters made a modest living in Liverpool, England. But it was only when they exploded on the global scene and were able to tap a vast international market for recordings and performances before large audiences that their incomes soared. Were it not for the global transportation and distribution at their disposal, they would have spent their careers in relative anonymity in Liverpool. Most important, however, was that the Beatles were not unique. They were joined at the top of the income distribution by prominent sports figures and other entertainment personalities. Without jet aircraft, these income outliers would have numbered far less.

EDUCATION'S GINI

Globalization's superearner trend is even threatening to reach down to the area of our labor force least prone to income inequality— education. Teaching has been local and lecture audiences small. Salaries have reflected the economics of one on one or, at most, one on several hundred. But that is about to change. Superprofessors at some of our major universities have already gone online, reaching many thousands at a time. It is about to become a teaching world quite different from being bottled up in local classrooms. It may take awhile before such free lectures become sources of revenue for universities,

with eventually much of that money ending up as incomes of the superprofessors, which would accordingly move up education's Gini.

STOCK PRICE DOMINATES

But outranking globalization and the superearners in importance as
drivers of inequality has been the growth of stock price–influenced
incomes. Portfolio management and investment banking vie for the
top-paying industries according to data from the Bureau of Labor
Statistics (BLS). As can be seen in Exhibit 11.1, the correlation between the Gini coefficient and the ratio of the S&P 500 stock price
index to the average hourly earnings of production workers is, un-
surprisingly, quite significant as stock price gains have greatly out-
distanced the rise in production worker wages, matching the pattern
of the Gini coefficient. But what has invited the attention of headline
writers in recent years is the extraordinary rise in chief executive officer (CEO) compensation, especially when compared with average
production worker wage.[9, 10] The rise in the ratio of stock prices to
average nonexecutive wages over the past half century is reflected in
the declining share of gross domestic income earned by nonexecutive workers compared with the share of those whose income relates
importantly to capital income—dividends, interest, rent, stock option grants, and capital gains (although the last is not included in the
calculation of the Gini coefficient). Compensation data clearly show
that the value of a CEO's total compensation package is closely tied
to the aggregate market value of the firm.[11]

Having served on fifteen boards in the quarter century prior to
joining the Fed, often on the boards' compensation committees, I
observed firsthand how the system worked. "Directors who determine executive salaries argue," I wrote in 2007,[12] "that key decisions

by CEOs leverage vast amounts of [a company's] market value. In global markets, the difference between a right move and an almost right move might represent hundreds of millions of dollars, whereas a generation ago, when the playing field was much smaller, the difference would have been in the tens of millions. Boards reflecting this view feel pressed by competition to seek the 'very best' CEO, and are obviously willing to pay what it takes to acquire the 'stars.'" I should have added that second-best choices were available at a lower package of compensation, but the reason they are second best is that their average success rate has been a shade lower than the top pick. But given the aggregate market size of the average large firm, the implication of that higher success rate, more often than not, readily swamps the pay differential required to get top tier talent. I would be remiss if I did not point out that decisions of boards of directors do not always follow "best practice." I discuss my experiences on boards, which were not always pleasant, in *The Age of Turbulence* (pages 423–36).

I have not joined any boards since I left the Federal Reserve, but while it appears that the authoritarian power of CEOs that I observed for a quarter century (from 1962 to 1987) prior to my Fed tenure has markedly diminished, an increasing number of major companies are becoming quasi-"government-sponsored enterprises." The quality of governance, if anything, has deteriorated as a consequence. If not reversed, the growth in the quality of our workforce will start to slow.

THE SCHOOLING ECHO

At the end of World War II, the skills conveyed by American educational institutions were extolled throughout the world. Students from all over the globe prized coming to the United States for an education they believed they could not get at home. Our university degrees were avidly sought, and indeed that remains largely true to this day. But our primary and secondary education systems have lagged. The 1995 Trends in International Mathematics and Science Study (TIMSS) reported data on the global status of American students that came as a shock. It and comparable measures of the shortfalls of our K-12 education system prodded changes that, apparently, have improved student performance somewhat in recent years.

But is the echo of deteriorating schooling two decades ago as yet evident in the income-earning capabilities of those educated in that environment? Now, almost fifteen years later, we would expect some evidence of deteriorating quality of education being exhibited in a slower pace of economic performance, most specifically in productivity and its marginal proxy, real incomes. The data, however, exhibit no such trend. The ratios of income for households headed by fifteen- to twenty-four-year-olds to those headed by thirty-five- to forty-four-year-olds and those headed by forty-five- to fifty-four-year-olds remain stable through 2011. This suggests that education failures may yet turn up in deteriorating performance on the part of our workforce, and I must admit it is hard to imagine otherwise. But the evidence is not yet convincing, suggesting that other areas of economic distortions are at the root of income inequality.

JOB MARKET IMBALANCE
AND THE H-1B SUBSIDY

This, however, does not mean that there is no distortion in the overall labor force. Many employers report difficulty in hiring the job skills they need, and indeed that concern is mirrored in the ratio of recent job openings to new hires, which in March 2013 was as high as it was in 2007, a period when labor markets were far tighter and all categories of workers were in short supply. This suggests that the skill structure of the workforce overall does not match the needs implied by the complexity of our capital infrastructure, most specifically in areas of high-tech industry.

One area of economic policy that has received far less attention than it should is immigration reform. It is more likely than most policy issues to stabilize income inequality by opening up our skilled labor force requirements to the large pool of skilled workers abroad who show significant willingness to fill in our gaps in skills and, most important, at a significantly lower pay level. The barrier is clearly the H-1B immigration restrictions that protect (and subsidize) our high-income earners from the pressures of global wage competition.

As I noted earlier, the share of GDP that accrues to finance and insurance has more than tripled since the end of World War II (from 2.4 percent in 1947 to 7.9 percent in 2012). These jobs today are among the highest paid in the nation, in part because they are protected by immigration quotas that restrict entry of competitors who, were they allowed, would press such compensation and the Gini coefficient lower. Demand for visas for skilled workers (H-1Bs) "has exceeded supply every year since 2003, when," as the *Economist* noted, "Congress slashed the number of visas on offer by two-thirds." Compounding the problem posed by numerical limits on employment-based visas and green cards, employers are disincentivized to pursue skilled foreigners in the first place, owing to a lengthy and expensive process required to "show that they have tried and failed to find a suitable American for the post."[13] It is difficult to overemphasize the importance of long overdue reform.

IN SUMMARY

The degree of income inequality comes down primarily to the battle between asset values and the wage levels of the bulk of our workforce. Growing inequality can be viewed as the outcome of the shares of gross domestic income captured in competitive markets by labor and capital. In the early years following World War II, labor was dominant. With the rest of the world barely recovering, import competition was rarely seen. The power to strike and shut down a company gave labor the edge at the bargaining table. The world began to change when the lowly West German Volkswagen, a small and inexpensive car, first came to our shores in volumes. American car making was heavily concentrated in big powerful cars of the time and did not seem to need to worry about small, seemingly niche markets.

But an even more telling blow to American global market hegemony was the devastating 1959 strike that shut down the American steel industry for 116 days. Domestic steel users, previously shunning imported steel products as inferior, were forced to finally try them. Steel buyers, as I recall, were pleasantly surprised at the quality of the steels that came from abroad to fill the void. It was the beginning of the end of America's vaunted unrivaled supremacy in the postwar world steel market. The American Iron and Steel Institute (AISI) switched from being a strong supporter of free trade (the United States was a large exporter of steel) to a proponent of a "control imports" policy. I sadly recall when the AISI approached Townsend-Greenspan to help them in their lobbying strategy. We declined. We had ten major steel companies as clients at the time. I saw the handwriting on the wall and began to diversify my company's client base.

Globalization was mounting, as were our imports. We slipped from producing nearly half the world's GDP immediately after the war to averaging less than 30 percent since 1980. Imports of goods rose from 2.5 percent of GDP in 1947 to 14.6 percent in 2012 (Exhibit 11.2). Labor unions' share of the workforce began to decline. Strike activity fell off rapidly. The share of national income going to corporate profits, after trending downward since the postwar years, began to trend upward in the early 1980s—and stock prices followed. With that rise came increased income inequality. That trend continued until the onset of crisis in 2008. The decidedly probusiness environment before 2008 was nurtured by euphoric booms in quick succession between 1993 and 2006. Political opposition to the probusiness environment was muted.

What can be done to end and possibly reverse the society-wrenching rise in income inequality? Having the United States withdraw from global competition is a nonstarter. It would succeed only in reducing the overall level of economic activity, both here and abroad. It would threaten the status of the dollar as the still undisputed world reserve currency. Similarly, constraining the secular rise in stock prices and the ratio of capital stock to labor input would have a similar effect. Taxation of upper income groups is limited. By 2009, according to the CBO, already more than 94 percent of individual income tax liabilities were levied on the top 20 percent of household income earners, up from 65 percent in 1979.

SEQUESTERS

But the onset of crisis created a deep schism between Democrats and Republicans, leading to the most recent "fiscal cliffs," inadvertent sequesters, and a general breakdown in necessary legislative cooperation.

This breakdown appears to have resulted indirectly from the

half century of a near 10 percent annual rate of increase in social benefits under the sanction of *both* major political parties and, since 2001, tax cuts that eliminated the fiscal flexibility that historically had been essential to fund budget solutions acceptable to all parties.

As I noted in Chapter 9, the rise in benefits has crowded out capital investment at a virtual dollar-for-dollar rate that, in turn, has significantly lessened our rate of economic growth. The unintended and ironic consequence has been a suppression of our capacity to fund future social programs. In retrospect, I have concluded that had we grown those benefit programs in line with the growth of nominal GDP since 1965 (6.8 percent per year), rather than at an actual annual rate of 9.4 percent,[14] we would have advanced social welfare goals, albeit more slowly than contemplated, but without undermining America's growth engine, arguably the ultimate source of social benefits.

TWENTY-TWENTY

Retrospection, of course, is always twenty-twenty. As I reminisced in Chapter 9, in the early 1960s fiscal policy was perceived as too structurally tight, engendering "fiscal drag" that was believed to be limiting economic growth. I do not recall any worries of overdoing the policy remedy: tax decreases and spending increases. In fact, federal government net savings remained in surplus between 1959 and 1966. We failed, however, to fully recognize the contractionary effect of benefit programs on gross domestic savings and, as a consequence, on economic growth.

That growth slowdown of the last half century has left us with much less room for further expansion of entitlements, especially given the limits to further retrenchment in discretionary spending programs. Reversing our current direction is clearly economically feasible. Unless we do so, we will be risking another wrenching financial crisis. The size of our fiscal problem is reflected in the dramatic rise in the proportion of spending that has been borrowed in recent years rather than funded with taxes. That proportion had risen from zero in fiscal year 2001 to 45 percent in early 2010, and was a still problematic one fifth in 2013.

Even bringing deficits down to a level that only stabilizes the debt-to-GDP ratio implies a permanent slowing of spending and/or a major rise in revenues from current levels. Political constituencies have gotten used to not only a certain flow of new benefits but also a continued expansion of existing benefits as well. Many of those in Congress who are constantly pressing for tax cuts are confronted with the inconvenient fact of having already sanctioned the benefit surge that now has to be financed.

A TURNAROUND

As difficult as it may appear, a turnaround of policy of the magnitude required has ample historic precedent. For example, Sweden's highly praised welfare state ran into a crisis in 1990 and has since initiated a major reversal of course. Government's share of GDP declined markedly from 1993 to 2012. Sweden brought its government accounts into balance. Its economy became competitive. They know there is still much to be done, but the *Economist,* following an extensive analysis of Sweden's and other Scandinavian economies' revival, concluded, "The world will be studying the Nordic model for years to come."[15]

The performance of the Scandinavian countries is by no means unique in demonstrating the incredible power of market competition. China, scarcely to be compared with democratic Sweden, nonetheless has demonstrated the remarkable economically recuperative powers of deregulating markets and allowing competition to flourish. And one cannot but admire the extraordinary tenacity of Margaret Thatcher, who lifted Britain from its malaise in the 1980s.

Regrettably, since 2009, the United States has been moving in the opposite direction. Our expansionary policy response to the 2008 crisis failed to restore precrisis growth for reasons I raised in Chapter 7. The Dodd-Frank Wall Street Reform and Consumer Protection Act enacted July 21, 2010, has created a pall of uncertainty over financial markets (see Chapter 5). There is no doubt that the euphoria driving the dot-com and housing bubbles bred much fraud, much of which, I suspect, to date, has gone undetected. We will never be able to fully prevent such wrongdoing. Its malignant roots are too deeply embedded in our nature.[16] So is our inbred sense of justice in seeking to punish wrongdoers. But regulatory punishment of bubble malfeasance, beyond proven criminal fraud, which of course should be vigorously prosecuted, does little to restore our economy to where we would like it to be. Revenge may be soul satisfying, but it is rarely economically productive.

COMPETITION

The fundamental driver of capitalism is competition. The unbroken line of success of China in recent decades, the so-called Asian Tigers a generation earlier, and West Germany coming out of World War II have all been predominantly the result of removing impediments to competition. The great contribution of the classical economists— Adam Smith and his followers—was to show how supply and demand interact to form a price system that directs resources to the needs most valued by consumers. To be sure, the proofs of these economic principles were in the context of individuals acting in their own long-term self-interest. Nobody, in the late eighteenth century or ever since, has *fully* believed that assumption, but nonetheless we conclude that it is close enough to the real world for these economically novel eighteenth-century paradigms to be credible.

ELASTICITY

Freedom of entry to markets creates high elasticity of supply (where a small price increase induces large increases in supply). High elasticity of supply thwarts monopolies (single sellers).[17] A loss of market power of individual sellers enhances the ability of markets to set prices that achieve the mix of production of goods and services most desired by consumers.

The theoretical demonstration of competition as the primary driver of capitalism is reinforced by strong empirical evidence. In Chapter 10, I demonstrated the highly statistically significant relationship between competition and the broadest measure of relative global economic success, real per capita GDP. Although competition works mainly through creating market flexibility, it also depends on a conviction on the part of market competitors that the price and wage outcomes of transactions that compose "competition" are "fair."

PUBLIC VERSUS PRIVATE
SECTOR ELASTICITY

In private organizations, one aspect of creative destruction that we experience is the painful process of cost cutting necessitated by a squeeze on profit margins. Companies have no choice. Public institutions, however, not subject to bankruptcy, are less concerned about getting the lowest price or cost than is a private institution. Public institutions directly and indirectly have access to sovereign credit and taxpayer funds. The response to price change of a private business ranges from high to modest. The response of a government, on the other hand, ranges from modest to none.

I observed this process first hand as Federal Reserve banks presented proposals, as required, to the Federal Reserve Board to replace the buildings that had almost all gone into operation at the start of the Federal Reserve System in 1914. I recall during the recession of 1989 that large numbers of commercial real estate properties were selling at substantial discounts. But Reserve bank building proposals were invariably for *new* buildings, despite their far greater cost. New buildings were recommended because Reserve bank buildings were presumed unique in that they needed an extra large vault in the basement. Virtually all Reserve banks eventually ended up with new, more costly buildings.

I often wondered whether the process would have been handled differently in the private sector. As diligent as we were at the Federal Reserve about saving taxpayer money, it is still the case that public budgets are *chosen* to be restrained, while private budgets are forced to do so by limited available resources.[18]

This is a classic case of inelastic demand and supply creating higher prices. I chose this example in particular because the people who were making these decisions were truly dedicated to keeping costs down. But subliminally they also knew that government was different from the private sector, where companies had to cope with the fact that funds might not be available to fund such projects under any circumstances.

If the Federal Reserve restricted its demand to new buildings only, prices of new buildings would rise relative to old ones. Restricting its choices, public sector demand for space was more price inelastic than in the private sector, where an institution, if forced by limited funds, might have found a previously unexplored alternative in refitting an older building with a vault, employing fewer real resources and increasing the elasticity of supply. In instance after instance, in my experience, government programs are far more price inelastic than comparable cases subject to private market competition. They produce a higher price and use more resources than would typically be the case in the private sector, while at the same time increasing the utility of our capital stock only modestly compared with the private sector model.

THE MARKET ADJUSTMENT PROCESS

Are free markets in general capable of adjusting more quickly to economic shocks than controlled markets? This is not an easy question to answer given the paucity of useful data, but in my experience, several noteworthy examples suggest that the answer is yes:

1. The 1973–74 oil shock,[19] when companies forced to the wall reduced demand far more than most analysts expected, especially given the earlier history of inelastic demand for oil with respect to price;
2. A widespread notion in the late 1970s that bringing inflation down was too costly in terms of unemployment, a view that was proved mistaken;

3. Medicare Part D, where drugs turned out under competition
   proved to be far less costly than previous experiences had
   indicated, though as some contend, the original cost estimates may have been elevated.

Health care, especially under government fee-for-service subsi-
dization, is an important case in point. Neither supply nor demand
for medical services appears to respond to price change as readily as,
say, the demand and supply at our corner grocery store. First, ease of
entry for medical professionals is encumbered by a long and expensive period of schooling and certification. Hence, the supply of medical professionals does not easily respond to unexpected increases
in demand. The result is higher prices. Similarly, physicians do not
leave medicine very readily as the price of their services falls. In short,
supply of medical services is relatively inelastic. The demand for
medical services is also highly inelastic, conceivably more so than
their supply. When confronted with serious illness, medical care is
given our highest priority. Where subsidized, as in Medicare, demand is particularly unresponsive to price because it becomes a virtually free good to beneficiaries. Price generally does not inhibit
individual patients.

This tendency is more or less evident in all goods and services
whose supply, and especially demand, is affected by government-
dependent private businesses. The result is less demand and supply elasticity in markets that governments attempt to favor.
Government-dependent companies and services are particularly
prone to politically determined entry—subsidies, guarantees, char-
ters, price supports, controls, leases on government land, and all
such government-sponsored actions that prevent markets from
functioning in a fully flexible manner. When markets are flexible,
monopolies cannot raise prices.

Of course, not all government policies promote increases in nonmarket-determined use of a product or service. Government is, on occasion, on the side of restraining market demand—promoting reduction in tobacco usage and innumerable drugs and foods, for example. But for the most part, government sponsorship promotes the use of products and services which, in conjunction with choosing political favorites (cronies), engenders inelastic demand and/or supply, artificially raising prices and lowering production, and in the end, reducing standards of living.

CREATIVE DESTRUCTION

The dark side of capitalism is that wealth[20] is created only when obsolescent technologies and companies are allowed to fade out and are replaced. There is inevitable pain in this process. Only economic growth, low unemployment, and new job availability can assuage the economic angst, at least in part. There is no way to fully eliminate the pain experienced by those who are the market casualties of creative destruction. If standards of living are to rise, productivity must grow. But that requires that the "new" are constantly displacing the "old" low-productivity capital assets and the jobs associated with them. Government policies that try to limit the pain and stress of economic adjustment by propping up stagnant or failing low-productivity companies against the pressures of creative destruction suppress economic growth and, ironically, in the end the jobs that the economically displaced were seeking. In recent years, too many companies that should have been allowed to fail (and restructure) or shrink have been propped up by regulation or tax payer–funded bailouts.

It is economic growth that is essential to new job creation.

Businesses hire, not out of the goodness of their souls, but because they have no other choice in periods of economic growth. Economic growth requires economic flexibility to alter a company's mix of resources. It implies creative destruction. The purpose of competitive excellence is to be a survivor. But if there is a survivor of the battle of competition, there must also be a casualty. Pain is thus a regrettable by-product of creative destruction and economic progress. Economic growth that creates new job openings does assuage the pain of job loss, but only up to a point. Through much of the twentieth century, we sought ways to contain the pain of the capitalist process. The most universally advocated was job retraining for job losers. In 1992, President Bill Clinton, however, described such government initiatives at the time as a "confusing array of publicly funded training programs."[21] Regrettably, my experience is that the political issue is not the outcomes of job training programs but whether the politician who advocates them gains electoral popularity as a result. This is the reason why there have been so many different overlapping job training programs on the books that lost their relevance years ago and should have been discarded. Community colleges appear to be doing a much better job (see *The Age of Turbulence,* page 402).

CAPITALIST "FAIRNESS"

Following the Civil War, criticisms of the "fairness" of markets began to surface when highly subsidized, newly built railroads were able to expand across the Great Plains to the West Coast, leaving the unsubsidized competitors of the railroads (stagecoaches and riverboats) unable to profitably follow them and compete for farmers' business west of the Mississippi. It added to the already widespread discontent among those farmers suffering high shipping rates charged by these railroad monopolies. It was that sentiment that eventually led to the Interstate Commerce Act of 1887, the first federal law in the United States to regulate private industry.[22]

By and large, early nineteenth-century markets were dominated by agriculture, whose pricing was largely local and competitive (almost all, of course, east of the Mississippi). Government's role in this process, as I noted in Chapter 6, was largely restricted to enforcing contracts and, in later years, antitrust and pure food and drug laws. But the world of virtually wholly free markets changed with the advent of the Great Depression and the New Deal, especially the National Industrial Recovery Act. It dictated prices and wages until it was struck down by the Supreme Court in 1935. A slew of regulatory agencies were spawned in those years that exist to this day and are best known by their acronyms: SEC, FDIC, CCC, NLRB, FHA, FCC, and many others.

Markets in the United States prior to the Civil War were generally considered "free" and, in the context of the ethos of the time, therefore "fair." Even today, when we shop at a retail store where prices are listed, we can either choose to forgo the purchase or pay the list price. Alternatively we can haggle on the issue of price. But in the end, the transaction is voluntary, and this matters in a society that believes there are rights to property as well as person. Indeed, we define a "free market" as a market where the vast majority of transactions are deemed by both sides of the transaction as voluntary and not subject to coercion by monopolists or the state. If we do not have enough money, we do not buy. But we do not expect the retailer or any other private individual to supply our needs for free. The principle extends all the way from the corner grocer to the purchase of homes and industrial companies. Very few consider these voluntary exchanges to be other than "fair."[23, 24]

Many agree that free markets do maximize the material values sought by consumers, but it is a system not of one citizen, one vote but of one *dollar,* one vote, and hence a value system skewed in favor of the wealthy. In that same sense, it is considered "unfair." There is probably no system by this reckoning that is both productive and fair. Capitalism's inequality of wealth, of course, reflects the variations of economic talent among our populations, and the prevalence of inherited wealth. As I note in Chapter 1, the propensity to favor children and relatives over strangers passes wealth within a family from one generation to another. Moreover, wealthy individuals concentrate charity on those institutions that support the values of the givers.

Since its inception in the late eighteenth century, the capitalist system thus has always been considered "unfair" by part of our population. Critics, ranging from Karl Marx and William Jennings Bryan in the nineteenth century to the Latin American economic populists of the twentieth century, have always argued that as a consequence of economic power, standards of living are "unevenly" distributed. But none of these critics have proffered a system that, when tried, has produced the material standards of living that capitalism has produced, *even for our lowest income recipients.*

LIVING TOGETHER

Our current political clash over the extent of the size of our government—the size of our welfare state—and economic fairness has been brewing at least since the New Deal of the 1930s. The roots of the issue of economic fairness, rarely discussed outside the halls of academia, date back to the long-simmering debate about who among the multitude of economic participants in the interconnected capitalist production process has valid claims on shares of its output. To this day, it remains an issue in dispute. The socialist movement that emerged in the nineteenth century, to a greater or lesser extent, held that the output of a market economy is jointly produced and that the product each individual produces cannot be disentangled from the total. In effect, all producers are equally indispensable to the creation of the whole. The higher incomes received by some individuals are not theirs by right. Therefore, duly elected government should be the custodian of the national income and the arbiter on how it is distributed. This was the implicit substance of William Jennings Bryan's Cross of Gold speech, which riveted the nation in 1896. Karl Marx went further and argued that much of national income was not only unearned but the product of the exploitation of the working class by the capitalist class. Even though Marxism has been widely rejected as an explanation of the way democratic capitalist systems work, "fairness" of income distribution continues to be a matter of fierce debate.

Classical and neoclassical economists argue that in a free competitive market, incomes earned by all participants in the joint effort of production reflect their marginal contributions to the output of the net national product. Market competition ensures that their incomes equal their "marginal product" share of total output, and are justly theirs. That view largely prevailed in most of the developed world through the nineteenth century and through World War I. The income tax, as a potential purposefully redistributive vehicle, did not emerge in the United States until 1913.

Former French conservative prime minister Édouard Balladur was dismissive of free-wheeling market competition when he analogized the process to one governed by the law of the jungle, a highly pejorative but eloquent description. "What is the market?" he asked. "It is the law of the jungle, the law of nature. And what is civilization? It is the struggle against nature." We cannot get around the fact that there is a Spencerian "survival of the fittest" aspect to market adjustments. We can no more change that than we can change its root: human nature. Such a view of the economic world dominated much of nineteenth-century America and beyond. It is not an accident that Charles Darwin and Herbert Spencer, with their stark views of human nature, dominated much of the discourse of the second half of the nineteenth century. The values of self-reliance and rugged individualism square with that starkly deterministic view of economic life. We can choose to buffer the competition's "losers" from the extremes of suffering and want, but we cannot eliminate the competition and the trade-off between productivity and such buffering.

WE MUST CHOOSE

The choice we are being forced to make is simply this: What type of society do we wish to live in? One in which self-reliance is the ethos, where government has little role aside from setting the legal conditions of political freedom, such as the rights of minorities spelled out in the first ten amendments to the U.S. Constitution? Or a society and government whose primary function is to "entitle" citizens beyond the individual freedoms defined in our constitution, providing all forms of income transfers crafted to elevate the least privileged members of society to equality of opportunity, if not equality of economic outcomes? In short, do we wish a society of dependence on government or a society based on the self-reliance of individual citizens? Which, if either, given human nature, is the most efficient in serving the society as a whole? This is at the root of the political debate between a welfare state and something far short of that.

With increasing economic abundance through the nineteenth

and twentieth centuries, the inherent economic necessity of the prudence associated with an ethos of self-reliance began to fade and morph into our current age of entitlements. But the conflict within each of us between dependence and self-reliance is made even more acute by the tyranny of economic arithmetic. We cannot expect to consume virtually all of current production and still create everrising standards of living. The math doesn't work.

THE POLITICAL RESPONSE: TOO BIG TO FAIL

As we've seen, the events of 2008—a record postwar collapse of economic activity and the historically unprecedented breakdown in the ability of a number of financial markets to operate (money market mutual funds, commercial paper, and trade credit, for example)—spawned a rapid political response that invoked massive bailouts and reregulation based on the presumption that these heretofore extremely rare economic outcomes were to become commonplace in the future. While deeply worrisome, this unprecedented response should not have come as a surprise. Economic policy had morphed since Paul Volcker and his Federal Reserve embarked on his then-very controversial tightening of monetary policy in 1979 that tilted the U.S. economy into its greatest recession of the postwar years. The Fed's goal: *future* economic stability. The reasoning was the same behind the Resolution Trust Corporation's gutsy decision to incur the wrath of Congress when in 1989 it began auctioning the remnants of the deteriorating illiquid inventories of the 747 failed savings and loans at deeply discounted prices, an action that eventually saved the American taxpayers many tens of billions of dollars.

Both the Fed and the RTC sought long-term benefits for the American economy at significant short-term political cost. That type of trade-off appears no longer acceptable. Today's policy makers are no longer allowed to incur short-term risks to increase the probability of success in achieving long-term gains. The consequence has been the emergence of a notion that, prior to 2008, had lain largely dormant in the backwaters of economic policy: that a business, especially a financial institution, had become "too big to fail" (TBTF). Its collapse, it is argued, could, because of its interconnectedness with critical sectors of the economy, bring down large segments of our economy along with it. Coupled with the current heavy bias toward government responding with a "solution" to every conceivable shortcoming of our economy, real or imagined, the doctrine of TBTF is a recipe for economic stagnation.

IN THE AFTERMATH

As I noted in Chapter 7, an immediate broad activist financial response to the Lehman collapse was necessary to stabilize America's fractured markets after its largest structural rupture in eight decades. But instead of backing away and allowing markets to rebalance in early 2009, we counterproductively, under the auspices of the Dodd-Frank Act, designated a number of financial businesses as "systemically important." Although the Dodd-Frank Act explicitly says it is focused on eliminating financial institutions that are "too big to fail," it does not.[25] How can government, having recently bailed out a number of banks, ever allow an institution designated as "systemically important" to fail? At the end of this road is crony capitalism (see page 266).

Propping up "zombie companies" (as near bankrupt companies

have come to be known) diverts part of the nation's savings from funding productive technologies to continuing the support of the obsolescent technologies of our less productive "systemically important" firms. Productive firms that are well run do not seek or need government support; hence, designation as TBTF is superfluous. It matters only to those behemoths that are less productive. JPMorgan was pressured in 2008 to take unneeded bailout money because regulators worried that unless the bailouts were seen as an all-encompassing program of assistance, irrespective of need, failing firms would also refuse to accept such unprecedented assistance for fear of being permanently labeled second rate.

Our bankruptcy statutes, with all of their shortcomings, have been a major contribution to the flexibility and success of our economy for generations. Once financial markets had stabilized and debtor-in-possession financing became feasible, these zombie banks should have been put through the normal time-tested process of balance sheet restructure rather than the more politically responsive procedures of the postcrisis years. Guarantees with sovereign credit are an addicting narcotic. This is especially the case when their heavy costs (in terms of lessened competitiveness) are delayed and, even then, insidiously hard to isolate in clear view. Federal credit guarantees accordingly in recent years have become regulators' solution of choice for most financial problems. But unscored and largely unnoticed is their negative effect on economic flexibility, so critical to economic growth.

As I noted in Chapter 5, seventeen systemically important financial institutions (SIFIs) have been designated by at least one major regulator as too big to fail, effectively rendering them guaranteed by the federal government. But I fear that even sound banks that are able to compete and survive in the roughest times on their own, if designated as too big to fail, with time will succumb to the awareness that if they take foolish risks, they will not be subjected to extreme punishment by markets. This means that even more scarce savings of the nation will be diverted to support less-productive institutions, both financial and nonfinancial, depriving funding from productive technologies. I emphasize in Chapter 9 that when the U.S. government runs a deficit *ex post*,[26] some other sector of the American economy must be deprived of resources of an equal amount. Alternatively we would need to borrow the equivalent from foreign savers to fund those who are too big to fail. Those companies *should* be allowed to fail and, if necessary, liquidate.

As has occurred with Fannie Mae and Freddie Mac, the market has already accorded these TBTF institutions subsidized funding. This is evident in the cost of funding of large banking institutions relative to competing smaller institutions not favored with subsidized borrowings. As I noted in Chapter 5, IMF researchers in a recent working paper estimated "the overall funding cost advantage of [global] SIFIs as approximately 60 bp in 2007 and 80 bp in 2009."[27] The top forty-five U.S. banks in this study exhibited about the same degree of support as the global average. I also referenced Federal Reserve research that estimated the comparable market subsidy to Fannie Mae and Freddie Mac of 40 bp.[28] In competitive financial markets, 40 bp to 60 bp is a very large advantage.

Such a market-based subsidy will enable a bank or other financial intermediary to attract part of the nation's savings to fund its operations, even if its policies and portfolio, unsubsidized, would fail. Even more worrisome, the market players are beginning to conjecture that, in the event of the next crisis, most of the American financial system effectively would be guaranteed by the U.S. government.

The net effect of the politics of the financial crisis, especially in the form of the Dodd-Frank Act, will be to lower the long-term path of the nation's productivity and hence growth in standards of living still further. Regrettably, a slowdown in productivity growth from the path it would have otherwise taken is not politically visible before it will become obvious in a permanent loss of share of global GDP.

THE "UNTHINKABLE"

Prior to the bailout of Bear Stearns, and later General Motors, Chrysler, and AIG, the notion that a large iconic American *nonbank* corporation would not be allowed to fail was rarely embodied in anybody's risk management template.[29] Few envisioned a major corporation (aside from Fannie Mae and Freddie Mac) being too big to fail. Virtually all risk managers perceived the future as largely determined by competitive markets operating under a rule of law—until 2008, that is.

Henceforth it will be exceedingly difficult to contain the range of possible policy activism in the face of even a modest economic disruption. Short of a significant credible shift in policy direction, promises of future government restraint will not be believed by markets. That became evident, postcrisis, in the failure of elevated risk spreads on liquid long-term debt to return to pre-2007 levels.[30] Uncertainty and the variance it adds to potential outcomes of actions by private firms makes the world an economically riskier place.

TIMES HAVE SURELY CHANGED

On May 10, 2012, JPMorgan, America's largest bank, reported a loss of $2 billion that resulted from a failed hedging operation.[31] The loss barely reduced JPMorgan's net worth. Common shareholders of the bank suffered a loss. Depositors of the bank and taxpayers did not. Nonetheless, Jamie Dimon, JPMorgan's CEO, was called to testify before the Senate Banking Committee. As a director of JPMorgan between 1978 and 1987, I was aware of numerous sizable losses that made shareholders unhappy. But I do not recall any bank regulator publically commenting on the issue, or the JPMorgan CEO being called to testify. The loss was an issue solely between JPMorgan's shareholders, its board, and management.

Yet the world has so changed that this recent loss was implicitly considered a threat to taxpayers. Why? Because of the poorly kept secret of the marketplace that JPMorgan will not be allowed to fail any more than Fannie and Freddie have been allowed to fail. In short, JPMorgan, much to its chagrin, I am sure, has become a de facto government-sponsored enterprise no different from Fannie Mae prior to its conservatorship. When adverse events depleted JPMorgan's shareholder equity, it was perceived by the market that its liabilities were effectively, in the end, taxpayer liabilities. Otherwise why the political umbrage and congressional hearings following the reported loss?

Many, if not most, of the seventeen systemically important American banks are market competitive and in no immediate prospect of failing to meet their obligations. History tells us, however, that eventually such dependence on government protection, as I noted earlier, will dull their competitive drive, which can eventually lead to those institutions' becoming wards of the state.

CRONY CAPITALISM

Crony capitalism emerges when government has wide discretion in controlling markets and favors some private practitioners over others. Those companies effectively become well-compensated tools of a state that shields them from the winds of creative destruction. The quid pro quo is important political support from the private firm. They have all of the important characteristics of companies that are too big to fail.

My earliest memory of what we now call crony capitalism is President Eisenhower's famous retirement speech on the dangers of the emergence of a military-industrial complex. Today crony capitalism's effect on modern global markets is undeniable. Such firms dominate the economy of Russia, where fealty to President Putin counts greatly. Widespread publicity regarding relatives of China's political leaders who have accumulated large fortunes, allegedly owing to their political connections, has been an embarrassment to the Communist Party. Crony capitalism in its various guises affects almost all countries to a greater or lesser extent. The World Bank attempts to measure and rank countries by the degree to which government has "control of corruption"—a major aspect of which is cronyism. At the top of their list of crony capitalists for 2010 were Venezuela, Russia, Indonesia, China, India, and Argentina. The least afflicted are the Scandinavian countries, Switzerland, New Zealand, and Singapore. "Cronyism" is rare in the United States because our press would pounce on any evidence of the type of blatant cronyism that exists in Russia. Nonetheless, we need to be vigilant.

THE RIGIDITIES OF ENTITLEMENT ECONOMICS

The rise of the role of government in the United States has coincided with, and is doubtless a cause of, increasing market rigidity. Competitive flexibility is a necessary characteristic of an innovative growing economy, and we are at the edge of losing it. According to the World Economic Forum, we have fallen in competitive rankings from first to seventh since 2008. The momentum of innovation of past generations is still working its way through large segments of our economy, but we are increasingly living off the seed corn of past harvests, and unless we reverse the inexorable increase in the role of government, we will surely lose our preeminence as the undisputed global economic leader.

The hegemony of the United States was evident to me as I spent more than two decades[32] in government when our country was still the undisputed "special nation." Our status was most evident in international gatherings at the IMF, the OECD, and meetings of the finance ministers and central bankers in Basel, Switzerland, and, in fact, all over the world. In recent years, that hegemony, according to Americans participating in recent meetings, has faded measurably. However, there is no apparent successor to the role of special nation. I believe we can regain our leadership role, provided we end our self-destructive policies. I will elaborate on this in the remaining chapters.

TWELVE

MONEY AND INFLATION

The spectacle of American central bankers' trying to press the inflation rate *higher* in the aftermath of the 2008 crisis is virtually without precedent. The only previous case I can recall was during the 1930s. The gold standard was abandoned in 1933 because it seemed to be depressing the general price level and inhibiting recovery out of the Great Depression. More important, the restrictive nature of gold undermined the fiscal flexibility required by the New Deal's welfare state.

After a century and a half of stable prices (when the dollar was convertible into silver and gold), fiat money[1] price inflation took hold.[2] Between 1933 and 2008, the Consumer Price Index of the BLS increased more than fourteenfold, an average annual rise of 3.4 percent. Most of the rest of the developed world abandoned gold during the 1930s and had inflation experiences similar to that of the United States. Central banks were as a consequence ceded the role of controlling the supply of money, and hence prices. Most economists at that time embraced the notion that the long-term growth rate of real GDP was facilitated by "a little inflation," and accordingly, central bankers made it their goal to keep the *rate* of inflation down rather than to keep the *level* of prices unchanged.[3] That policy, of course, acquiesced in an ever-rising price level.

In both the ancient and modern worlds, gold and silver have been universally accepted as means of payment. Their values are perceived as intrinsic and, unlike every other form of money, they do not need the further backing of credit guarantees by a third party. I have always found the status of these precious metals in our societies puzzling.[4] But by the seventeenth century, gold and silver had started to become too bulky to handle in the normal course of business. That gave rise to paper currencies and eventually bank deposits (see Box 12.1).[5] Originally, bank money was promises to redeem a note on demand in gold or silver; but it soon became apparent that sovereign government promises to pay *eventually*, rather than on demand, still made these fiat monies acceptable, within limits, as a medium of exchange.

But because they are acceptable as a medium of exchange, in addition to facilitating transactions, they can also serve as a store of value. The amount of cash needed to physically facilitate transactions is almost always quite small—amounts hung up in mail float, for example. The rest of money balances along with a large number of other assets—bonds, stocks, and even homes—are held as a store of value.

BOX 12.1: REDEEMABLE PAPER CURRENCY

As trade volumes mounted, the physical quantities of precious metals required for transactions became infeasible and by the seventeenth century, paper currency emerged in the form of "warehouse receipts" (banknotes) for stored gold. Among London goldsmiths, the warehousers of gold, paper promises to pay in gold rapidly began to displace the metal itself. It soon became obvious to the goldsmiths that much of the gold laid idle most of the time, and because gold is fungible, they realized they could lend out any part of their gold. One depositor's gold was indistinguishable from that of another depositor. Whose gold they lent out did not matter. They could issue far more warehouse receipts than they had warehoused gold. Fractional reserve banking was born.

Clearly, the average length of time gold deposits laid idle in storage determined the extent to which warehouse receipts could be expanded beyond the actual amount of gold deposits. The longer gold depositors left their bullion idle, the larger the proportion of gold "currency" that could be safely loaned out. The well-established goldsmiths soon found that because withdrawals of stored gold in any month was only a modest fraction of what they held, they could safely re-lend 50–80 percent of their gold without fear of being unable to meet the withdrawals of any depositor. The goldsmiths eventually became today's commercial bankers and their gold reserves were replaced by commercial bank deposits at central banks. This principle, in modern guise, holds to this day.

THE HOLDING PERIOD

The average holding period between acquisition of a money and its use to purchase a good, service, or asset is, of course, determined in the end by the person's propensity to save. A person living hand to mouth has no ability to save, and their holding period for money, of necessity, will be quite short. At higher income levels, holding periods for all forms of assets, money included, are quite long. In all cases, money, the data show, will be held only so long as people do not expect it to lose a noticeable part of its value—that is, so long as they don't expect product prices to rise inordinately. Only when idle store-of-value balances are spent do prices rise. In the case of extreme price rise, money holders figuratively rush for the exits; the average length of the currency's holding period collapses, and hyperinflation takes hold. Symmetrically, when people increase their holding period for money balances, by definition, spending and prices fall. But so do interest rates, in an extension of Keynes's liquidity preference paradigm.

FIAT CURRENCY

It is the variability of money-holding periods that has played so large a role in the history of fiat money and finance in general, and, as we shall see, in the structure of models of the financial sector. The soon-to-be United States financed its Revolutionary War, starting in 1775, with paper money ("Continentals"), which people initially accepted in payment for goods and services. It was used, for example, by General Washington to buy goods and services for his fledgling army.

For a while, most recipients of those proceeds apparently respent them at much the same pace they did with gold before the hostilities began. (That is, the average holding period of the currency was apparently relatively stable.) But the huge volume of fiat issuance (nearly $250 million) engulfed the market and recipients soon found themselves with more paper money than they needed and presumably began to increase their consumption expenditures and asset buying, shortening the overall average holding period. People soon began to spend the currency as quickly as they received it. Their average holding period collapsed. Within three years, the purchasing power of the Continental had fallen to less than a fifth of its face value. By the spring of 1781, valueless, it ceased to circulate. It was not, so to speak, "worth a Continental."

It is not surprising that when adopted, the Constitution of the United States reflected a hard money ethos. United States currency in circulation through the first six decades of the nineteenth century was confined to gold and silver coin, as well as banknotes redeemable for specie, such as those issued by the First and Second Banks of the United States.

Our history, however, appears to confirm that people are still willing to hold fiat money paper despite losing up to, say, 5 percent or even 10 percent a year in purchasing power. But beyond that, fiat money holders evidence increasing unease, especially if their incomes are not rising commensurately. When the fiat money printing presses speed up, money holders bail out.[6] As money turnover accelerates, the currency becomes increasingly unacceptable. In the extreme—the Brazilian financial crisis of 1993–94 comes to mind—the holding period shrinks rapidly as prices explode to the time it takes to accept funds and then unload them.[7]

THE CHOSEN

This raises a second issue of money and finance: From whom are people willing to accept money in exchange for goods, services, and assets? Anybody can create money simply by issuing a personal IOU, but can he or she get anybody else to accept it as payment for goods or other financial instruments? Sovereign nations with taxing power have proved the most credible purveyors of fiat money, reflected in their ability to float fiat money debt (IOUs) at interest rates lower than any creditor in their private sectors. Thus, governments or their central banks can print money and expect it to be held by the public as a store of value for an extended period of time—much longer than Continentals, but far shorter than gold or silver. Hence, governments can run budget deficits because they are able to find willing buyers for their notes and bonds.

MONEY MATTERS

The nature of fiat money, as well as the means to keep fiat money inflation in check, in recent years has never been in doubt. As the iconic Milton Friedman once perceptively asserted, "inflation is always and everywhere a monetary phenomenon."[8] In fact, it could not be otherwise because prices are traditionally defined in units of money, such as cents per pound and dollars per square foot. While "price" is unambiguously defined, or nearly so, money, in the sense that Friedman used the term, regrettably is not. What economists seek is a universally accepted medium of exchange. If prices are indeed defined in units of money, we should be able to find some statistical measure of money such that, when it rose faster than an economy's capacity to turn out goods and services, prices rose; and when money growth was negative relative to the capacity to produce, prices fell.[9] In short, we want a measure whose numerator is money (or any financial instrument[10]) and whose denominator is capacity. I call the ratio unit money supply.

MONEY CHOICES

There are several series that can be credibly used for the denominator (capacity) of unit money supply. All, more or less, convey the same result. What constitutes money, or more exactly, a universal transaction balance, has been far more elusive.

There has never been any doubt that currency has to be part of any transaction balance. Currency and coin for modest-sized transactions have always been acceptable as payment for goods and services. A potential problem arises because of the very large American dollar currency holdings abroad, currently two fifths of the total.[11] Foreign holdings of U.S. checkable, time, and savings deposits, however, account for less than 5 percent of total deposits. Overall, subtraction of foreign holdings of currency and deposits does not materially affect the trends of unit money supply. Accordingly, I have stayed with the more historically available data on money supply as published by the Federal Reserve.

I tested a number of choices for money supply and even a number of debt instruments as a substitute for money. The measures of money supply most economists use are variations of what we call M1, M2, and M3. M1 comprises currency, traveler's checks, demand deposits, and other checkable deposits. M2 is equal to M1 plus savings deposits, small-denomination time deposits, and retail money funds. The broadest measure, M3, adds to M2 institutional money funds, large-denomination time deposits, overnight and term repurchase agreements, and overnight and term eurodollars. Publication of M3 was discontinued by the Federal Reserve in 2006 but can be approximated with data from other sources.

The data strongly suggest that the measure of money supply that, when divided by capacity, most closely follows price is Milton Friedman's choice: M2. Both the narrower M1 and broader M3 measures do poorly relative to M2 in tracing price movements.

I use the price for personal consumption expenditures excluding food and fuel, long favored by the Federal Reserve, to represent U.S. domestic prices more generally.[12]

A TIGHT FIT

The closeness of fit of unit M2 and price over the decades is impressive (see Exhibit 12.1). From 1909 to 1933, prices exhibited little long-term trend, as was the case reaching back over the previous century. But from the onset of fiat money in 1933 to date, prices have risen at an annual rate of 3.4 percent on average. Unit M2 rose by an identical 3.4 percent annually. The two series parallel each other through World War I (1917 to 1918), the turbulence of the early twenties, the stability of 1925 to 1929, the Great Depression, World War II (1941–45), the postwar "moderate" inflation (1946 to 1969), and most of the rapid inflation between 1969 and 1991. But starting in the late 1980s, unit M2 seemed to have lost its closeness of fit to the price level. Banks had become fearful that their capital positions were inadequate, inducing them to restrain lending. I described the economy at the time as confronting "fifty mile-per-hour headwinds."[13] Provisions for loan losses as a percent of loans rose to a then-postwar high.

The breakdown of M2 spawned a flurry of analyses. I found that the most credible was published several years later in an interesting joint paper by economists at the New York and Dallas Federal Reserve banks, which concluded that M2's historic tie to inflation and economic growth had become unhinged and that "depository institutions' capital difficulties during the late 1980s and early 1990s can account for a substantial part of the deterioration in the link between M2 and inflation and economic growth. With these problems now behind us, the link between M2 and economic growth has strengthened."[14] Although price inflation did slow somewhat as unit money supply stagnated, I still find the money supply to price relationship of that period puzzling.[15]

Money supply, of course, does not directly translate into price. That occurs only when M2 is drawn upon for the purchase of goods and services. Money velocity is the number of times M2 is turned over to facilitate the transactions that make up nominal GDP (see Exhibit 12.2). The ratio of price to unit money supply is the virtual algebraic equivalent of what economists call money velocity, the ratio of nominal GDP to M2.[16] As can be seen in Exhibit 12.3, my alternative measure of money velocity (see footnote 16) can be explained by the degree of inflationary pressure on the economy (the operating rate), the level of short-term interest rates, and equity prices. The greater the degree of inflationary pressure, the more likely people will be to accelerate their turnover of transaction balances; the higher the interest rate or rate of return on equity, the more likely people are to hold income-earning assets in lieu of cash, thereby reducing M2 and raising money velocity. Combining these determinants of money turnover with money itself portrays an even closer historical fit to the general price level (Exhibit 12.4). Thus, in summary, money supply is by far the dominant determinant of price over the long run, but in the short run other variables are important as well.

Given all the other evidence of suppressed demand, money

velocity in 2012 not unexpectedly was at its lowest level in more than a half century.

MONEY AND PRICES IN FOREIGN ECONOMIES

In most foreign countries, unit money supply and price moved in patterns similar to those in the United States, though with far less tightness of fit. In countries with substantial international trade, import prices materially affect the general price level and hence blur the relationship between price and *domestic* unit M2. But the most dramatic example of the inflation-money link outside the United States occurred in Brazil between the first quarter of 1993 and the third quarter of 1994, when the country's fiscal and financial breakdown led to a near 150-fold increase in prices and a 180-fold increase in unit money supply.

THE LOAN/MONEY MULTIPLIER

Central bankers in London, Frankfurt, Tokyo, and Washington have responded to the aftermath of the 2008 crisis with a massive expansion of their balance sheets. The Fed more than tripled the size of its assets between late 2008 and mid-2013. Nine tenths of the U.S. expansion was funded by the Fed's creation of central bank money: currency and reserve balances (the monetary base) held by depository institutions at the Fed. Those commercial and savings banks are currently being induced by the Fed to hold the bulge of reserve balances by paying an interest rate of 25 basis points on those funds.[17]

When the banks decide to lend their reserve balances to bank customers, they first have to set aside additional capital and loan loss reserves as insurance against default on the new loan. I estimate that during the years 1995 to 2007, the amount set aside (the monetary base divided by M2) averaged 12 percent of the loan (see Exhibit 12.5)[18]. But fear-gripped lending officers have been setting aside a much higher percentage of loan acquisitions since the Lehman collapse—26 percent in 2012 and more than 30 percent as of mid-2013. Loan officers in recent years have obviously become quite leery of lending to other than the soundest borrowers.

Virtually all of the proceeds of new loans are spent on inventories, capital equipment, cars, homes, and a variety of goods and services.[19] The retail stores, contractors, and all other recipients of the new spending deposit their funds into one or more banks. Those banks, in turn, after their necessary set-asides, relend them to customers who proceed to spend the borrowed funds.[20]

In short, the initial Fed deposit (or currency issuance) ends up financing a long series of ever-diminishing new loans, cumulating to a multiple of the Fed's original central bank money injection. That process continues until the individual bank set-asides cumulate to the size of the original reserve balance injection.[21] How long it takes to complete the multiple cycles of lending depends largely on the size of the set-asides that consecutively drain off the reserve balance. The larger the set-aside, the smaller the loan multiplier. Given the current near-record size of the set-asides and the rapid rate of spending loan proceeds, most of the loan multiplication process presumably takes less than six months after the initial injection of Fed reserves. Moreover, the pace of decline affects Fed policy. If policy requires a steady *level* of central bank assets, the Fed will need to replenish the reserve balances as they are converted to bank loans and currency.

REDUCING THE FED'S BALANCE SHEET

The ratio of M2 to the monetary base in mid-2013 matched its all-time low in 1940. The Fed, of course, is fully aware that the current amount of central bank money eventually needs to be reined in and, presumably, plans to reduce it prior to the onset of market pressure to do so. The simplest means is to sell Fed assets, almost wholly Treasury notes, bonds, and mortgage-backed securities. This, the conventional procedure by which the Fed tightens credit, will induce a significant rise in interest rates.[22]

The next most effective measures to absorb large amounts of reserves are a hike in reserve requirements and/or issuance of Federal Reserve bills. Again, interest rates would doubtless rise. But latter initiative, however, would require legislation that, in today's climate, would be politically precarious for the independence of the Fed. Unless the economy unexpectedly moves quickly into high gear, any credit tightening will, as usual, run into considerable political opposition. It always has.

FEAR AND THE FUTURE

One of the themes of this book is that fear induces a far greater response than euphoria. Accordingly, asset prices and other fear-sensitive financial variables move far more rapidly when falling than they do when rising. Thus, while the collapse in the money multiplier was sharp and deep following the 2008 crash,[23] its recovery is apt to be gradual. There's not much history to give us guidance to recovery. But what we have most likely suggests that the pattern of recovery would be that which followed, for example, from 1952 to 1963. That represented a near doubling of the money multiplier, spread over the course of eleven years. That would suggest a rate of increase in unit money supply and hence in prices, through 2017, averaging more than 7 percent per year. A similar pace of rise in the multiplier between 1918 and 1930 yields an implicit annual rate of price rise from 2012 to 2017 of 6 percent.[24] Given so few comparable periods during the past century, such forecasts need to be viewed as illustrative simulations only. It is easy to contemplate price acceleration, with today's Federal Reserve balances unchanged, ranging from 3 percent per annum to double digits over the next five to ten years. Interest rates under any scenario will rise, as will arguments that the Fed's tightening was premature.

The Fed somewhat surprisingly weathered virtually all assaults on its authority following the crisis of 2008. Approaching its one hundredth anniversary, it has a long history of resilience to political forays.

THIRTEEN

BUFFERS

Not a day goes by that does not reveal deterioration in some aspect of our nation's public infrastructure, followed by a call for immediate action. The average age of highways and streets, as estimated by the Bureau of Economic Analysis, has increased from sixteen years to twenty-five years since the early 1970s. To those of us who have to drive over our increasingly pockmarked streets, numbers shouldn't be necessary. Sewer systems and public hospital buildings have aged similarly. Even our national parks are falling behind in maintenance.

But the most visible aging of government assets, and possibly the most consequential, is that of our military. Had we not had excess manufacturing capacity and infrastructure as we entered World War II, we could not have countered our enemies with overwhelming capacity to produce. The size of budget deficits that prevailed during the war was a measure of the extent to which we marshaled the savings of the private sector to help fund the purchase of war materials. But in order to get consumption down and savings up, rationing proved necessary.

Since the end of the war, the average age of military buildings and other facilities has tripled. If there is such a thing as a poster child of aged military equipment, it surely must be the fleet of B-52s, the long-range strategic bomber. It has a long distinguished history. As I wrote in 1952, "The long-range intercontinental bomber tasks will be in the hands of a new swept-wing eight-jet bomber now undergoing test—the B-52."[1] Its latest version, the B-52H, whose final production run ended in 1964, did yeoman service as recently as 2003 in Iraq. It is scheduled to remain in service beyond 2040. I am certain that there are innumerable current B-52 pilots whose fathers, and conceivably grandfathers, flew earlier models of this renowned aircraft. There are still eighty-five H models, fitted with modern avionics, in our active inventory.

The aging of naval ships has gained even greater prominence in the press. Our aircraft carriers are expected to have a fifty-year service life, and many of them are well up in nautical adulthood. I hesitate to include the USS *Constitution* ("Old Ironsides"), the oldest commissioned warship afloat, a wooden-hulled frigate celebrated for its exploits in the War of 1812. It is in a class of its own. It was first deployed in October 1797 and most assuredly is the most renowned piece of military equipment still in our inventory. Its propulsion system is identified by the navy with mock seriousness as 42,710 square feet of sail on three masts.

If "Old Ironsides" is the oldest naval vessel in our arsenal, the newest, scheduled to be delivered in 2015, is the aircraft carrier *Gerald R. Ford,* the first in the Ford class of carriers that are being added to the aging Nimitz and Enterprise class carriers. I can think of no more appropriate tribute to my old boss, President Ford, than to have a leading edge of our military power named after him.

The Abrams tank, the main battle tank of the army, is more than thirty years old, as is the Bradley armored infantry carrier. Much of the army's equipment, however, is new, fashioned largely for its operations in Iraq and Afghanistan. Some of it, such as the large special trucks engineered to meet the devastation of roadside mines in many sensitive combat areas, may not be relevant in the future.

It is not quite clear, however, how important the aging is to our national security. It all depends on a forecast of who our enemies are going to be five to fifteen years from today. Most analysts believe that the probability of head-to-head superpower confrontations like those that dominated the first four decades following World War II is very small, but no one seems sure. Our military structure cannot significantly change quickly—the very long delivery lead times preclude it. But the type of military hardware we procure in the years immediately ahead will depend very much on our longer-term balance of power perspectives.

The issue of equipment aging divides military and political tacticians and will likely continue to do so for the intermediate future. I would hope that this debate is not resolved by another conflict in which American military capabilities are sorely tested.

SO, TOO, THE PRIVATE SECTOR

The private sector has not been immune from the aging of infrastructure. Since the 1970s, the average age of manufacturing industry assets, for example, has increased from under eleven years to more than sixteen years. Similar aging is evident in wholesale trade, utilities, and air transport.

The share of private nonresidential buildings in real GDP has been in long-term decline since 1981, and those buildings are not being replaced, probably reflecting the slowdown in growth of the working-age population (fewer workers, fewer buildings), as well as the recent increased discounting since 2008 of expected incomes from very long-lived assets.

THE TASK AHEAD

There can be little doubt that a major modernization of our infrastructure is long overdue. It is easy to demonstrate the time and motor fuel wasted in traffic jams owing to failure to keep road capacity growing in line with the number of vehicles on the road. But fixing the public infrastructure is no easy task. Funding is the major obstacle. Our fiscal position is daunting. To balance the budget, we need to raise revenue by a fourth or cut outlays by a fifth, or some combination of the two. We are unlikely to get close to balancing the budget even within ten years. Increasing federal outlays on infrastructure will increase the deficit (negative savings) and must be matched, *ex post,* by a comparable rise in savings less capital investment by households and private business or by increasing our rate of borrowing from abroad. To the extent that increased deficit spending curtails capital investment in other sectors, it is a depressant to economic growth in the short term and productivity in the long term. But unaddressed is the question of the effect of infrastructure on productivity. Rising outlays on infrastructure will, of course, increase nominal GDP, which, in turn, should increase the level of gross domestic private savings, but not nearly enough to be significant.

We are no longer the nation that we were coming out of World

War II, which built a visible public (and private) infrastructure while still diverting a large part of our GDP to Cold War defense. We did it then by maintaining a savings rate out of household income of 10 percent. Today, as I've noted, that rate is in low single digits.

THE LARGER ISSUE

Our infrastructure deficiencies are part of a larger problem confronting the United States—the amount of our resources we set aside for contingencies. There are some inventories that sit unused for years—the Strategic Petroleum Reserves, for one. Some resources we produce stand idle for protracted periods and may in fact never be used: vaccine stockpiles for epidemics that never happen and dykes along rivers that never reach flood levels. By far our largest standby asset is, of course, our military.

Such assets serve as guarantees against, for example, foreign invasion, flu epidemics, tsunamis, and hurricanes, none of which are predictable and may never happen. They nonetheless require the building up of buffers of idle resources that are not otherwise engaged in the production of consumable goods and services. They are employed only if and when a crisis emerges. Such buffers address contingencies that range from uncertain but repetitive to rare and unpredictable. The former are insurable because they offer a reasonably steady rate of return to insurers. The latter are not.

Individual fires cannot be predicted, but they happen often enough for almost all cities to create and fund fire departments, whose cost is tantamount to insurance premiums. Health emergencies are not predictable but are also sufficiently repetitive to create health insurance, hospitals, and ambulances. The buffer may encompass expensive building materials (for example, special steels) whose earthquake flexibility is needed for only a minute or two every half century, or lightning rods that could be struck every month, or every decade.

The most visible insurables are life and property. I suspect that the higher the standard of living, the larger the share of GDP that originates in private insurance. Long-term uncertain risks have indeterminate probability distributions and are hence not insurable. Only risks on which actuaries can put a numerical probability are insurable. Risks that are highly variable imply too unstable a rate of return.

The choice of funding buffers is one of the most important decisions that societies must make, whether by conscious policy or by default. If policy makers, private and public, choose to buffer their populations against every conceivable risk, the nation's current standards of living would, of necessity, decline. Funding such "investments" requires an increase in savings and, accordingly, a decline in immediate consumption. Resources can be put to active use or on contingency standby status, but not both at the same time. Buffers are a dormant investment that may lie idle and seemingly unproductive for most of their lives. But they are included in our total real fixed assets (and real net worth) statistics. It is no accident that earthquake protection of the extent employed in Japan, for example, has not been chosen by less prosperous countries at similar risk of a serious earthquake. Those countries have either explicitly or implicitly chosen not to divert current consumption to fund such an eventuality. Haiti, a very poor country, has not yet fully recovered from its 2010 earthquake. It had neither built a protective infrastructure like Japan's nor has it had resources to recover on its own. Buffers are largely a luxury of rich nations. Only rich nations have the resources to protect their populations against events with extremely low probabilities of occurrence.

How much of its ongoing output should a society wish to devote to fending off once-in-fifty or one-hundred-year crises? How is such a decision reached, and by whom? While the decisions of what risks to take remain predominantly with private decision makers,[2] the responses to low-probability events such as the Japanese earthquake and tsunami of 2011 have been largely government scripted. Although formal data are not available to gauge the depth and quality of our standby buffers, the aging and deterioration of our fixed capital stock, both public and private, is ample evidence that a subclass of those assets, standby buffers, is also in a state of decline.

FOURTEEN

THE BOTTOM LINE

When I was first contemplating the substance of this book, I was fully aware that a basic assumption of classical and neoclassical economics—that people behave in their rational long-term self-interest—was not wholly accurate. Moreover, the crisis of 2008 had impelled me to reassess my earlier conclusion that our animal spirits were essentially random and hence impervious to economic modeling. I was amazed, however, during the early months of this venture at just how many supposedly random variables were explained by statistically highly significant regression equations. Many, if not most, economic choices, the data show, are demonstrably stable over the long run for as far back as I can measure. My list is long, though doubtless, incomplete.

MODEL BUILDING

Producing a fully detailed model is beyond the scope of this book. But such a model would include a number of variables reflecting those verities of human nature that reveal long-term economic stabilities. Among them are time preference (and interest rates), equity premiums, corporate earnings–price yields, and, since the nineteenth century, the private savings rate. They reflect the outer limits to fear and euphoria that define the dynamics of the business cycle. For forecasting purposes they can be assumed to continue trendless in the future.

In addition, there are those stabilities that are not inbred, such as the sum of social benefits and gross domestic savings as a percent of GDP. Other forecast stabilities include the size of the workforce—those potentially in the workforce have already been born—and average hours worked.

Owing to the vagaries of human nature, forecasting will always be somewhat of a coin toss. But I believe if we appropriately integrate some of the aspects of animal spirits' systematic behavior, constrained by market forces reflecting the imperatives of double-entry bookkeeping identities, we should importantly improve our forecasting accuracy. Euphoria will always periodically produce extended bull markets that feed off herd behavior, followed by rapid fear-induced deflation of the consequent bubbles.

These models should embody equations that, when possible, measure and forecast systematic human behavior and corporate culture. Regrettably, we have too few relevant historical observations that yield confident insights into the way financial markets behave, though we know a great deal more than we did before the 2008 crisis.

But we are far removed from the halcyon days of the 1960s, when there was great optimism that econometric models offered new capabilities to accurately judge the future. Having been mugged too often by reality, we forecasters appropriately express less confidence about our abilities to look beyond our immediate horizons. We will forever need to reach beyond our equations to apply economic judgment. Fortunately, most of our intuitive insights, when subject to the discipline of a syllogism, apparently do conform to reality.

We may never approach the fantasy success of either the Oracle of Delphi or Nostradamus, but we can surely improve on the discouraging performance of the past five years.

INTROSPECTION

This journey of analysis has finally come to rest in a place I could never have contemplated when I first began to recalibrate my economic views in light of what the crisis of 2008 was telling us about ourselves. America started out in the glorious aftermath of an early post–World War II era when we took the lead in setting up a new international financial system based on the U.S. dollar as well as an International Monetary Fund, World Bank, and GATT.[1] As I noted in Chapter 11, it was not until the 1960s that we turned our national benevolence to the less well off within our own borders and set in motion an inexorable rise in social benefits to persons. Since its inception with Social Security in 1935, the social benefits program had barely demonstrated much momentum until Medicare was enacted in 1965 and benefits embarked on their unrelenting rise from 4.7 percent of GDP to nearly 15 percent of GDP by 2012. As I noted in Chapter 9, had we kept social benefits' *share* of GDP to a still large 4.7 percent, as best I can judge, little of the fiscal chaos we are now experiencing would have found its way to the front burner of public policy. Especially disturbing is the fact that the retirement of the baby-boomer generation, the recipient of a large share of the benefits, has just begun.

But we have sadly learned that social benefits, never contemplated in a significant role of government before the Depression of the 1930s, have developed a whole infrastructure of political constituencies in support of every new entitlement. Trust funds for social benefits were crafted to mirror fully funded private pension plans. Contributions to trust funds plus interest and, since 1984, taxes on benefits, however, have fallen far short of full funding of benefits, according to the funds' official actuaries. But even the federal government's efforts to finance all of these programs on at least a pay-as-you-go basis have also fallen short, to a point where a fifth of federal government outlays (especially benefits) have to be borrowed in financial markets. The source of those funds is almost wholly private domestic savings and whatever savings we can borrow from abroad.

Postwar current account surpluses reflected the unmatched generosity of America. Exports of abundant grains[2] from America's heartland and industrial materials and capital goods were shipped from our shores in 1947 and 1948. But starting in 1982, the surplus ran out and we began instead to have to borrow from foreign businesses, individuals, and governments to supplement our diminishing flow of domestic savings. Those borrowings have created a net American debt to the rest of the world valued currently at nearly $5 trillion. As our government budget deficits rose, gross domestic savings fell pari passu. The cause of our diminished flow of gross domestic savings, as I document in Chapter 9, is demonstrably government social benefits to persons.

Gross private domestic savings as a share of GDP have been remarkably stable reaching back to 1870 (see Exhibit 9.5). It remains the primary source of funding of American gross domestic investment—the source of productivity growth and standards of living. Personal consumption expenditures, by definition, add nothing to our capital stock and hence nothing to our future standards of living.

Yet social benefits, almost all of which are consumed, as I demonstrate in Chapter 9, have been a virtual dollar-for-dollar diversion of private savings flows from private fixed capital investment to personal consumption expenditures. As CBO data demonstrate, owing in part to the continued rise in income inequality, the highest quintile of income earners accounted for 94 percent of individual income tax liabilities in 2009, up from 64 percent in 1981.[3] That quintile has been a major source of funding for the rise in benefits. The average savings rate of the top quintile is approximately 10 percent to 15 percent of income,[4] but I calculate that the *marginal* savings rate of this group is triple that, as I document in Chapter 9. Household savings as a percent of disposable personal income have declined from approximately 10 percent in the mid-1970s to less than half of that in 2013.[5] The unexpected outcome of the switch from savings funding investment to financing consumption has been the significant decline in the growth rate of GDP and the erosion of household middle incomes.

American business, however, *is* doing well. Cash flow has risen significantly, not because the economy is robustly expanding (it has not) but because business costs are under control, with competitively and technologically suppressed hourly wage costs of production workers rising less than 2 percent annually during the past couple of years, and even less in real terms (see Box 14.1). This weakness reflects, in part, the remarkable decline in private sector union participation. The evidence confirms that collective bargaining does increase union wage premiums. Public unions have also come under stress as diminished tax revenues increasingly press on state and local employee earnings.

But even our still vibrant corporate sector seems hardly likely to continue thriving unless the pall of uncertainty is lifted and a far greater proportion of its abundant cash flow is invested in capital outlays. This is especially important because, with government outlays constrained by deficits, the only significant source of self-generating spending is private business that, with large unused cash flows, has resources to expand (see Box 14.2). American innovation continues to edge out global competition, but the diminishing rates of GDP and multifactor productivity gains—the latter our measure of the extent to which innovation contributes to a higher growth rate—are worrisome.

BOX 14.1: THE MISMATCH

The increasing shortfall of adequate skills to match the ever-rising needs of our workforce has led in recent years to a shift in the composition of capital investment toward labor-saving equipment. That has pressed many semiskilled workers' wages lower as robots take over routine though still complex tasks. Pressure on highly skilled workers' wages has been less, especially given the limited quotas for competitive high-skilled immigrants.

With, as I noted in Chapter 8, an apparently inbred upper limit to human IQ, are we destined to have an ever smaller share of our workforce staff our ever more sophisticated high-tech equipment and software? Even taking into account population growth, do we ever reach the point when all we have left is a small handful of especially talented people who can create and operate the newer technologies?

Technology rarely moves at the same pace as the educational capabilities of a workforce. While there is an upside limit to the average intellectual capabilities of a population, there is no upper limit to the complexity of technology. This implies an ever greater need of automation where robots' simulated intellectual capabilities must begin to have the capacity (taught by human beings) that we have yet to imagine.

The gap between job openings and new hires in an increasing number of occupations raises the specter that, at our best, we may not have the capability to educate and train students up to the level increasingly required by technology to staff our ever more complex capital stock. The median attainment of our students just prior to World War II was a high school diploma. That level of education at the time, with its emphasis on practical shop skills, matched the qualifications, by 1950s standards, for a reasonably skilled job in a steel mill or auto-assembly plant. The mass of our labor force then was still dominated by high school graduates and less. On-the-job training filled what education holes still existed. These were the middle income jobs of that era.

But the skill level required of today's highly computerized technologies cannot be adequately staffed with today's median skills. Moreover, much of what absorbed labor a half century ago has been displaced by robots and more advanced forms of labor-saving technologies. It is in this context that the seeming failure of our primary and secondary school systems (K to 12) in recent years raises concerns about levels of future productivity growth.

BOX 14.2: THE MULTIPLIER

It is always difficult to envision the source of recovery or decline in economic activity when such a large proportion of that activity is endogenous, that is, determined solely by responses to the initiatives of others. The reason for the current suppressed economic environment is that inflowing orders are themselves reflecting incoming orders of others. How does an economy exit self-reinforcing stagnation? Fortunately, not all order placements are in response to other players in the economy. For example, a company with a new invention decides to build a new plant to manufacture widgets for which there is yet a market. The activity of building the new plant increases the stream of endogenous orders that are set off by the initiative of the new investment. That process, duplicated many times over, will enlarge the flow of endogenous orders that will carry the total economy to higher levels. This is the famous economic multiplier at work.

LOOKING BACK

The most problematic trend that has emerged from this crisis is the doctrine of "too big to fail" (TBTF). As I explain in Chapter 5, the role of finance is to allocate the savings of a society toward funding the most promising cutting-edge investments. TBTF aborts that process and economic growth and is rapidly spawning an American crony capitalism. I have come to a point of despair where, if we continue to make banks wards of the state through TBTF policies, I see no alternative to forcing banks to slim down to below a certain size threshold where, if they fail, they will no longer pose a threat to the stability of American finance.

LOOKING AHEAD

I have purposely refrained from the type of long-term forecast that I made six years ago for the year 2030 in *The Age of Turbulence* because it required, then and now, an assumption that there would be no "governmental restrictions against competition in domestic markets" (page 467). I cannot make such an assumption currently yet cannot think of a credible alternative assumption.

Integrating evidence of how people responded during the recent years of extreme economic stress has furthered economists' understanding of financial and economic relationships during periods that almost all of us have rarely, if at all, experienced. We have learned a great deal about tail risk and risk aversion generally. Bubbles seem more understandable, as does the fragility of markets. The exercise is scarcely complete, but I believe economists now have gained access to a vast array of data that no generation has had before. Those newly available data have allowed me to answer the question that I put to myself in Chapter 1: "We humans appear a truly homogenous species. But at root, what are we?" The answer, I now tentatively conclude, at least from an economist's perspective, is that we are driven by a whole array of propensities—most prominent, fear, euphoria, and herd behavior—but, ultimately, our intuitions are broadly subject to reasoned confirmation.

That reason persuades me and most economists to conclude that modern industrial capitalism, despite earlier excess enthusiasm of what it could accomplish, has been the most effective form of economic organization ever devised, a fact attested to by the remarkable gains in material well-being and life expectancy that it has produced since its emergence during the eighteenth-century Enlightenment.

But at its core is creative destruction, a system of winners and losers. If we wish to achieve ever higher levels of productivity and standards of living, there is no alternative to displacing obsolescent low-productivity facilities with facilities embodying those technologies at the cutting edge. Arithmetic requires it. But there is the inevitable hardship imposed on significant segments of our workforce who lose their jobs and often their homes in that process of displacement.

POLITICAL SCHISM

The conflict of goals has manifested itself most visibly in recent battles over American federal budget priorities. These battles have exposed a schism in our national electorate that is unprecedented in our postwar experience. The political conflicts we are currently experiencing reflect the fiscal, monetary, and regulatory paths on which we find ourselves. The angst has had profound effects on long-term business investment confidence, as reflected in suppressed investment in assets with life expectancies over twenty years (see Chapter 7). Following its collapse, hopefully home building is on an important rebound. But at its latest reading (June 2013), single-family housing starts were still only a third of where they were at their peak of seven years ago.

We need to lift the burden of massive new financial regulation that is becoming increasingly counterproductive (see Chapter 5). Overall business capital expenditures, as a share of cash flow, need to continue to rise from their lowest readings since the Great Depression of the 1930s. If we remove the pall of uncertainty on business and investors and merely return equity premiums to near normal, the rise in stock and other asset prices will do more to galvanize our recently moribund job market than any currently proffered government program (see Chapter 4). Moreover, we need to increase the level of bank lending currently suppressed by the lethargic demand for funds and the perceived need of banks to protect their equity capital (see Chapter 12).

I recognize that such a reversal will put us back into a mode of elevated creative destruction and rejuvenated animal spirits. I see no alternatives, given human propensities that are prone to excess. I see no way of removing periodic irrational exuberances without at the same time significantly diminishing the average rate of economic growth and standards of living. There was no irrational exuberance in the Soviet Union and none in today's North Korea. But there was, and is, a depressed standard of living. Rising standards of living require innovators who have unlimited expectation of success and perseverance no matter how many times they fail. Thomas Alva Edison in particular comes to mind. Exuberance (the propensity for optimism) is required—even if at times it runs to excess.

Our fractional reserve financial structure is inevitably a source of instability. That can be readily addressed, however, by expanding the level of capital requirements of our banks and other financial intermediaries by more than currently contemplated. In doing so, we can remove many of the threats of an unstable financial system. Had large capital buffers been in place in 2005 and 2006, extensive losses would have nonetheless occurred, but they need not have toppled the financial system. With adequate capital, no contagious defaults could have arisen. For some banks, "adequate" equity capital requirements, however, may be too high to produce a competitive return on equity. They will have to shrink or liquidate. But high capital requirements, I strongly suspect, will also nudge the ratio of net income to assets higher in the process, leaving net income as a percent of capital in line with history's remarkable period of stable returns to equity (see Chapter 5).

THERE *MUST* BE A BETTER WAY

Our highest priority going forward is to fix our broken political system. Short of that, there is no viable long-term solution to our badly warped economy. In America we are being pulled apart politically in ways unrivaled since the aftermath of the 1929 crash.

Fortunately, modern societies have finally abandoned as unworkable the various economic models of socialism that were so popular a century or more ago. But we need to recognize that welfare states, unless contained, have proven similarly trouble prone. Even the long-vaunted welfare model of Sweden has felt the need for a significant overhaul.[6]

Democratic societies such as ours require a broad and deep adherence to a set of principles that are not subject to compromise. As I noted in Chapter 10, for Americans it is our Bill of Rights. But if 300 million people are to live in relative peace and tranquillity, most every other legislative initiative must be subject to compromise. If every debate were on a matter of uncompromisable principle, we could never reach agreement on a functioning set of laws to which virtually the whole society could adhere. Such a condition happened once in this country and it led to wrenching internecine warfare. For the nation's first nearly three quarters of a century, the festering inconsistency of adhering to the principle that "all men are created equal" yet condoning slavery finally exploded with, and was resolved by, a civil war. Our nation has since fought its way through two world wars, a Great Depression, a constitutional crisis leading to the resignation of a president, and most recently a Supreme Court ruling to determine the outcome of a presidential election.

My first realization of a striking shift in our politics was brought to my attention by the staunch conservative three-term senator from Utah, Robert Bennett. He feared that despite his strong approval ratings, his 2010 reelection bid was by no means secure. In his 2004 reelection, Bennett won 69 percent of the vote. His problem, as he stated it, was unexpected contenders for his Senate seat from his political *right*. It was my first awareness of what later came to be known as the Tea Party, a political movement that emerged in 2009 and became a powerful force in the 2010 election.

THE STAKES

Both uncompromising sides of our ongoing debate on fiscal and other issues need to recognize that financial crisis lurks should we fail to resolve our deeply disruptive fiscal imbalance. And that imbalance is far greater than the official data portray (see Box 14.3). Differences even of the current magnitude are not new in this country, but as I noted in Chapter 10, we seem to have lost our legislative ability to reach across the aisle to find common ground for solutions. At risk is the status the American economy has held as the preeminent world economic power for more than a century.

BOX 14.3: CONTINGENT LIABILITIES

Throughout most of American history, a private bank or firm under stress was expected to either save itself or file for bankruptcy. Government bailouts were almost never on the table. That ethos remained largely intact into the twenty-first century. Even Fannie Mae and Freddie Mac were "officially" not too big to fail as late as 2006. The bailout premise cracked in 2007 and was eviscerated in 2008. The general current expectation in most markets is that large financial institutions and some iconic nonfinancial firms, in trouble, would be rescued by the government. Virtually overnight the liabilities of much, if not most, of finance, along with some nonfinancial debt, became de facto contingent liabilities of the U.S. government (including the Federal Reserve).

For decades, American sovereign debt has always been a potential, but rare, source of support for private financial intermediaries (Continental Illinois) and nonfinancial firms (Lockheed). But the recent bailout of General Motors and Chrysler has underscored a future willingness on the part of government, as an almost routine policy initiative, to backstop private business far more generously. Central banks in developed countries, more generally, have also made it clear by their actions in 2008 and since that in the event of a future pending default of the private financial system, they will step in and provide as much credit as is required to prevent such defaults and their associated contagion. For finance, such guarantees ultimately lead to a collapsing and consolidating of much of the banking system into the central bank. This has in fact already occurred to the banking systems of the southern Eurozone. Moreover, expansions in a central bank's assets and monetary base have always created increases in money supply (transaction balances) (see Chapter 12) that, with a long lag, almost invariably ignite the general price level.

POLITICAL WASHINGTON

My introduction to "political Washington" came in the 1960s when I was first invited to the dinners that were hosted by the *Washington Post*'s Katharine Graham, pundit Joseph Alsop, and others. To my recollection, the invitees to these dinners were ritualistically half Democrats and half Republicans. Today, attendance at similar dinners is predominantly a 95 to 5 percent split, with either Democrats or Republicans in the majority.

A NECESSARY IMPERATIVE

The bias toward unconstrained deficit spending is our top domestic economic problem. During the 1920s and earlier, budget deficits were avoided because there was a fear that they would immediately engender financial distress and inflation. That view, of course, was uninformed and soon was set aside as deficits arose and the sky did not fall.[7] But the fact remains that the only way to get permanently lower tax rates is to lower spending. We are fooling ourselves if we believe otherwise. I acknowledge the possibility, or even probability, that we may not be able to solve the social benefits dilemma without some form of crisis that would reset the political incentives toward restraint. But wise heads may preempt such an outcome. I miss the likes of Senators Howard Baker, Bob Dole, Daniel Patrick Moynihan, and Lloyd Bentsen, whose wisdom is sorely needed in today's halls of Congress.

So long as the pall of economic uncertainty that created the severe retrenchment of long-lived investments persists (see Chapter 7) and fiscal policy remains in stalemate, inflation is most likely to remain contained. But as economic uncertainty eventually lifts, driven by our propensity for optimism, so will business activity, inflation, and interest rates. But as our experience in the second half of 1979 demonstrated, change can happen unexpectedly and rapidly.[8] If late 1979 is any criterion, inflationary crises will engender seminal changes in fiscal policy and politics.

Contemplating a return to years of balanced government budgets does currently seem a bit of a stretch. Moreover, even if we can retain America's century-long gross domestic private savings rate that ranged mostly between 15 percent and 20 percent of GDP, we still need to address how those savings will be invested in the future.

Despite its temporary breakdown in 2008, the U.S. financial system is still clearly in the forefront of global finance, as it has been since the end of World War I. Viable competitors to replace the U.S. dollar as the world's reserve currency are nowhere in sight. Russia's financial system has advanced from its Soviet legacy, but its capitalism is more "crony" than it is Adam Smith. China may someday develop highly advanced finance, but that will take many years of cumulative progress on its financial infrastructure and processes. Admittedly, however, our international status is not what it was.

But before I despair of the future, I need to remind myself that we have been here before. Consider the national psyche of the United States in 1940. We had just been through a near decade of economic stagnation. The future appeared bleak. America's greatness was in our past. Less than a decade later, the American economy was humming on all cylinders.

ACKNOWLEDGMENTS

This book would have barely gotten off the ground, and certainly would never have reached completion, were it not for the dedication of my three key assistants—Noah Hall, Jeffrey Young, and Katie Byers Broom. Noah deciphered and edited my illegible script through the many iterations of the book and contributed significantly to the research behind it as well, both quantitative and qualitative. Jeff conducted the majority of the countless statistical analyses that supported the narrative of the book and controlled the more than sixty exhibits displayed throughout. Katie researched many historical topics and accordingly compiled data series that allowed me to extend much of the book's pivotal investigations well into our past.

I am indebted to the large number of my former Federal Reserve Board colleagues who were most helpful in recollecting our shared experiences over my eighteen-year tenure. David Stockton in particular, since retired from the Board, was of immeasurable assistance in the early months of researching and writing this book until previous commitments to the Bank of England called him away. Pat Parkinson, also formerly of the Fed, has kept me abreast on the latest innovations of the derivatives markets. Peter Wallison and Brian Brooks enhanced my understanding of the legal intricacies of mortgage markets.

For the second time in seven years, Scott Moyers of Penguin Press shepherded me through the joys and agonies of book writing. His clarity of thought helped me structure the arguments of this effort. His colleague at Penguin Press Mally Anderson acted as the liaison between my team and all of the departments at Penguin that had a hand in turning our initial draft of the manuscript into, I trust, a polished, shelf-ready book. She also offered her own valuable editorial insights, particularly in the selection of in-text exhibits.

Finally, I owe my deepest gratitude to my wife Andrea, whose support and encouragement through pressured periods of writing was indispensable to my effort.

As I warned in *The Age of Turbulence*, there are errors in this book. If I knew where they were, I would have fixed them. But of the ninety thousand words, my probabilistic mind tells me some are wrong.

APPENDICES

Exhibit 1.1
Personal Saving Rate, 1897–2012

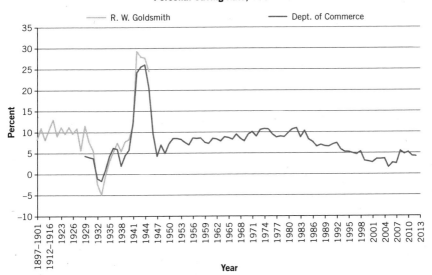

Source: R. W. Goldsmith, "A Study of Saving in the United States" (1955); U.S. Department of Commerce.

Exhibit 2.1

Ratio of Equity Capital to Assets in the Banking Sector, 1834–2012

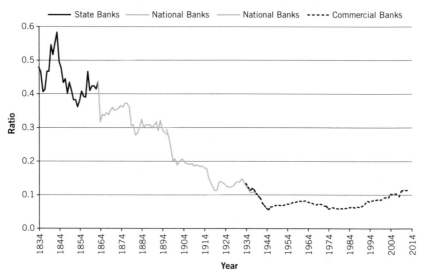

Source: Federal Deposit Insurance Corporation; Office of the Comptroller of the Currency; Federal Reserve Board.

Exhibit 3.1

Nominal Yields on 10-Year Government Debt, Average for 15 Countries,* monthly

Source: Various official data sources.

*The countries are Austria, Belgium, Canada, Denmark, Finland, France, Germany, Italy, the Netherlands, Norway, Spain, Sweden, Switzerland, the U.K., and the U.S.

Exhibit 3.2

Variance of Interest Rates: 10-Year Government Debt in 15 Countries,* monthly

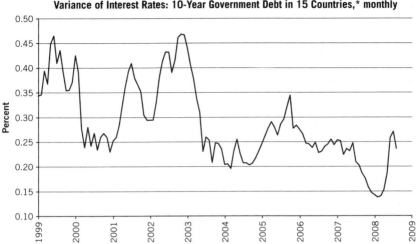

Source: Various official data sources.

*The countries are Austria, Belgium, Canada, Denmark, Finland, France, Germany, Italy, the Netherlands, Norway, Spain, Sweden, Switzerland, the U.K., and the U.S.

Exhibit 3.3

Dependent Variable (Time Period: Jan. 1991–Dec. 2005, 180 obs.)		
m/m %Δ in: CoreLogic Home Price Index (Seasonally adjusted, Single Family Combined, Distressed Included)		
Independent Variable(s)	**Coefficient**	**t-Statistic***
Freddie Mac 30yr Fixed-Rate Mortgage Rate, % p.a. (3 months ago)	–0.303	–9.111
Adjusted R-sq	**Durbin-Watson**	
0.604	0.159	

*t-statistic calculated using Newey-West HAC standard errors and covariance.

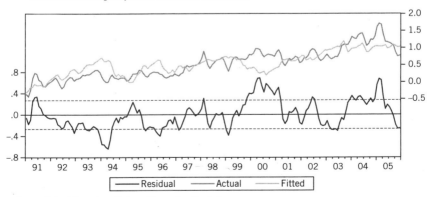

Source: Federal Home Loan Mortgage Corporation; Corelogic.

Exhibit 3.4

Monthly Changes in Home Prices, January 1977–March 2013

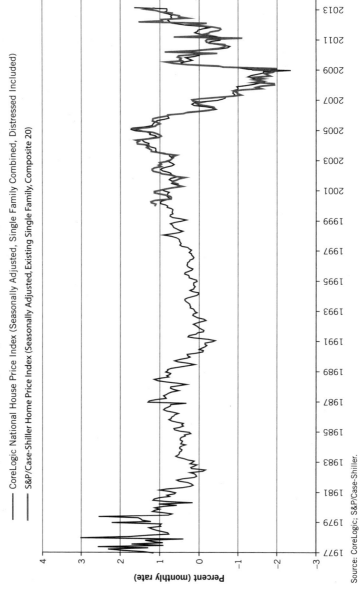

— CoreLogic National House Price Index (Seasonally Adjusted, Single Family Combined, Distressed Included)

— S&P/Case-Shiller Home Price Index (Seasonally Adjusted, Existing Single Family, Composite 20)

Source: CoreLogic; S&P/Case-Shiller.

Exhibit 3.5

Issuance of Subprime Mortgage-Backed Securities, Q1.1995–Q1.2013

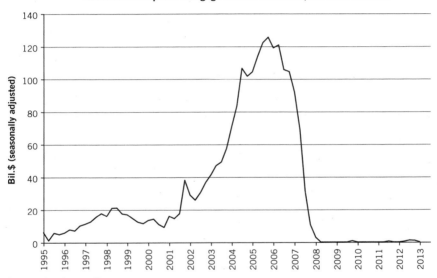

Source: Inside Mortgage Finance.

Exhibit 3.6
Holdings and Market Shares of Subprime Mortgage-Backed Securities by Fannie Mae and Freddie Mac, 2000–10

Year	Total subprime MBSs outstanding (billions of dollars)	Change in total subprime MBSs outstanding (billions of dollars)	Fannie Mae and Freddie Mac single-family private-label mortgages retained in their portfolios[a]			
			Change from end of previous year			*As percent of change in total subprime MBSs outstanding*
			Billions of dollars	As percent of total subprime MBSs outstanding	Billions of dollars	As percent of change in total subprime MBSs outstanding
2000	95.7					
2001	128.7	33.0	19.0	14.8	5.7	8.1
2002	198.9	70.2	24.7	12.4	40.1	40.5
2003	298.1	99.2	64.9	21.8	85.8	48.1
2004	476.4	178.3	150.6	31.6	28.6	14.5
2005	673.4	197.0	179.2	26.6	-10.2	-6.1
2006	840.4	167.0	169.0	20.1	-35.6	43.6
2007	758.8	-81.6	133.4	17.6	-34.0	20.7
2008	594.9	-163.8	99.4	16.7	-17.3	15.0
2009	479.5	-115.4	82.1	17.1	-9.5	13.1
2010	407.0	-72.5	72.6	17.8		

Sources: Federal Housing Finance Agency, *2010 Report to Congress*, LoanPerformance data, and author's calculations.

a. Fannie Mae publishes its subprime securities holdings for each year from 2002 to 2010. For 2001 the sum of subprime and alt-A holdings is approximately reported, with the division between them guided by shares of total outstanding subprime and alt-A mortgage-backed securities (MBSs). Freddie Mac publishes similar data for 2006–10. With minor assumptions, estimates are made for the sum of subprime and alt-A holdings for earlier years. The separation is made essentially to reflect the ratio of total outstanding subprime and alt-A MBSs.

Exhibit 3.7
Yield Spread of Bonds Rated CCC and Lower over 10-Year
Treasury Notes, daily, August 1988–June 2013*

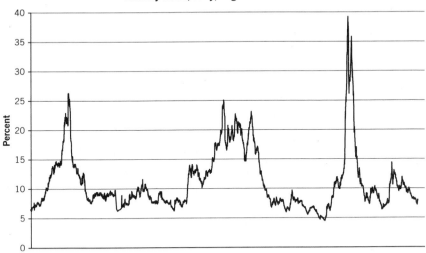

Source: Bank of America Merrill Lynch; Federal Reserve Board.

*Average yield on Bank of America high-yield cash pay bonds rated CCC and lower minus yield on 10-year Treasury notes at constant maturity.

Exhibit 4.1
Common Stock Earnings Yield, 1890–2012

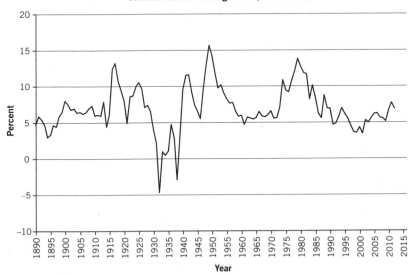

Source: Cowles Comm dividend yields converted to earnings yields using U.S. Interstate Commerce Comm railroad stock dividend payout ratios (1980–1946), S&P 500 As Reported earnings yield (1947–1987) and Operating earnings yield (1988–2012).

Exhibit 4.2
U.S. Equity Risk Premium, quarterly, 1957–2013

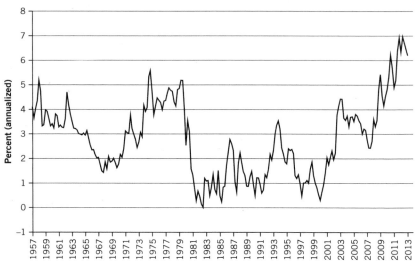

Source: J.P. Morgan

Exhibit 4.3
Yield Spread: S&P Industrials 10-Year BB+ Bonds less 10-Year Treasury Notes, quarterly

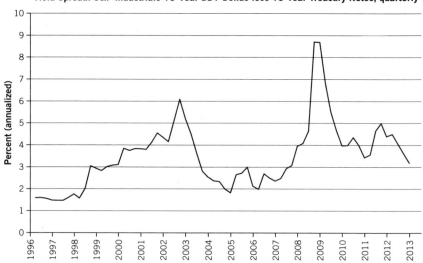

Source: Standard and Poor's; Federal Reserve Board.

Exhibit 4.4

Dependent Variable (Time Period: Q1 1975–Q1 2013, 153 obs.)		
Personal Consumption Expenditures (***SAAR, Bil.\$) / Disposable Personal Income (SAAR, Bil.\$)		
Independent Variable(s)	**Coefficient**	**t-Statistic***
Household (incl. NPOs) Stock Net Worth (Period Avg, Bil.\$) / DPI	0.0209	9.66
Household (incl. NPOs) Homeowners' Equity (Period Avg, Bil.\$) / DPI	0.0308	6.35
Household (incl. NPOs) All Other Net Worth (Period Avg, Bil.\$) / DPI	0.0188	2.63
6-Month Certificates of Deposit (% p.a./100) (3 quarters ago)	−0.3752	−9.56
[**Adjusted PI / DPI] (2 quarters ago)	0.2666	2.30

Adjusted R-sq	**Durbin-Watson**
0.903	1.089

*t-statistic calculated using Newey-West HAC standard errors and covariance.
**Adjusted PI = (0.9*Wages and Salary Disbursements) + (1.0*Personal Current Transfer Receipts)
    + (0.6*All Other Personal Income).
***Seasonally adjusted annual rate.

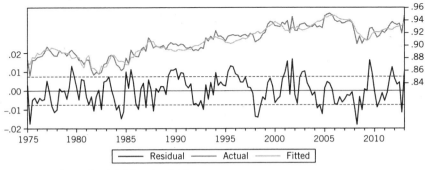

Source: Federal Reserve Board; U.S. Department of Commerce.

Exhibit 4.5

1953–2012 average:

> (Personal Savings (PS) + Interest + Transfers) ÷ Disposable Personal Income (DPI) = 0.0983
>
> Household Net Worth (NW) ÷ DPI = 4.99

$PCE \div DPI = (DPI - PS - Interest - Transfers) \div DPI = 1 - 0.0983 = 0.9017$

PCE from equities (PCE_E) = 0.0214 x NW, annually

PCE_E = 0.0214 x NW (period average)

> = 0.0214 x (NW ÷ DPI) x DPI

> = 0.0214 x 4.99 x DPI

> = 0.1068(DPI)

$(PCE_E \div DPI) + (PCE_{DPI} \div DPI) = PCE \div DPI$

$(PCE \div DPI) - (PCE_E \div DPI) = PCE_{DPI} \div DPI$

> → 0.9017 − 0.1068 = 0.7949

$PCE_E \div PCE = 0.1068 \div 0.9017 = 0.1184$

Therefore, $PCE_{DPI} \div PCE = 1 - 0.1184 = 0.8816$

Exhibit 4.6

Dependent Variable (Time Period: Q1 1970–Q4 2012, 172 obs.)		
ln [Real GDP / Real GDP (4 quarters ago)]		
Independent Variable(s)	**Coefficient**	**t-Statistic***
ln [**Corp & Home Equity, Period Avg (1 quarter ago) /	0.127	9.691
**Corp & Home Equity, Period Avg (5 quarters ago)]		
Adjusted R-sq **Durbin-Watson**		
0.419 0.364		

*t-statistic calculated using Newey-West HAC standard errors and covariance.
**Domestic holdings of domestic corporate equities and foreign corporate equities, at market value.

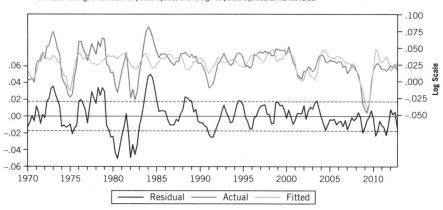

Source: U.S. Department of Commerce; Federal Reserve Board.

Exhibit 4.7

Dependent Variable (Time Period: Q1 1993–Q1 2013, 81 obs.)		
Real Pvt Nonres Fixed Invst (SAAR, Bil.Chn.2005$) / Pvt Nonres Fixed Assets (2005 = 100)		
Independent Variable(s)	**Coefficient**	**t-Statistic***
S&P 500 (1941-43=10) / Pvt Nonres Fixed Invst Price (SA, 2005 = 100) (1 quarter ago)	0.473	19.044
Nonfarm Operating Rate (SA, % of capacity) (3 quarters ago)	0.165	6.118
Structures' share of nominal Pvt Nonres Fixed Invst	6.332	4.517
Adjusted R-sq **Durbin-Watson**		
0.946 0.585		

*t-statistic calculated using Newey-West HAC standard errors and covariance.

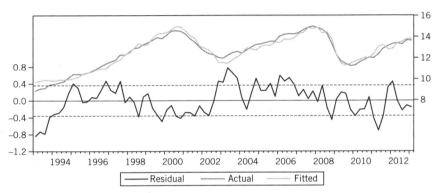

Source: U.S. Department of Commerce; Standard and Poor's; Federal Reserve Board; author's calculations.

Exhibit 5.1

500 Largest American Corporations: Average CEO Pay to Average Market Value, 1960–2010

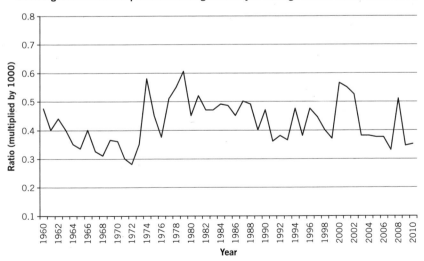

Source: Steven N, Kaplan. "Executive Compensation and Corporate Governance in the U.S.: Perceptions, Facts and Challenges." Chicago Booth Paper No. 12-42, July 2012.

Exhibit 5.2

Share of Finance and Insurance in GDP for the U.S., 1947–2012

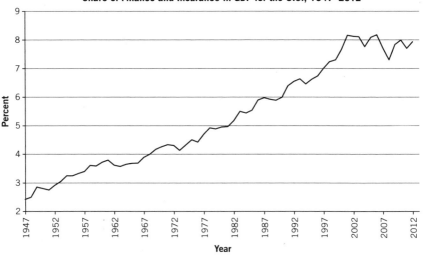

Source: U.S. Department of Commerce.

Exhibit 5.3

Price of 5-Year Credit Default Swaps[a] (Basis Points[b])

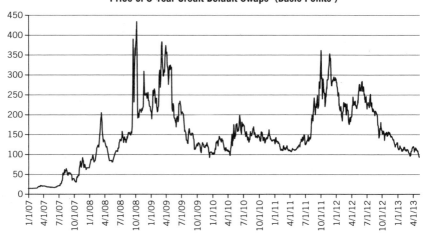

Source: Author's calculations; Bloomberg.

a. Unweighted average prices of CDSs issued by Bank of America, Citigroup, Goldman Sachs, JPMorgan, Wells Fargo, and Morgan Stanley.

b. Hundredths of a percent of the notional value of the underlying swap contract.

Exhibit 5.4

Equity-to-Assets Ratios at FDIC-Insured Commercial Banks, Q4.2004–Q1.2013

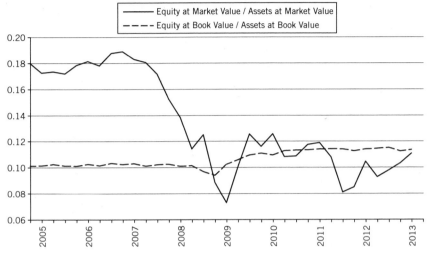

Source: Federal Deposit Insurance Corporation; Bloomberg; author's calculations.

Exhibit 5.5

CDS and LIBOR-OIS Spreads at Various Maturities

September 2009, March 2010, and April 2013

Basis Points

Maturity	September 15, 2009	March 31, 2010	April 22, 2013
CDS			
10 years	133	121	176
5 year	135	117	128
3 year	137	98	82
1 year	134	69	34
LIBOR-OIS			
3 months	12	11	16
1 month	7	8	8

Sources: British Bankers' Association, Bloomberg (CMA New York), and Reuters.

Exhibit 5.6

Ratio of Net Income to Equity in the Banking Sector, 1869–2011

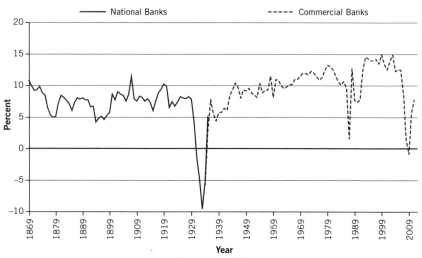

Source: Federal Deposit Insurance Corporation; U.S. Department of Commerce.

Exhibit 7.1

Private Fixed Investment in Structures as a Share of Total GDP
quarterly, 1947.Q1–2013.Q1 (with NBER recessions shaded)

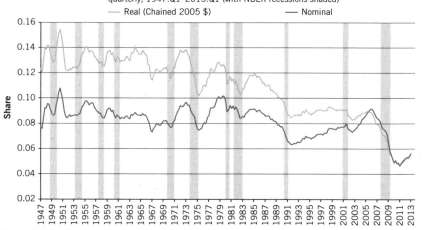

Source: U.S. Department of Commerce; National Bureau of Economic Research.

Exhibit 7.2

Capital Expenditures as a Share of Savings

plotted through 2012

—— [1] Nonfarm Nonfinancial Corporate Business: Capital Expenditures / (Internal Funds + IVA)
—— [2] (Gross Private Domestic Fixed Nonresidential Investment + Private Inventory Change) / [2] Gross Business Saving

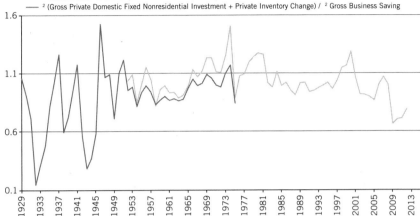

1. Federal Reserve Board.
2. Historical Statistics of the United States.

Exhibit 7.3

Dependent Variable (Time Period: Q1 1970–Q4 2012, 172 obs.) In [US Nonfinancial Corporate Business: Capital Expenditures / Cash Flow]		
Independent Variable(s)	**Coefficient**	**t-Statistic***
In [1 + (**Cyclically Adjusted U.S. Federal Deficit / GDP)] (1 quarter ago)	−4.208	−12.327
Nonfarm Operating Rate (Seasonally adjusted, %) (1 quarter ago)	0.0527	9.640
**Deficit & Cyclically Adjusted U.S. Treasury Spread: ***30yr–5yr (% p.a.) (1 quarter ago)	−0.0844	−6.977
Adjusted R-sq **Durbin-Watson**		
0.722 0.825		

*t-statistic calculated using Newey-West HAC standard errors and covariance.
**Adjusted to decrease multicollinearity between independent variables.
***20yr Treasury substituted for 30yr Treasury prior to Q2 1977.

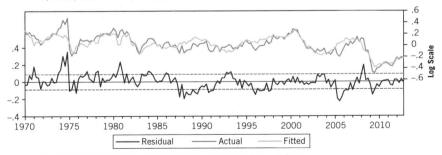

Source: U.S. Department of Commerce; Federal Reserve Board; author's calculations.

Exhibit 7.4

Dependent Variable (Time Period: Jan. 1985–Dec. 2012, 336 obs.)		
In [Single-Family Housing Starts (SAAR, Thous.Units)]t		
Independent Variable(s)	**Coefficient**	**t-Statistic***
CoreLogic Home Prices, Distressed Excl (SA, Jan.2000=100) [current / 3yr moving avg]	1.400	5.954
Civilian Unemployment Rate: 16 yr + (SA, %)	–0.0618	–5.280
Total Vacant Housing Units (Period Average, Thous)	–0.00013	–10.976
Homeownership Rate (%)	0.1023	7.760
Freddie Mac 30-Year Fixed-Rate Mortgage Rate (%)	–0.0636	–5.691
Adjusted R-sq	**Durbin-Watson**	
0.900	0.294	

*t-statistic calculated using Newey-West HAC standard errors and covariance.

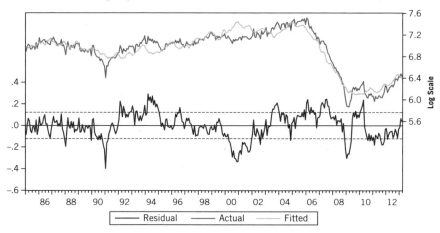

Sources: U.S. Department of Commerce; Corelogic; U.S. Department of Labor; Federal Home Loan Mortgage Corporation.

Exhibit 7.5
Yield Spreads (%, average*), 1900–2012

— U.S. Treasury Obligations: 30yr–5yr (Monthly, Mar. 1977 – Dec. 2012)
— U.S. Treasury Obligations: 20yr–5yr (Monthly, Apr. 1953 – Dec. 1978)
— High Grade Corporate Bonds: 30yr–5yr (Annually, 1900 – 1955)

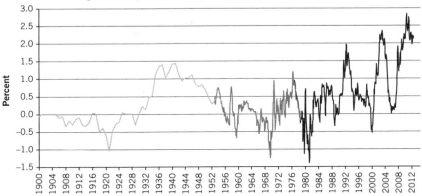

Source: Federal Reserve Board; National Bureau of Economic Research.

*Historical high grade bond yields are annual averages, U.S. Treasury yields are monthly averages.

Exhibit 7.6
Real Private Domestic GDP (SAAR), quarterly, Q1.2000–Q1.2013

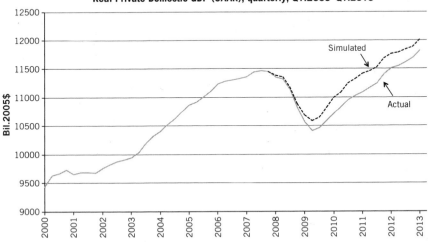

Source: U.S. Department of Commerce; author's calculations.

Exhibit 7.7

Real US Output Gap (as % of Real Potential GDP)

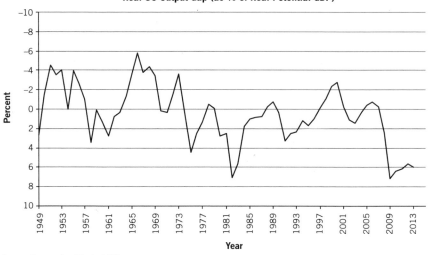

Source: Congressional Budget Office.

Exhibit 7.8

Re-Default Rate of Modified Loans: 60 or More Days Delinquent

— 3 Months After Modification — 6 Months After Modification
- - - 9 Months After Modification — 12 Months After Modification

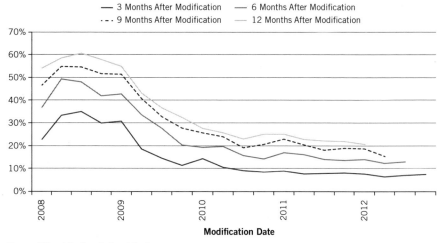

Source: Office of the Comptroller of the Currency.

Exhibit 8.1

CBO Forecasts of Productivity Growth vs. Actual Productivity Growth in the 10 Years Prior

—— CBO's Projection of Potential Nonfarm Business Output per Hour Average Annual Growth Rate Over the Following 5 Years
—— Actual Average Annual Growth Rate of Real Nonfarm Business Output per Hour for the 10 Years Preceding the Quarter of CBO Publication

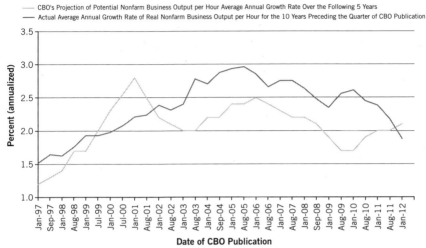

Source: Congressional Budget Office; U.S. Department of Labor.

Exhibit 8.2

Ratio of Real Output per Hour: Nonfarm Business/Total Business
quarterly, Q1.1947–Q1.2013, both series are seasonally adjusted, and set to 2005=100

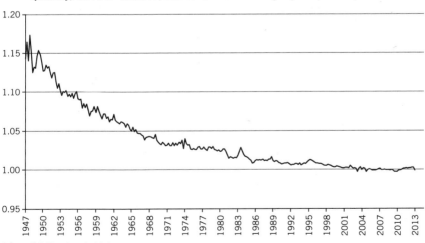

Source: U.S. Department of Labor.

Exhibit 8.3

Real Output per Hour of Nonfarm Business: annual rate %chg over 15 years ago

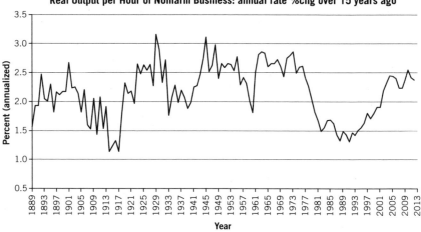

Source: J. W. Kendrick, "Productivity Trends in the United States" (1961); U.S. Department of Labor.

Exhibit 8.4

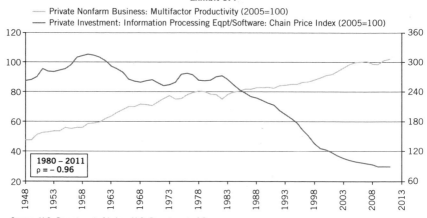

Source: U.S. Department of Labor; U.S. Department of Commerce.

Exhibit 8.5

U.S. Consumption: Selected Nonfuel Mineral Commodities,* Crude Oil, and Other Liquid

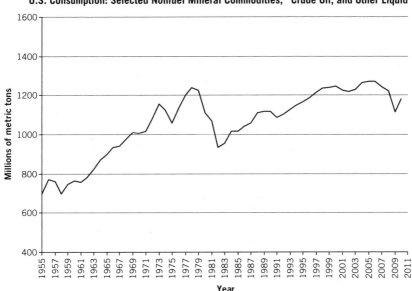

Source: U.S. Geological Survey.

*Bauxite, alumina, cement, clays, copper, gypsum, iron ore, iron and steel scrap, lime, nickel, phosphate rock, silicon, sulfur, and tin.

Exhibit 8.6

Kilograms per Real Dollar of Goods Shipped by Vessel and Air, 1953–2012

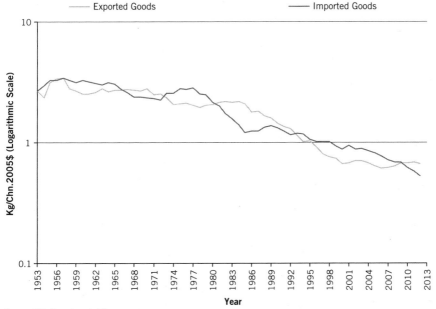

Source: U.S. Department of Commerce.

Exhibit 8.7

──── Estimated Weight of Real Goods Output (based on weight-to-value ratio of imports)
──── U.S. Consumption of Selected Nonfuel Mineral Commodities, Crude Oil, and Other Liquids

Source: U.S. Department of Commerce.

Exhibit 8.8

──── U.S. Inventions Patent Issuance (thousands)
──── Gross Additions to Synthetic Nonfarm Business Productivity Stock

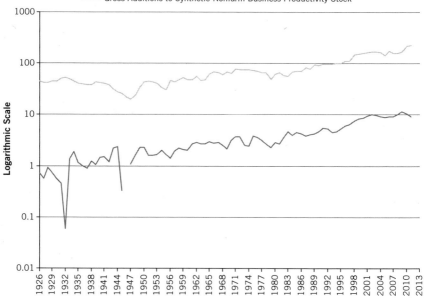

Source: U.S. patent and Trademark Office; author's calculations.

Exhibit 9.1
In [Government Social Benefit Payments to Persons (Bil.$)]
(showing average annual growth rates by presidential administration)

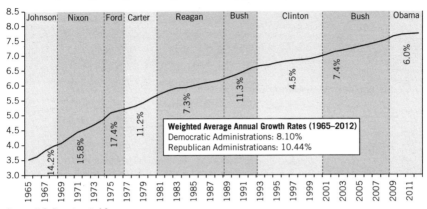

Source: U.S. Department of Commerce.

Exhibit 9.3

Savings by Sector (As % of GDP)	1965	2012	'12 less '65
Gross Domestic Saving	22.04	12.88	−9.16
DomDomestic Business	10.87	13.14	2.27
Undistributed Corporate Profits with IVA & CCAdj	4.90	4.60	−0.30
Consumption of Fixed Capital	5.97	8.54	2.56
Hou Households (incl NPIs)	7.18	5.10	−2.08
Net Saving	5.94	3.13	−2.81
Consumption of Fixed Capital	1.24	1.97	0.73
Government	3.98	−5.35	−9.33
Federal Government	2.21	−5.95	−8.15
Net Saving	0.45	−6.85	−7.30
Consumption of Fixed Capital	1.76	0.90	−0.85
State and Local Government	1.77	0.60	−1.18
Net Saving	0.91	−0.82	−1.73
Consumption of Fixed Capital	0.87	1.42	0.55

Savings Reconciliation (As % of GDP)	1965	2012	'12 less '65
Gross Domestic Saving	22.04	12.88	−9.16
less: Net Lending (or Net Borrowing [−])	0.86	−2.98	−3.83
less: Capital Transfer Payments to the Rest of the World	0.00	−0.04	−0.04
plus: Statistical Discrepancy	0.21	0.26	0.05
equals: Gross Domestic Investment	21.38	16.16	−5.22

Federal Government (As % of GDP)	1965	2012	'12 less '65
Net Federal Government Saving	0.45	−6.85	−7.30
Federal Government Current Receipts	16.82	17.11	0.29
Personal Current Taxes	7.10	7.30	0.20
Collected from Top 10% Income Bracket	3.40	5.68	2.29
Collected from Bottom 90% Income Bracket	3.71	1.61	−2.09
Collected from Top 20% Income Bracket	4.39	6.84	2.45
Collected from Bottom 80% Income Bracket	2.71	0.46	−2.26
Taxes on Corporate Income	3.84	1.87	−1.97
Contributions for Federal Government Social Insurance	3.16	5.98	2.82
All Other Current Receipts (incl Federal Reserve Banks)	2.72	1.96	−0.76
Federal Government Current Expenditures	16.37	23.96	7.59
Federal Defense Consumption Expenditures	7.03	4.49	−2.54
Federal Nondefense Consumption Expenditures	2.10	2.27	0.17
Federal Government Social Benefit Payments to Persons	3.79	11.32	7.53
Federal Grants-in-Aid to State & Local Governments	1.00	2.98	1.99
All Other Federal Government Current Expenditures	2.45	2.90	0.45

State and Local Government (As % of GDP)	1965	2012	'12 less '65
Net S&L Government Saving	0.91	−0.82	−1.73
S&L Government Current Receipts	9.25	13.19	3.94
Personal current taxes	0.92	2.14	1.22
Taxes on corporate income (excl S&L Reserve Banks)	0.27	0.31	0.03
Contributions for S&L Government Social Insurance	0.11	0.11	0.00
Federal Grants-in-Aid to State & Local Governments	1.00	2.98	1.99
All other S&L government current receipts	6.96	7.65	0.69
S&L Government Current Expenditures	8.34	14.02	5.67
S&L Consumption Expenditures	6.98	9.76	2.78
S&L Government Social Benefit Payments to Persons	0.92	3.53	2.61
All Other S&L Government Current Expenditures	0.44	0.72	0.29

Total Government (As % of GDP)	1965	2012	'12 less '65
Net Government Saving	1.36	−7.67	−9.03
Government Current Receipts	25.08	27.32	2.24
Personal Current Taxes	8.02	9.44	1.42
Taxes on Corporate Income	4.11	2.18	−1.93
Contributions for Government Social Insurance	3.27	6.10	2.82
All Other Current Receipts (incl Reserve Banks)	9.67	9.61	−0.07
Government Current Expenditures	23.72	34.99	11.27
Federal Defense Consumption Expenditures	7.03	4.49	−2.54
Nondefense Consumption Expenditures	9.08	12.03	2.95
Government Social Benefit Payments to Persons	4.71	14.85	10.14
All Other Government Current Expenditures	2.89	3.62	0.74

Total Government (As % of GDP)	1965	2012	'12 less '65
Total Contributions for Government Social Insurance	3.27	6.10	2.82
Federal	3.16	5.98	2.82
State and Local	0.11	0.11	0.00
Total Government Social Benefit Payments to Persons	4.71	14.85	10.14
Federal	3.79	11.32	7.53
State and Local	0.92	3.53	2.61

Exhibit 9.4
Gross Private Saving

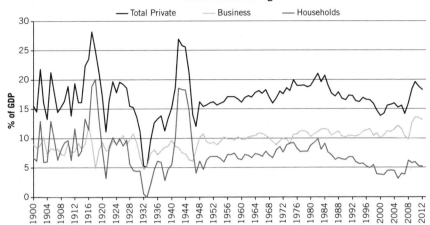

Source: R. W. Goldsmith, "A Study of Saving in the United States" (1955); U.S. Department of Commerce.

Exhibit 9.5
Gross Domestic Saving

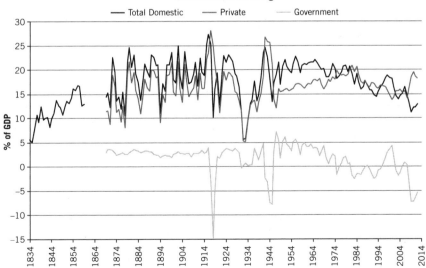

Source: R. E. Gallman, "Gross National Product in the United States, 1834–1909" (1966); R. W. Goldsmith, "A Study of Saving in the United States" (1955); U.S. Department of Commerce.

Exhibit 9.6

Share of Personal Consumption Expenditures Attributable to Net Worth

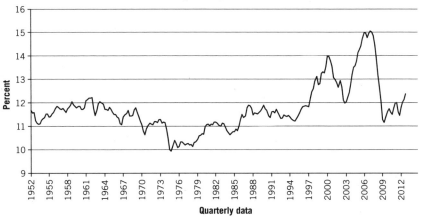

Source: U.S. Department of Commerce; Federal Reserve Board; author's calculations.

Exhibit 9.7

— Sum: Government Social Benefits Payments to Persons + Gross Domestic Saving
— Gross Domestic Saving (Private and Public)
— Government Social Benefits Payments to Persons

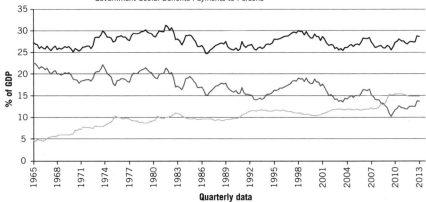

Source: U.S. Department of Commerce.

Exhibit 9.8

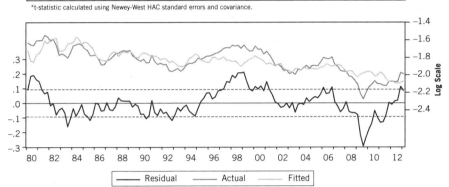

Dependent Variable (Time Period: Q1.1980–Q1.2013, 133 obs.)		
ln [Gross Domestic Saving / GDP]		
Independent Variable(s)	**Coefficient**	**t-Statistic***
ln [1 + Real 10yr Treasury Yield]	6.927	8.363
Adjusted R-sq	**Durbin-Watson**	
0.615	0.227	

*t-statistic calculated using Newey-West HAC standard errors and covariance.

——— Residual   ——— Actual   ——— Fitted

Source: U.S. Department of Commerce; Federal Reserve Board.

Exhibit 9.10

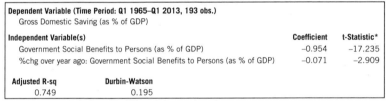

Dependent Variable (Time Period: Q1 1965–Q1 2013, 193 obs.)		
Gross Domestic Saving (as % of GDP)		
Independent Variable(s)	**Coefficient**	**t-Statistic***
Government Social Benefits to Persons (as % of GDP)	–0.954	–17.235
%chg over year ago: Government Social Benefits to Persons (as % of GDP)	–0.071	–2.909
Adjusted R-sq	**Durbin-Watson**	
0.749	0.195	

*t-statistic calculated using Newey-West HAC standard errors and covariance.

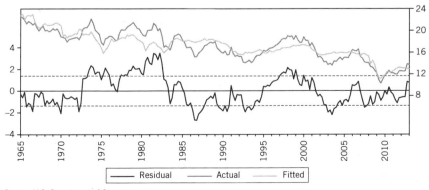

——— Residual   ——— Actual   ——— Fitted

Source: U.S. Department of Commerce.

Exhibit 10.2
Assets of European Central Bank

Source: European Central Bank.

Exhibit 10.5

× denotes emerging markets.

● denotes developed markets.

Source: International Monetary Fund; World Economic Forum.

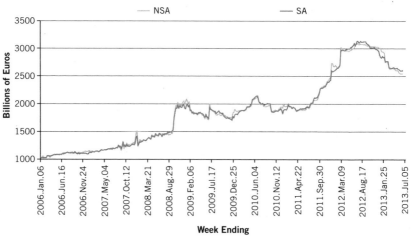

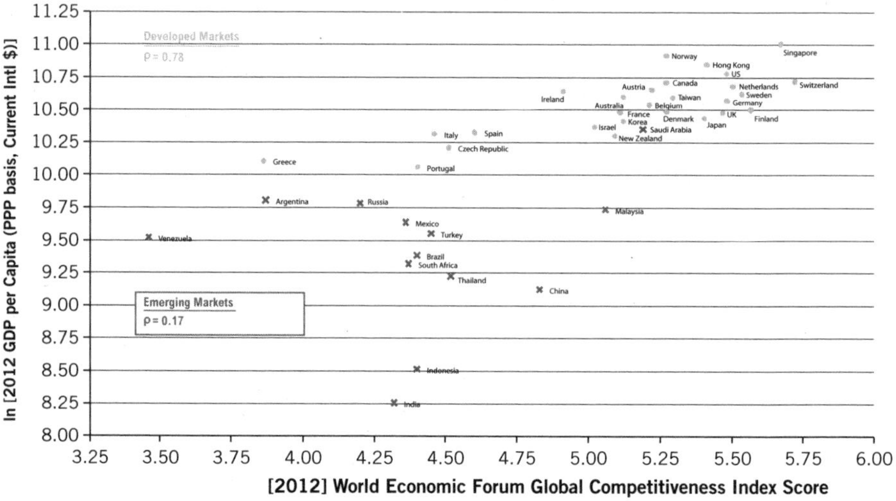

Exhibit 10.6

Distribution of 112th Congress (January 3, 2011–January 3, 2013): Liberal vs. Conservative

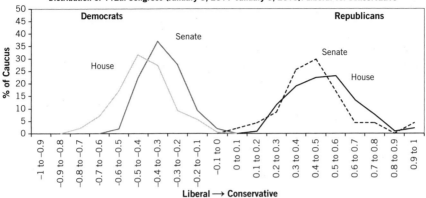

Sources: Voteview.com.

Note: Distributions include all people who served during the 112th congress.

Exhibit 10.7

Distribution of 56th Congress (March 4, 1899 – March 4, 1901): Liberal vs. Conservative

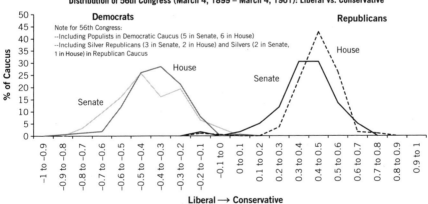

Source: VoteView.com.

Exhibit 11.1

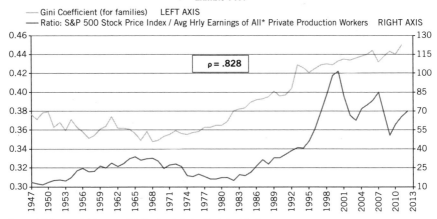

——— Gini Coefficient (for families)　　LEFT AXIS
——— Ratio: S&P 500 Stock Price Index / Avg Hrly Earnings of All* Private Production Workers　　RIGHT AXIS

$\rho = .828$

Sources: U.S. Department of Commerce; U.S. Department of Labor; Standard and Poor's.

*Prior to 1964, average hourly earnings are those of production workers in goods-producing industries only.

Exhibit 11.2

——— Imports of Goods as % of GDP　　——— Real Imports of Goods as % of Real GDP

Percent

Source: U.S. Department of Commerce.

Exhibit 12.1

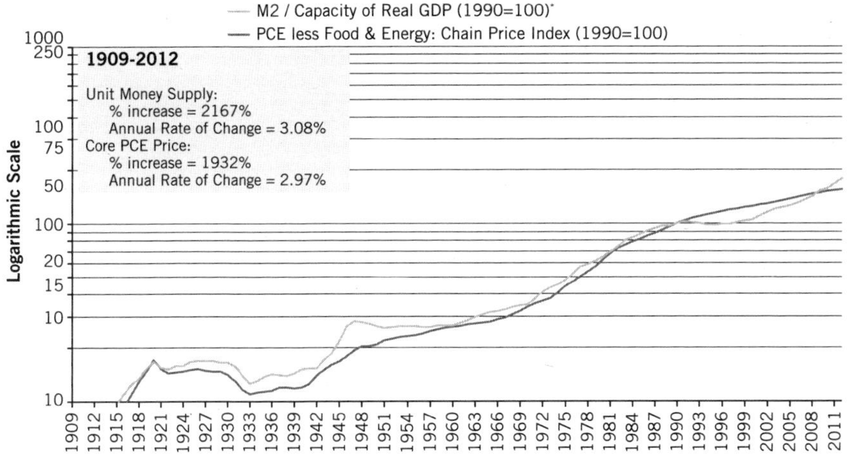
M2 / Capacity of Real GDP (1990=100)*
PCE less Food & Energy: Chain Price Index (1990=100)
1909-2012
Unit Money Supply:
% increase = 2167%
Annual Rate of Change = 3.08%
Core PCE Price:
% increase = 1932%
Annual Rate of Change = 2.97%
Logarithmic Scale
1000
250
100
75
50
100
20
15
10
10
1909
1912
1915
1918
1921
1924
1927
1930
1933
1936
1939
1942
1945
1948
1951
1954
1957
1960
1963
1966
1969
1972
1975
1978
1981
1984
1987
1990
1993
1996
1999
2002
2005
2008
2011

Source: U.S. Department of Commerce; Federal Reserve Board; author's calculations.

*See footnote 9 of Chapter 12 (pages 373–74) for derivation of estimate of capacity.

Exhibit 12.2

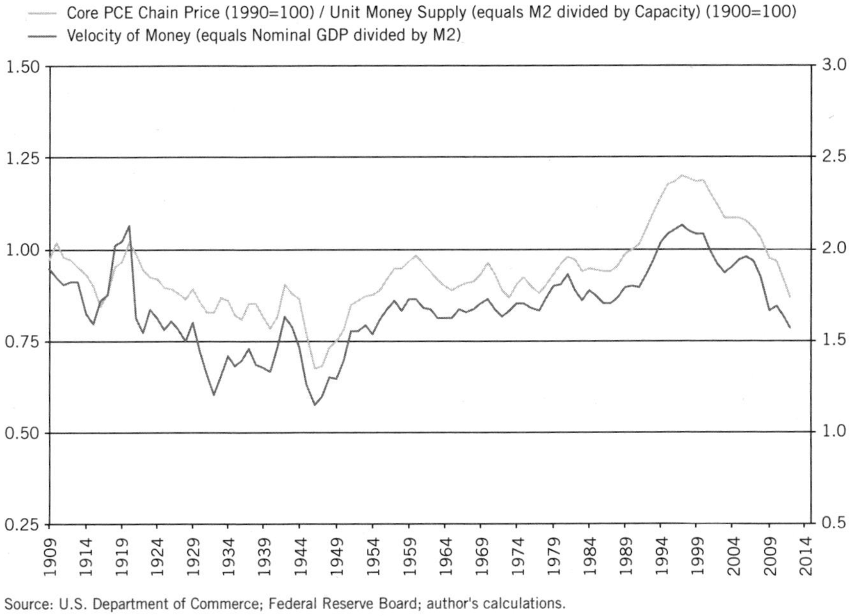
Core PCE Chain Price (1990=100) / Unit Money Supply (equals M2 divided by Capacity) (1900=100)
Velocity of Money (equals Nominal GDP divided by M2)
1.50
1.25
1.00
0.75
0.50
0.25
3.0
2.5
2.0
1.5
1.0
0.5
1909
1914
1919
1924
1929
1934
1939
1944
1949
1954
1959
1964
1969
1974
1979
1984
1989
1994
1999
2004
2009
2014

Source: U.S. Department of Commerce; Federal Reserve Board; author's calculations.

Exhibit 12.3

Dependent Variable (Time Period: 1909–2012, 104 obs.) [Core PCE Chain Price / (M2 / Capacity)] (1990=1.0)		
Independent Variable(s)	**Coefficient**	**t-Statistic***
**3-Month Treasury Bills, Secondary Market (% p.a.)	0.0169	4.82
***S&P 500 (1941-43=10) / GDP (Bil.$)	0.4314	3.68
Dummy (equals 1 from 1990 through 2012)	0.2021	7.30
Operating Rate, Total Economy (%)	0.0032	2.19

Adjusted R-sq	**Durbin-Watson**
0.723	0.513

*t-statistic calculated using Newey-West HAC standard errors and covariance.
**Linked to 1yr corporate bond yield prior to 1934.
***Cowles Comm/S&P common stock composite prior to 1921.

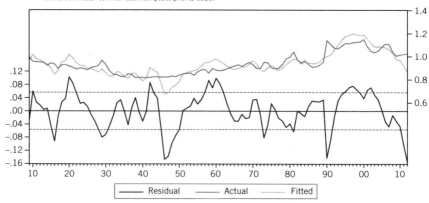

Source: U.S. Department of Commerce; Federal Reserve Board; Standard and Poor's; The Cowles Commission; D. Durand, "Basic Yields of Corporate Bonds, 1900–1942" (1942); author's calculations.

Exhibit 12.4

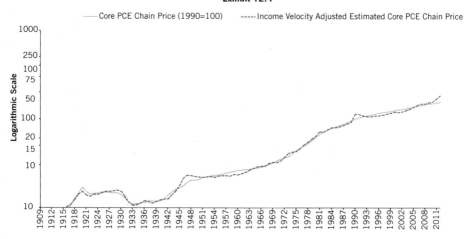

Source: U.S. Department of Commerce; author's calculations.

Exhibit 12.5

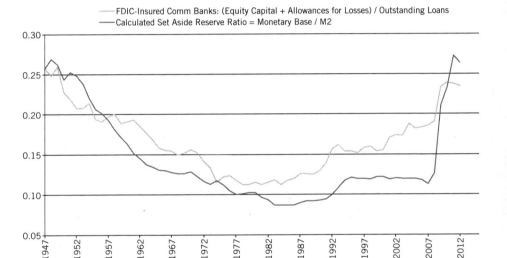

FDIC-Insured Comm Banks: (Equity Capital + Allowances for Losses) / Outstanding Loans
Calculated Set Aside Reserve Ratio = Monetary Base / M2

Source: Federal Deposit Insurance Corporation; Federal Reserve Board.

NOTES

INTRODUCTION

1. 13 (3) was subsequently altered by Dodd-Frank.
2. Wolfowitz, incidentally, was the father of Paul, who became president of the World Bank. I was deeply moved when Paul asked me to write a note to his children about the grandfather they never knew.
3. As I note in Chapter 4, I believe asset price causation is underrepresented in most models.
4. Effective management that marries human labor and engineering, for example, does require insights into how people interact in the hierarchy of all business organizations, but it is a minor part of nonfinancial decision making.
5. IMF, *World Economic Outlook,* April 2007, p. xii.
6. I mumbled, "I can't believe we could have a once-in-a-century type of financial crisis without a significant effect on the real economy globally."
7. Christina Romer and Jared Bernstein, "The Job Impact of the American Recovery and Reinvestment Plan"; January 9, 2009.
8. John M. Keynes, *The General Theory of Employment Interest and Money* (Whitefish, MT: Kessinger Publishers, 1936/2010), pp. 161–62.
9. *Fortune,* March 1959. It was not my finest hour. Stocks continued to rise for years.
10. Undaunted, almost four decades later, I opined that on rare occasions, "fear, whether irrational or otherwise, grips participants and they unthinkingly disengage from risky assets in favor of those providing safety and liquidity. The subtle distinctions that investors make, so critical to the effective operation of financial markets, are abandoned."

(Statement before the Committee on Banking and Financial Services, U.S. House of Representatives, October 1, 1998)

11. Regression analysis per se measures only the association between variables and the probability that that association is other than by chance. Economic judgment must be applied to indicate causation.

CHAPTER 1: ANIMAL SPIRITS

1. An economic model based on the "economic," that is, rational, man is surely a first approximation. Even Adam Smith, the founder of modern economics, in *Wealth of Nations* (1776) recognized that reality does not quite fully fit his great insights of the way markets function and self-interest creates wealth.

2. I have always been intrigued by where such epiphanies originate. I know introspectively that if I accumulate a large amount of seemingly unrelated information, in time, new ideas will pop into my head that organize and draw conclusions from that store of information. I have no awareness of the internal process that, apparently, percolated in the frontal lobe of my brain in a process that reminds me of the workings of an impenetrable black box from which ideas flow without antecedents.

3. Daniel Kahneman, *Thinking, Fast and Slow* (New York: Farrar, Straus and Giroux, 2011) p. 4.

4. Colin Camerer (Cal Tech) and George Loewenstein (Carnegie Mellon), *Behavioral Economics: Past, Present, Future* (October 2002), pp.1–2.

5. Sidney Homer and Richard Sylla, *A History of Interest Rates,* 3rd ed. (New Brunswick, NJ: Rutgers University Press, 1991).

6. The choice offered to the children was either to eat one marshmallow immediately or abstain in return for two, fifteen minutes later.

7. Thorstein Veblen, *The Theory of the Leisure Class: An Economic Study of Institutions* (1899).

8. Ori Heffetz of Cornell University conducted an imaginative test of Veblen's thesis when he separated consumption of goods and services on the basis of their visibility to others. His analysis notes that "income elasticity is . . . higher if a good is visible and lower if it is not." In passing, Heffetz underscores the historical stability of the propensity in quoting from Plato: "Since . . . appearance tyrannizes over truth and is lord of happiness, to appearance I must devote myself." Ori Heffetz, "A Test of Conspicuous Consumption: Visibility and Income Elasticities," *The Review of Economics and Statistics* 93, no. 4 (November 2011).

9. Dorothy S. Brady and Rose D. Friedman, "Savings and the Income Distribution," *Studies in Income and Wealth*, NBER (1947), pp. 247–65.

10. Sample surveys of U.S. consumer income and outlay have been published periodically by the U.S. Department of Labor and its predecessors since 1888. I collected data from twenty-one surveys from 1888 to 2012. The raw survey data appeared to have no consistent pattern until I exhibited each income bracket's ratio of spending to income against each particular year's average family income. Then, like Brady and Friedman, for all twenty-one surveys, the ratio of spending to income for those households with a third of the nation's average income concentrate around 1.3 (that is, spending exceeds income by 30 percent). The spending/income ratio then falls eventually to about 0.8 at double the average income level.

11. Other propensities—time preference, competitiveness, home bias, and optimism—relate to a far greater extent to people reacting individually to changes in their external environment.

12. Without outside guidance of one form or another, reality is too complex for the average person to handle. To function at all, most people require an instruction manual on how to respond to the myriad decisions required every minute of every day, from deciding what to wear to how to behave in any gathering.

13. It is revealing that the most drastic penalty for misbehaving prisoners is to place them in solitary confinement.

14. Daniel Kahneman, p. 255.

15. In some rare cases for those seeking status in their society's pecking order, a higher price is an attraction to buy, though it might validly be argued that the product being purchased has a joint value including the value of a perceived rise in status achieved by exhibiting the resources to buy.

16. Letter to Dr. H. L. Gordon (May 3, 1949 - AEA 58–217) as quoted in Walter Isaacson, *Einstein: His Life and Universe* (New York: Simon & Schuster Paperbacks, 2007), p. 113.

CHAPTER 2: THE CRISIS BEGINS, INTENSIFIES, AND ABATES

1. Short-term debt as a share of total liabilities was close to the lowest levels since the end of World War II. Liquid assets relative to short-term liabilities were at exceptionally high levels historically, and the market value of net worth as a ratio to liabilities was close to its highest level in decades.

2. The closest example was the shutting down of the call-money market for one day at the height of the panic of 1907.

3. Hugo Bänziger, "Money Market Funds Need New Global Standards," *Financial Times* (November 5, 2009). Bänziger was chief risk officer at Deutsche Bank at the time.

4. Trade finance soared to 600 basis points over Libor, effectively shutting down global trade. Exports fell sharply in unison in every major trading center. Goods in transit backed up, leaving long lines of ships at ports, unable to unload their canceled cargos. The backup was immediately evident everywhere. As a consequence, global industrial production was cut back sharply.

5. More than 4 percent of the nation's seven thousand commercial banks failed or were assisted during 2009 and 2010, while all four major investment banks were on the ropes.

6. *Global Shadow Banking Monitoring Report 2012;* Financial Stability Board; November 18, 2012.

7. Alan Greenspan, "The Evolution of Bank Supervision." Paper presented at American Bankers Association, Phoenix, October 11, 1999.

8. Allen N. Berger and David B. Humphrey, "Bank Scale Economies, Mergers, Concentration, and Efficiency: The U.S. Experience." Working Paper 94–25. Wharton Financial Institutions Center (June 1994).

9. *FDIC Quarterly Banking Profile,* 2nd Quarter, 2006, p. 3.

10. I often maintained that because of this complexity, policy makers had to rely on an international "invisible hand" to bring equilibrium to such undecipherable markets. The high level of market liquidity appeared, erroneously, to confirm that the system was working.

11. In their excellent book, *This Time Is Different: Eight Centuries of Financial Folly* (Princeton, NJ: Princeton University Press, 2011), Ken Rogoff and Carmen Reinhart effectively documented the dangers of leverage.

12. In mid-September 2007, when home prices were still close to their highs, I did fear that the heavy overhang of vacant homes for sale would induce a significant price decline. (See Krishna Guha, "Greenspan Alert on US House Prices," *Financial Times,* September 16, 2007.) But I had no expectation that prices would fall an additional 28 percent for a total decline of 33 percent from peak to trough, the largest decline ever.

13. From the end of 2002 to the end of 2007, commercial banks did add $277 billion (a 27 percent addition to equity capital), but it was clearly not enough to address what was about to occur.

14. Gerald P. Dwyer, "Credit Ratings and Derivatives," Federal Reserve Bank of Atlanta, August 2009.

15. The Securities and Exchange Commission has argued against reserves not tied to specific loans because such leeway can affect reported earnings to shareholders. (True.) Company earnings have always been subject to shifting earnings from one quarter to the next. But such manipulation over the long run is obviously restrained by the underlying profitability of the firm. We will have to live with profit manipulation being constrained by outside audit.

16. See data in Chapter 4.

17. FOMC transcripts of May 1995, pp. 32–33.

18. Alan Greenspan; "Global Challenges." Remarks at the Financial Crisis Conference, Council on Foreign Relations, New York, July 12, 2000.

19. The term "regression" derives from an early (nineteenth-century) application of this technique. It concluded that the heights of descendants of tall ancestors tended to *regress* toward the mean of their distribution.

20. A D-W in excess of 2.0 (extremely rare in economic time series) indicates negative serial correlation.

21. The t-statistic for an independent variable is calculated by dividing the variable's regression coefficient by the standard error of that coefficient.

22. The independent variables in this regression are (1) the cyclically adjusted federal budget deficit as a percent of GDP, (2) the nonfarm business operating rate, and (3) the spread between the yields on 30-year and 5-year U.S. Treasury obligations. See Chapter 7 for a discussion of the relevance of this regression.

CHAPTER 3: THE ROOTS OF CRISIS

1. For a more detailed explanation see Alan Greenspan, *The Age of Turbulence* (New York: Penguin Press, 2007), chapter 20.

2. I had always been skeptical of such estimates. The state of disrepair in that most advanced economy of the Soviet bloc just didn't square with the numbers. Having much of my life compared visual economic landscapes with statistics on standards of living, there was no way East Berlin, and by extension East Germany, had developed living standards anywhere close to those of West Germany. As a member of the President's Foreign Intelligence Advisory Board in 1985, and being assigned to a project that brought me in close contact with upward-biased Soviet economic statistics, I could imagine that East Germany was not immune from the central planning bias. After the fall of the

Berlin Wall it was exposed by more accurate appraisals of economic performance.

3. Foreign direct investment in China, for example, rose gradually from 1980 to 1990, but then rose thirty-ninefold by 2007, and contrary to global trends, moved higher through the crisis of 2008.

4. IMF, *World Economic Outlook,* April 2007, chap. 5, p. 162.

5. Although the decline in global interest rates indicated, of necessity, that global saving intentions were chronically exceeding global intentions to invest, actual global saving and investment rates in 2007, over all, were only modestly higher than in 1999. This observation suggests that the uptrend in the saving intentions of developing economies was being tempered by investment intentions in the developed world. That weakened global investment was a major determinant in the decline of global real long-term interest rates was also the conclusion of a March 2007 Bank of Canada study. (See Brigitte Desroches and Michael Francis. "World Real Interest Rates: A Global Savings and Investment Perspective," Bank of Canada Working Paper 2007–16, Ottawa, March 2007.)

6. The path of the convergence is evident in the unweighted average variance of interest rates on ten-year sovereign debt of fifteen countries. That average declined markedly from 2000 to 2008 (Exhibit 3.2). The variance of the logarithms of the fifteen long-term interest rates exhibits similar trends.

7. For example, "Finance and Economics: Houses Built on Sand," *Economist,* September 15, 2007, p. 104.

8. IMF, *World Economic Outlook,* April 2008, chap. 3, p. 113.

9. For the period 1991 to 2005, the $R^2 = .57$ and the adjusted t-value for mortgage interest rates is a highly significant -8.7.

10. Neither survived the crisis intact as an ongoing firm.

11. That many of the investors were European was confirmed by the heavy losses on U.S. mortgages reported by European investors. Euroarea banks, for example, exhibit a very high ratio of residential mortgage-backed securities write-downs to the residential mortgage loans they hold (IMF, *Global Financial Stability Report,* October 2009, p. 10). The size of the buildup of subprime securities holdings abroad, during the bubble years, is unclear. The U.S. Treasury's annual Foreign Holdings Survey reports that by the end of 2006, foreign investors held $386 billion of privately issued U.S. mortgage-backed securities, some of which were commercial mortgage-backed securities, compared with $125 billion in 2002. By 2012, the total had reached $716 billion.

12. In October 2000, HUD finalized a rule "significantly increasing the GSEs' affordable housing goals" for each year from 2001 to 2003 (Office of Policy Development and Research, 2001). In November 2004, the annual housing goals for 2005 and beyond were raised still further. Goals are still being set.

13. The size of the commitments was tied to the size of the GSEs' portfolio of mortgage assets.

14. Federal Housing Finance Agency, *2008 Annual Report to Congress* (revised), Historical Data Tables 5b, Part 2, and 14b, Part 2 (originally published May 18, 2009, and updated to include a significant reclassification effective September 3, 2009). Before the revision, I estimated the share at less than 30 percent. Data newly reclassified by Fannie Mae account for almost all of the revision.

15. Mortgage Bankers Association

16. Early Payment Defaults (EPDs): mortgages that go into ninety plus days delinquency or full default status within the first year.

17. Inside Mortgage Finance Publications, *The 2009 Mortgage Market Statistical Annual,* vol. I: "Mortgage Originations by Product," p. 4; vol. II: "Non-Agency MBS Issuance by Type," p. 13.

18. The remaining 20 percent was being held by investors presumably unwilling to sell them at prevailing market prices.

19. That extraordinarily receptive market arguably was driven to excess by purchases by Fannie and Freddie to meet their HUD obligations.

20. Alan Greenspan, "The Crisis," Brookings Papers on Economic Activity, Spring 2010, p. 242.

21. After all, self-amortizing conventional mortgages had been designated by Basel II to be sufficiently safe for regulated financial institutions to put up regulatory capital at only a fraction of the requirements on unrated claims on corporate lending.

22. Alan Greenspan, testimony, "Government-Sponsored Enterprises." Committee on Banking, Housing, and Urban Affairs, U.S. Senate; February 24, 2004.

23. Federal National Mortgage Association 10-K for fiscal year ended December 31, 2004. Filed on December 6, 2006; p. 146.

24. These covenants are restrictions put on a borrower by a lender that might, for example, restrict other borrowings, the level of working capital, or debt service cover.

25. Brown Brothers Harriman, where I worked in the summer of 1947, was a case in point. They eschewed the speculative markets of the dot-com and housing booms and therefore remained solvent. But their

asset growth during those years hardly compared with that of Citi or JPMorgan.

26. Michiyo Nakamoto and David Wighton, "Citigroup Chief Stays Bullish on Buy-Outs," *Financial Times*, July 9, 2007.

27. That outcome was most stark when interest rates on savings and loan (S&L) liabilities (mostly short term) rose sharply in the early 1980s, dramatically increasing the institutions' cost of debt. Interest rates on new mortgages also rose, but because the maturity of the mortgage assets was quite long, only the few newly issued mortgages of the S&Ls increased their income. The income from the vast majority of their mortgages was unchanged. The effect was to squeeze earnings, and much of the industry filed for bankruptcy as a consequence.

28. Alan Greenspan, Remarks at the Economic Club of New York, February 17, 2009.

CHAPTER 4: STOCK PRICES AND EQUITY STIMULUS

1. Warren Buffett, perhaps the most successful investor of my generation, recently told me that he has followed that strategy for decades.

2. Interest rates, after all, in the fifth century B.C. were similar to those of modern times. I know of no other "time series" that has exhibited such stability.

3. Panic selling is an integral part of any bear market. But panic buying, excluding short covering, is rarely evident during bull markets. As the data show, the rate of price increase in bull markets tends to be importantly less than the average pace of decline in bear markets.

4. Rick Ferri, "Index Fund Portfolios Reign Superior," *Forbes*, August 20, 2012.

5. While bear markets are far more implosive than bull markets are expansive, the number of days of stock price decline is far lower than the number of days of rise. Daily stock prices since 1955, after factoring out their long-term uptrend, fell 4 percent less often than they rose, and average daily declines were 4 percent larger than average daily gains.

6. The five-year maturity is long enough to eliminate expected business cycle fluctuations.

7. Unlike spending from wages and salaries, spending of capital gains requires a comparable increase in household debt, or a smaller increase in other assets than would otherwise have been the case.

8. The range is wide, however. An estimated 16 percent of consumption

expenditures was attributable to changes in capital values during the first quarter of 2006, and as low as 10 percent during the fourth quarter of 1974.

9. Regression analysis over the years 1985 to 2012 indicates that a 5 percent rise/fall in prices will generate a change in starts of plus or minus 7.4 percent (Exhibit 7.4).

10. To estimate the overall effect of changing asset prices on total GDP would be a simple job merely of adding up the effects of asset prices on personal consumption expenditures and private and municipal capital investment. But that does not account for interaction between sectors.

11. The market value of U.S. companies, foreign companies, and homes rose by an annual average of 8.1 percent, 14.4 percent, and 6.1 percent, respectively.

12. Regrettably, there were few chairwomen in those days.

13. Alan Greenspan, "Stock Prices and Capital Evaluation," in *American Statistical Association, 1959 Proceedings of the Business and Economic Statistics Section* (American Statistical Association, Washington, D.C., 1959), pp. 2–26.

14. This was a precursor to "Tobin's q," promulgated by James Tobin of Yale in 1969.

15. Some corporations use the weighted average of debt and equity capital.

16. For this calculation I include inventory change with fixed investment.

17. Net borrowing (which includes issuance of new stock) is equal to the net increase in liabilities less the increase in assets other than capital investments. This statistic is equivalent to what the Federal Reserve's Flow of Funds account calls the "financing gap."

18. Operating earnings less interest payments, and a few other adjustments, equals pretax earnings.

CHAPTER 5: FINANCE AND REGULATION

1. Much of this chapter has been expanded and updated from an earlier article, "The Crisis," which I wrote for the Brookings Panel on Economic Activity (Spring 2010).

2. Moreover, it is a matter of ongoing dispute as to whether the outcomes of free markets are "just," an issue I will address in Chapter 11.

3. I have witnessed too many stock and commodity price booms and crashes that exhibit very similar psychology-driven paths of expansion and contraction.

4. Alan Greenspan, "We Will Never Have a Perfect Model of Risk," *Financial Times,* March 16, 2008.

5. Although depreciation is a debit on the income statements of households and businesses, the savings available to fund investment (household savings and business cash flow) are gross of that loss. Depreciated assets (for example, houses or plant and equipment, depending on which sector is being considered) have incurred a loss in value from regular use that does not materialize into an actual deduction from cash flow. (Any assets that have been completely depreciated are replaced, a realized cost that is already reflected in consumption expenditures and thus lower gross savings.)

6. Including the Federal Reserve, technically a financial intermediary.

7. Increased financial income shares of GDP are evident in the United Kingdom, Netherlands, Japan, Korea, and Australia, among others. The world's most rapidly expanding (and increasingly market-oriented) economy, China, reports a rise in financial intermediaries' share of GDP from 1.6 percent in 1980 to 5.5 percent in 2012.

8. The net foreign demand for U.S. financial services has grown significantly but has been largely offset by net imports of insurance services.

9. A recent study finds a markedly above-average rise in the salaries of those employed in finance since 1980. (See Thomas Philippon and Ariell Reshef, *Wages and Human Capital in the U.S. Financial Industry: 1909–2006,* NBER Working Paper 14644, January 2009.)

10. *Economist,* "Number-Crunchers Crunched," February 13, 2010.

11. Household financial assets, which reflect most of the holdings of insurance and pension funds, can be taken as a proxy for the assets of the economy to be managed at a fee. The ratio of household financial assets to disposable personal income did rise through 2000, but has been trendless since.

12. Alan Greenspan, "Dodd-Frank Fails to Meet Test of Our Times," *Financial Times,* March 29, 2011.

13. The Dodd-Frank Act reorganized the use of the 13 (3) authority.

14. Alan Greenspan; "Technology and Financial Services" (speech, Journal of Financial Services Research and the American Enterprise Institute Conference in Honor of Anna Schwartz, Washington, D.C.; April 14, 2000).

15. Yields on riskless longer maturities can fall below short-term riskless rates if tight money convinces investors that future inflation will be less and funds availability more.

16. Sidney Homer and Richard Sylla, *A History of Interest Rates,* 3rd ed. (New Brunswick, NJ: Rutgers University Press, 1991), p. 340.

17. Clearly that was not the case for the savings and loan industry that had assumed interest rates would remain low forever. They did not. Their predominantly short-term funding costs rose dramatically in the early 1980s. The return on their mortgage portfolios, however, rose only modestly. Nearly 750 S&Ls failed in the years following.

18. A normal distribution reflects the probability of events that approximate coin-tossing outcomes.

19. Immediately subsequent to Lehman, a number of investment firms constructed probability distributions of outcomes employing, as the negative tail, data based on the post-Lehman experience. Using Monte Carlo simulations and other techniques, they concluded, not unexpectedly, that the probability of a financial crisis as severe as the one that followed the Lehman default was much higher than indicated by models in which risk is more normally distributed. Such evidence suggests that the probability of the onset of what was previously thought to be a "hundred-year flood" is higher than once in a century.

20. The higher the level of market participants' capital, the greater the degree of liquidity. The larger the restrictions on the mobility of collateral, the less the needed capital. The larger the size of the combined equity of market participants, the larger the pool available to fund narrow bid-asked spreads.

21. Sebastian Mallaby, *More Money Than God: Hedge Funds and the Making of a New Elite* (London: Bloomsbury, 2010).

22. See endnote 15 in Chapter 2 regarding the SEC's position on generic bank reserves.

23. Although Gramm-Leach-Bliley repealed the Glass-Steagall Act of 1933, the mandatory separation of commercial and investment banking had essentially already been nullified more than a decade earlier. An April 1987 court ruling had legalized an interpretation of Glass-Steagall that enabled bank holding companies to have affiliated investment banks. These affiliates that came to be known as Section 20 affiliates had become ubiquitous well before the passage of Gramm-Leach Bliley. The important contribution of Gramm-Leach-Bliley was the significant reduction of costs of engaging in both commercial and investment banking activities, achieved by repealing the barriers and red tape associated with Section 20 affiliates. The repeal of the Glass-Steagall Act in fact changed very little. From the enactment of Gramm-Leach-

Bliley in 1999 to the Federal Reserve's acceptance of Goldman Sachs and Morgan Stanley as financial services holding companies at the height of the crisis, no applications to employ the greater powers were forthcoming. That forbearance apparently reflected a desire to stay clear of the Federal Reserve's regulatory embrace.

24. The seller of a CDS insures the holder of a particular debt instrument against loss in the event of default. Prices of CDSs are thus the most sensitive measure of the probability of bank default.

25. For five-year contracts, the average annual price of insurance was 0.14 percent of the notional amount of the underlying swap instruments.

26. Of course, in retrospect that proved to be insufficient compensation for the risk that was eventually revealed.

27. As fear of contagion from the European sovereign debt crisis mounted in the spring of 2010, CDS and LIBOR/OIS spreads rose markedly.

28. When, during the crisis, such assets appeared about to fail, sponsoring companies, fearful of reputation risk (a new insight?), reabsorbed legally detached affiliates at great loss.

29. See endnote 23 (pages 355–56).

30. Rates of return crashed during the first half of 2009, with declines matched (on an annual basis) only by those in the Depression years 1932–34. Both cases reflected a rare sharp breakout from the historical range, resulting mostly from large write-offs on previously extended loans.

31. Gary H. Stern, "Addressing the Too Big to Fail Problem." Statement before the Committee on Banking, Housing, and Urban Affairs, U.S. Senate, Washington, D.C., May 6, 2009.

32. Wayne Passmore, "The GSE Implicit Subsidy and the Value of Government Ambiguity," *Real Estate Economics,* vol. 33, no. 3 (2005), pp. 465–86.

33. Kenichi Ueda and Beatrice Weder di Mauro, "Quantifying Structural Subsidy Values for Systemically Important Financial Institutions," IMF Working Paper, May 2012.

34. The FDIC has experienced large losses in the value of assets taken over in resolution during the last five years.

35. At the end of 2007, Lehman Brothers had thirty-one times; Bear Stearns, thirty-four; and Citigroup, eighteen.

36. Partnership capital is often lost to a partnership when partners retire. Corporate capital is far more stable.

37. With rare exceptions it *has* proved impossible to identify the point at

which a bubble will burst, but its emergence and development *are* visible in credit spreads.

38. Alan Greenspan, "Banking Supervision." Speech before the American Bankers Association, Washington, D.C., September 18, 2000.

39. In 1903, O. Henry (W. S. Porter), who had more than a passing relationship with banking shenanigans, wrote in "A Call Loan" about a fictional bank examiner from the Office of the Comptroller of the Currency who was obsessed with the collateral backing a $10,000 loan. Such detailed scrutiny is exceptionally rare in today's larger banks.

40. Having served on JP Morgan's board for a decade just before my joining the Federal Reserve, I had an extended insight into the effectiveness of that company's counterparty surveillance of Citicorp, Bank of America, Wells Fargo, and others, relative to the regulatory surveillance by Federal Reserve banks.

CHAPTER 6: SCHOONER INTELLIGENCE AND THEN SOME

1. Willard Long Thorp, *Business Annals,* National Bureau of Economic Research, 1926.

2. First published in 1827.

3. One of the founders of the *Journal of Commerce* was the multitalented Morse, whose invention of the telegraph (and its extension to the transatlantic cable in 1866) undermined the competitive advantage of earlier "schooner" intelligence. Communication times collapsed (from the ten days it took a ship to bring information across the Atlantic to a matter of minutes).

4. On March 26, 1860, the *New York Herald* carried an announcement by the Central Overland California and Pike's Peak Express Company offering mail delivery from New York "to San Francisco in eight days. The first courier of the Pony Express will leave the Missouri River on Tuesday, April 3 at 5:00 pm, and will run regularly, weekly, hereafter, carrying letter mail only." The first lap of this relay between New York and St. Joseph, Missouri, was by telegram. But the line ended there.

5. The telephone (1876), and later, the wireless telegraph and radio, increased the scope and convenience of communications but reduced the time of transmission only modestly.

6. The Homestead Act, signed into law by President Lincoln on May 20,

1862, formally established an application and acquisition process by which any U.S. citizen (or intended citizen) could settle a 160-acre plot of federal land west of the Mississippi River. By 1934, the Homestead Act had transferred 10 percent of all U.S. lands from the government to individuals.

7. To close the loop of personal coincidences, the Conference Board was my first employer upon graduating from New York University.

8. Alvin Hansen: *Full Recovery or Stagnation?* (New York: W. W. Norton, 1938), and *Fiscal Policy and Business Cycles* (New York: W. W. Norton, 1941).

9. Klein ended up winning the Nobel Prize in Economics in 1980 for his contributions to computer-based econometric models.

10. The merger formed Global Insight, which was later acquired by IHS Inc.

11. Much of what follows is drawn from *The Age of Turbulence,* published in 2007.

12. The Ford administration did get enacted a one-shot tax rebate, which probably did not provide a large boost to the economy but also probably did little harm.

13. I was always impressed at the high quality of economists and economic research that was the defining characteristic of the Council of Economic Advisers. It was an economic consulting organization with one client: the president of the United States. Burton Malkiel was the CEA member who was officially in charge of coordinating the CEA's forecast with that of the U.S. Treasury and the president's Office of Management and Budget. (In 1973 [revised in 2007], Malkiel authored the bestseller *A Random Walk Down Wall Street* [New York: W. W. Norton].) Three agencies crafted the administration's official position on the outlook, though the CEA had more than equal influence.

14. See "Debt Matters" in Chapter 2, page 49.

15. Interestingly, in some quarters, the Federal Reserve has recently come under pressure in the wake of the crisis not to pursue more expansionary policies, at least those related to an expansion of its balance sheet.

Chapter 7: Uncertainty Undermines Investment

1. Residential building has recovered in part since mid-2012 but as of June 2013 remains well below its peaks of 2006.

2. This calculation, by including foreign earnings retained abroad, repre-

sents U.S. nonfinancial corporations' global consolidated cash flow, in which foreign retained earnings are net of capital investments of foreign affiliates. Corporate decision making, in my experience, is made on a worldwide basis.

3. Noncorporate investment as a share of gross savings in 2010 was the lowest in the postwar period, with the possible exception of one quarter in 1992.

4. The result is the same if motor vehicles and other somewhat shorter-lived consumer durables are included in investment.

5. Disposable personal income less personal consumption expenditures (less depreciation).

6. This is evidenced by the relationship between housing starts and the price of homes relative to their trailing three-year average (see Exhibit 7.4).

7. A clouded future will cause an existing homeowner to stay put and not take on the risk of a new home, but in addition, a large segment of households has chosen to switch to rentals (a short-term commitment). Of course, this swing reflects, in part, the sharp spike in home foreclosures.

8. Including both single-family and multifamily condominiums.

9. Long-lived structures, the mark of market expansion, were suppressed.

10. Real GDP barely declined in the "recession" of 1991 and not at all in 2001.

11. The rate of discount on expected returns from an investment tends to rise with maturity. This phenomenon is most visible in credit markets where yields on debt tend to increase with the maturity of the debt instrument—a rising "term structure," as it is commonly known.

12. The history of the spread since 1900 is depicted in Exhibit 7.5.

13. Taking into consideration only the change in output itself.

14. While unemployment among construction workers soared, by far most of the rise in unemployment reflected tepid demand economywide.

15. Although *short-lived* business equipment and software investment rose moderately in 2010 and 2011, U.S. overall private fixed investment has fallen far short of the level that history suggests should have occurred given the recent dramatic surge in corporate profitability.

16. Risk managers, especially in the financial sector, having badly underestimated negative tail risk prior to the crisis, have become increasingly uncertain of their ability to evaluate risk.

17. Prior to 2008, the only actual breakdown in market structure of which I am aware occurred for one day at the height of the panic of 1907.

18. Of which $649 billion had been expended through the end of 2011.

19. See chapters 3 and 4, as well as the later sections of this chapter, for evaluations of private equity stimulus and fiscal stimulus as contributors to economic recovery.

20. *Ex ante* (before the fact) and *ex post* (after the fact), terms largely attributed to Swedish economist Gunnar Myrdal, are widely used in macroeconomics to define the process by which disparate levels of intended savings and investment (*ex ante*) are brought into equality, *ex post,* through interest rates and other rates of return on assets. Although we have no direct measure of *ex ante*, we assume that if, at an interest rate, saving intentions exceed investment intentions, the rate of interest will fall until both savings and investment are brought into equality. Similarly, rates will rise in the reverse situation.

21. Thomas Huxley, "Biogenesis and Abiogenesis" (presidential address at the British Association, 1870).

22. Repeated experiments dealing with the real world produce the same results time after time. In economics, the conditions never stay stable long enough to produce an exact repetition.

23. The cracks in market structures had been repaired by then.

24. Such fears were clearly evident as the 1929 stock market bubble burst. There were innumerable consortiums of large investors and financial institutions that tried to stem the fall and failed.

25. Auction sales of wholly illiquid assets into a market devoid of bids will, almost without exception, be at prices for which the market will immediately pounce, as was the case with the RTC's novel auction initiative (see *The Age of Turbulence,* p. 117).

26. Chrysler had been bailed out by the federal government once before in 1980, but that incident apparently was not precedential.

27. The depression of 1896 was an exception.

28. Harold Cole and Lee Ohanian, "New Deal Policies and the Persistence of the Great Depression: A General Equilibrium Analysis," *Journal of Political Economy* 112, no. 4 (August 2004): pp. 779–816.

Chapter 8: Productivity: The Ultimate Measure of Economic Success

1. The combined profit margin of manufacturing, mining, and trade (Census Bureau) more than doubled during 1993 and 1994, and then peaked in 2000.

2. Price = (Average Hourly Labor Compensation / Output per Hour) – Other Unit Costs = Profit per Unit of Output Divided by price: 1 –

[Average Hourly Labor Compensation / (Output per Hour times Price)] – (Other Unit Costs/Price) = Profit Margin

3. To be sure, the BEA's nonfinancial corporate productivity growth rate was stronger, but it, combined with the reliable nonfarm business measure, implied an implausibly prolonged deeply negative rate of productivity growth for the whole of noncorporate business, and was hence disregarded.

4. The Federal Reserve's chief domestic economist at the time.

5. Laurence H. Meyer, *A Term at the Fed* (New York: Harper Collins, 2004), p. 125.

6. Real GDP actually grew during the recession years albeit at a subdued 1.8 percent annual rate from 2001 through 2003.

7. These five-year forecasts are statistically tied, significantly, to the average of the *previous* ten years.

8. See Chapter 10 on the issue of political culture and levels and growth of productivity.

9. A broader historical measure, of course, would include our farm workforce and its output—a major component of the U.S. economy into the early twentieth century. But two factors lead to the choice of examining the long-term trends in the nonfarm sector. First, the level of farm productivity tends to be far less than that of the nonfarm sector. And second, the share of our workforce devoted to farming has dwindled to around 2 percent (see Chapter 6), and the rapid replacement of low-output-per-hour farm workers with nonfarm workers imparted a rate of increase in national productivity heavily affected and distorted by the transfer of work from farm to nonfarm. But that came to an end in 2004, never to be repeated (Exhibit 8.2). Thus, tracing the nonfarm sector for long-term undistorted evaluation tends to be favored by economic forecasters.

10. An estimate for 1870 employs Angus Maddison's 1.92 percent annual rate of change between 1870 and 1913 to obtain a number consistent with the series published by John W. Kendrick and the BLS covering the period 1889 to 2012. (Angus Maddison, *The World Economy: A Millennial Perspective*. Development Centre of the OECD, 2001).

11. I suspect that this surprising degree of long-term stability reflects, in part, a large and slowly growing capital stock with an average age of more than twenty years. Obviously, the greater the average age, the slower the rate of turnover and the more stable the flow of imputed "services" from that stock relative to other factors of growth. The "services" emanate daily from our capital infrastructure—our buildings,

productive equipment, highways, and water systems, to identify just a few. And that relatively stable average age is itself reflecting the apparent stability of human time preference, a key animal spirit.

12. Virtually all of war-ravaged European plant and equipment was replaced with the newest technologies between 1950 and 1973.

13. See individual country data in Angus Maddison, *The World Economy: A Millennial Perspective*. Development Centre of the OECD, 2001.

14. The process of human adjustment to the real world may make it appear that, as a species, we are getting smarter. But that may reflect that the world in which we live is becoming ever more complex. The natural world had to seem more bewildering to people living one or two millennia ago. But raw intelligence at its highest levels appears little different now from our forebears of earlier millennia. For an interesting review of this controversial issue, see James R. Flynn's *Are We Getting Smarter* (Cambridge University Press; 2012).

15. The development of that paradigm is principally attributed to John W. Kendrick (National Bureau of Economic Research and George Washington University) and Robert Solow (Massachusetts Institute of Technology).

16. See, for example, Stephen D. Oliner, Daniel E. Sichel, and Kevin J. Stiroh, *Explaining a Productive Decade*. Finance and Economics Discussion Series, Federal Reserve Board, Washington, D.C., August 2007.

17. Almost all such projections also adjust labor input as measured by hours worked for the projected quality of the workforce, often proxied by average levels of completed education and other characteristics thought to be associated with labor quality.

18. This is a measure of the amount of capital consumed in the production process and, as such, weights a dollar of short-lived fixed capital expenditures (in terms of economic deterioration) more heavily than a dollar of long-lived fixed capital expenditures.

19. Output per Hour = MFP X $[\alpha(L/H) + (1-\alpha)(K/H)]$, where MFP = multifactor productivity, α = labor compensation/GDP, L = labor input, K = capital input, and H = hours.

20. Medicare and Medicaid are in-kind benefits; hence, by definition, they are "received" as consumption.

21. As a child in the 1930s, I was enthralled by the radio and film portrayals of *Buck Rogers in the 25th Century* (the *Star Trek* of my youth). Much of the future technology envisioned back then, in today's context, seems naive and uninformed.

22. Herman Kahn, *The Emerging Japanese Superstate: Challenge and Response* (New York: Prentice Hall; 1971).

23. Thomson Reuters 2011 Top 100 Global Innovator companies, November 15, 2011, http://top100innovators.com/.

24. The capital costs of robots are falling to the point where their equivalent wage per hour is becoming competitive with low-wage developing countries. The United States may continue to lose manufacturing jobs but not manufacturing business.

25. Nonetheless, some breakthroughs, such as the telegraph, are discontinuous, as has been the development of much information technology—notably, the emergence of the Internet.

26. I recall visiting in the 1960s a tall and narrow stamping plant built at the turn of the century. I was struck by its unusual shape. But it was only decades later that I learned that I had entered one of the last surviving relics of a certain aspect of America's industrial history.

27. Our current account deficit.

28. If, owing to market inefficiencies or regulation, competition is tepid, the degree of financial intermediation will be less and the *proportion* of accruing profits that are monopoly profits will be larger. (See discussion of crony capitalism in Chapter 11.)

29. This churning process that is driven by the relative price of assets is ongoing, continually tracing out what Joseph Schumpeter of Harvard labeled "creative destruction."

30. It is also not so for a highly regulated economy, or one rife with crony capitalism (see Chapter 11) which will, more often than not, direct savings into investments that do not offer rates of return high enough to effectively increase standards of living for all participants in the economy rather than for a favored few.

31. Stephen Oliner et al., *Explaining a Productive Decade,* August 2007.

32. Stacey Tevlin and Karl Whelan, "Explaining the Investment Boom of the 1990s," (Federal Reserve Board, March 2000).

33. *America: The Story of Us* (History Channel documentary).

34. In fact, much of today's reordering for inventories is conducted by computer programs that automatically send repurchase orders to suppliers.

35. Because the thin just-in-time supply chains reduce the amount of idle resources that companies require, those resources are partly replaced by a block of idle cash to be available when, for whatever reasons, the thin supply buffer breaks down. (See Gillian Tett, "Reality

Not Politics Dictates Corporate Cash Hoarding," *Financial Times,* January 18, 2013, citing analysis by Finn Poschmann of CD Howe Institute.)

36. The issue is somewhat mixed in that, for example, the metals content of ore can go in either direction.

37. The adjustment is in the prices that the BEA uses to convert nominal dollars of output to indexes of 2005 dollar purchasing power. As the quality of passenger cars, for example, improves with increasing technology, the Bureau of Labor Statistics, the source of most BEA prices, will adjust any rise in car prices to factor out changes in technology improvements from real inflation-related price increases.

38. Most important, these two separate indicators of the gross weight of GDP both exhibit historically flat trends over the past half century, and show a remarkably high relationship in year-to-year fluctuations. It is not clear, however, why the raw commodity weight is so low relative to that of the total output of goods. To be sure, there are many physical inputs, such as cotton, wool, and wood, that are not counted in the commodities measure, but the gap nonetheless seems inordinately wide.

39. Moore's law is the popular name for the prediction made by Intel cofounder Gordon Moore that the number of transistors per integrated circuit, or microchip, will roughly double every two years.

40. Since 2008, however, the share of global trade relative to global GDP has flattened.

41. Most fifteenth-century serfs tilled the same soil using the same tools and methods of their forebears. That resulted in nearly two millennia of stagnant output.

42. Angus Maddison. *The World Economy: A Millennial Perspective.* Development Centre of the OECD, 2001, p. 28.

43. I interpolate contiguous years to estimate a value for the end-of-year "stock" of productivity.

CHAPTER 9: PRODUCTIVITY AND THE AGE OF ENTITLEMENTS

1. President Barack Obama, remarks to the AARP convention in New Orleans, September 21, 2012.

2. AARP Commercial, MSNBC, September 18, 2012.

3. Sociologist Alice Fothergill (University of Vermont) conducted a study of the attitudes of recipients of aid during the 1997 Great Falls, North Dakota, flood. [Alice Fothergill, "The Stigma of Charity: Gender, Class, and Disaster Assistance." *The Sociology Quarterly,* vol. 44, no. 4, pp. 659–80 (2003).] Some recipients of aid following the flood that inundated New York City in late October 2012 in the wake of Hurricane Sandy expressed a similar sense of degradation. [Sarah Maslin Nir; "Helping Hands Also Expose a New York Divide," *New York Times,* November 16, 2012.]

4. "The Debt to Pleasure," *Economist,* April 27, 2013.

5. Private pension funds, on average, have not always been fully funded. A study by Goldman Sachs in 2011 indicated that between 2002 and 2011, the market value of private defined benefit plans of Standard and Poor's 500 corporations (U.S. plans only) ranged between 79 percent funded (2008) and 108 percent funded (2007).

6. Whether Social Security is fully funded or not has nothing to do with the security of payments to future beneficiaries. Benefits in either case are de facto fully guaranteed by the U.S. government. Because the federal government will cover any shortfall in the trust funds with general revenues, it is no longer conceivable that, as required by law, benefits will be cut in the event of a depletion of trust fund assets.

7. Pay-as-you-go funding requires only that current receipts of trust funds (contributions, interest, and, since 1984, taxation of benefits) cover current benefits. In this paradigm, contributions for social insurance or other taxes would have to rise sharply in line with the projected rise in benefits paid out to the retiring baby-boom generation. Full funding sets the payroll tax rates at fixed (higher) levels that will accumulate assets in the trust funds prior to the acceleration of benefits and then run them off as benefits rise. That smoothing effect creates an economically nondisruptive trust fund. The seventy-five-year (official) funding requirements fall somewhere in the middle owing to the fact that, under current projections, the trust funds become exhausted immediately beyond the seventy-fifth year.

8. The 2013 Annual Report of the Board of Trustees of the Federal Old-Age and Survivors Insurance and Federal Disability Trust Funds, p. 16.

9. The 1983 NCSSR was required to meet the seventy-five-year criterion—which it did, but only a year later the depth of the deficit of the seventy-sixth year again put the Social Security Trust Fund out of compliance.

10. The 2012 Annual Report of the Board of Trustees of the Federal Hospital Insurance and Federal Supplementary Medical Insurance Trust Funds, p. 3.
11. The trustees, I might add, included three incumbent cabinet secretaries.
12. Harry S. Truman, special message to the Congress Recommending a Comprehensive Health Program, November 19, 1945.
13. The BEA lists, under total government social benefits to persons, Social Security, Medicare, Medicaid, unemployment insurance benefits, veterans benefits, and other social benefits.
14. Dwight D. Eisenhower, State of the Union address, January 5, 1956.
15. John F. Kennedy, *Economic Report of the President,* January 1963.
16. Federal government savings (positive or negative), by the BEA's reckoning, is close to but not the same as budget surpluses and deficits.
17. The huge surge in stock market-related revenues temporarily propelled government savings into positive ground between 1996 and 2001.
18. To be sure, the cut in individual and corporate tax rates in 2001 and 2003 did lower federal receipts as a share of GDP somewhat. But by early 2013, as a result of "fiscal cliff" legislation, federal government tax receipts returned close to their historic range relative to GDP.
19. Contributions to social insurance had some association with benefits from 1965 to 1970 but then fell off abruptly thereafter. By 2012, contributions were little more than two fifths of benefits. Since 1970, they can just as readily be considered a generic payroll tax indistinguishable from any other form of tax receipt.
20. Since 1982, within the private sector, all of the crowding out of savings by consumption took place in the households subsector. Business savings edged higher. (See Exhibit 9.4.)
21. Gross savings are before charges for depreciation, and net savings are after such charges.
22. Richard Sutch, "Saving, Capital, and Wealth," *Historical Statistics of the United States,* millennial edition, 3; pp. 287–95.
23. Under full consolidation, domestic capital investment is necessarily equal to gross domestic savings plus new borrowed savings from abroad.
24. Gross savings as a share of GDP are, however, significantly positively correlated with interest rates (Exhibit 9.8).
25. For definitions of *ex ante* and *ex post,* see Chapter 7, note 20, page 360.
26. Federal Reserve banks, despite their "private" chartering, are a part of the federal government.

27. Corporate cultural restraints on capital investments I assume do not have a role in this process (see Chapter 4).

28. Adjusted for inflation.

29. The propensity to save out of household income has clearly been no match against the forces driving personal consumption. (Household consumption as a percent of income hovers between 90 percent and 95 percent.) The same pressures do not exist in the business sector, however, because business has no avenue to consume conspicuously. Its choice is not between consumption spending and saving, but largely between spending on capital assets; retiring debt and paying dividends to, and buying back stock from, shareholders.

30. There are, of course, statistical discrepancies in the published data.

31. All output has a claimant or owner. When claims to the GDP (wages and capital income) are summed, we obtain gross domestic income. Of necessity, it is equal in value to GDP.

32. Transactions can be classified as either capitalized or noncapitalized. Capitalized transactions are those that end up on the balance sheets of firms or of the economy as a whole. Noncapitalized transactions are consumption expenditures, which, once spent, disappear from our accounts.

33. Of course, if intentions to save in the private sector and among foreign lenders to the United States exceed *ex ante* U.S. funding requirements, there is no savings (and hence no investment) to be crowded out. In fact, the excess of savings intentions will tend to suppress interest rates and rates on other income-earning assets, thereby inducing some "crowding in"—that is, an increase of both savings and investment. Crowding in was particularly evident between 1998 and 2001 when the U.S. government was running a (rare) surplus. It was also the cause of the decline in interest rates in global markets from 2000 to 2005 (see Chapter 3, note 5).

34. The major problem with those surveys is that they depend on the tenuous recollection of people. Moreover, there is an apparent tendency to overestimate savings out of income, given what we know about the more accurate household savings totals from the Bureau of Economic Analysis and the Federal Reserve.

35. See Chapter 11 on measures of income inequality.

36. The upper quintile's effective tax rate fell from 17 percent of pretax income in 1981 to 13 percent in 2009. But the tax rate decline among the lower quintiles was much larger.

37. Had the slowdown in output per hour not occurred, average pretax household money income in 2011 would have been many thousands of dollars more than what was actually received.

38. The result also suggests that if benefits had risen only by 6.8 percent per year (in line with GDP growth) rather than 9.4 percent per year, gross domestic savings and the GDP growth rate would not have been importantly impaired.

39. Fortunately, through the spring of 2013, neither decreases in the dollar's trade-weighted exchange rate nor a rise in U.S. interest rates relative to foreign borrowing rates suggested that we had encountered borrowing difficulties. But such changes often happen unexpectedly with little advance notice.

40. Margaret Thatcher in an interview for *Thames TV This Week;* February 5, 1976: "Socialist governments traditionally do make a financial mess. They always run out of other people's money. It's quite a characteristic of them."

41. An ophthalmologist suggested to me that the prospective aging population will require, in the years ahead, a major increase in cataract removal procedures. But many ophthalmologists will retire with the baby boomers. Will we have adequate staff to cover that demand?

42. The hours worked are assumed to be those actually employed. The same people would be working in the counterfactual scenario, but, in 2011, at a higher level of output per hour. I further assume that the MFP residual is the same as calculated by the BLS.

CHAPTER 10: CULTURE

1. The group is officially called the G-10 governors, but it is actually made up of central bank governors of eleven countries: United States, United Kingdom, Canada, Germany, France, Italy, Belgium, Netherlands, Switzerland, Sweden, and Japan.

2. There was dissent, especially from Britain. Eddie George, the governor of the Bank of England, was skeptical. So was I.

3. For Ireland and Finland, the spread change during this period was slightly greater, at 106 and 112 basis points, respectively.

4. Gold was removed from U.S. circulation in 1933, but the Treasury offered unlimited gold convertibility to central banks.

5. There are thus two distinctly defined Eurozone areas: the north and the south. The ranking of credit risk spreads throughout the Eurozone at

mid-year 2012 was almost identical to the ranking of the level of unit labor costs (relative to that of Germany), suggesting that the higher labor costs and prices have rendered Euro-South less competitive and so more subject to credit risk. The more competitively priced net exports of the northern Eurozone participants, in effect, more than covered the rising level of net imports of the south. In short, since 1999, there has been a continuous net transfer of goods and services shipped from the north to the south. Northern Europe in effect has been subsidizing southern European consumption from the onset of the euro on January 1, 1999. It is not a recent phenomenon.

6. Kieran Kelly, "Greek Default Crisis Is All About Cultural Differences in the Eurozone," *Australian,* September 24, 2011.

7. The credits and debits of the central banks of the Eurozone against one another are TARGET2 balances. As such, any losses are against the ECB (not the creditor central banks) and are then distributed in proportion to the capital contributions to the ECB. See, for example, "The TARGET2 Settlement System in the Eurozone" by Gerald P. Dwyer of the Federal Reserve Bank of Atlanta (March/April 2012).

8. Many of the fiscal problems in southern Europe, of course, have reflected excessive leverage in their private sectors.

9. Calculations presume that all Eurozone currencies that locked into the euro's exchange rate on January 1, 1999, were competitive at that date.

10. A high savings rate, a measure of prudence, is a necessary but not a sufficient condition for high investment. An effective financial system that directs a nation's savings toward the funding of productive capital investments is also a requirement.

11. France, of course, has ties to both the north and the south.

12. Remarks by Mario Draghi at the Global Investment Conference, London, July 26, 2012.

13. The response was similar to what the U.S. Treasury did to help stop the run on Mexico's Tesobono and peso in late 1994.

14. It is difficult to determine the extent of a deutschmark premium relative to the euro in the event of a Eurozone breakup. There is little doubt that the Euro-South countries would be much weaker subsequent to a breakup. And given the weakening of the Euro-South legacy currencies, of necessity there will be an equal offset to northern strength because the consolidated euro exchange rates must "sum" to the value of the euro overall.

15. ECB assets are larger than those of the Federal Reserve.

16. Earlier in this chapter, I pointed to the sharp contraction of sovereign

bond spreads against the German bund leading up to the adoption of the Euro.

17. Mure Dickie, "Fukushima Crisis 'Made in Japan,'" *Financial Times,* July 5, 2012.

18. It is instructive that experiments with children, testing their ability to forgo available consumption in exchange for greater consumption in the future, showed a positive correlation between self-restraint and SAT scores (see Chapter 1). The choice of austerity now for greater future consumption is a clearly deeply inbred human trade-off.

19. Calculated slightly differently from gross domestic savings rates.

20. The correlation coefficient is .65, and the t-value of the 2011 savings rate regressed against per capita GDP is 3.3.

21. Of course, this conclusion more or less must be true owing to how we define a developing country relative to a developed country.

22. For details, see data on World Bank Web site (http://data.worldbank.org/data-catalog/worldwide-governance-indicators).

23. For details, see World Economic Forum *Global Competitiveness Report* (http://reports.weforum.org/global-competitiveness-report-2012-2013/).

CHAPTER 11: THE ONSET OF GLOBALIZATION, INCOME INEQUALITY, AND THE RISE OF THE GINI AND THE CRONY

1. Tom Brokaw, *The Greatest Generation* (New York: Random House, 1998).

2. The food aid that the United States gave to both its allies and adversaries following World War I, under the leadership of then-United States food administrator Herbert Hoover, was nonetheless substantial.

3. It had actually lessened between 1947 and 1968.

4. Enacted in June 1944, the GI Bill (officially titled the Servicemen's Readjustment Act) provided a number of benefits for World War II veterans, mostly assistance with tuition and living expenses for those pursuing further high school, college, or vocational education.

5. Nonetheless, work stoppages surged in the early 1950s.

6. Only 22 percent of married women were in the labor force in 1950 to bolster household income. Today, the figure is more than 60 percent.

7. The declining cost amortized over a two- or three-year period of robot "labor" had become highly competitive in terms of hourly cost with what had heretofore (1950s, for example) been middle income jobs.

8. Compensation per hour of private industry union workers dipped below that of nonunion workers in 2012.

9. The liberal Economic Policy Institute estimates a rise in the ratio of CEO compensation to production worker wage from 35 times in 1978 to more than 250 times in 2007.

10. The pattern of rising inequality that flattens in recent years is also evident in the spread between high- and low-earning industries that widened from 1990 to 2007 and then stabilized, as did the Gini coefficient.

11. Alan Greenspan, *The Age of Turbulence* (New York: Penguin Press, 2007), p. 426.

12. Ibid., pp. 425–26.

13. "Special Report on America's Competitiveness," *Economist*, March 16, 2013, p.11.

14. Of course, two and a half percentage points per year over forty-seven years yields triple the level of benefits by 2012.

15. *Economist*, Febraury 2, 2013, p. 9.

16. However, social norms have succeeded in suppressing it for the vast majority of us.

17. Elasticity of demand thwarts monopsonies (single buyers) as well. But monopsonies are rare, especially compared with far more prevalent monopolies of all types. John D. Rockefeller was the classic monopsonist when negotiating rail freight rates for his kerosene shipments in the 1890s. Finally challenged, he responded by exercising his control of the market for transportation of kerosene by switching from railroads to his own newly constructed pipelines. Moreover the consequent flattening of both supply and demand curves vis-à-vis price reduces deadweight loss, a classic measure of market inefficiency.

18. Fixed specifications for bank vaults dictated new buildings. Alternative and admittedly less convenient means of vault operations by a private company were cheaper, as were conceivably all such alternatives requiring a trade-off between security and cost. But such an evaluation, as I recall, was ruled out, given fixed specifications for a particular vault.

19. The crisis actually began in 1971 as crude oil pricing power shifted from the Texas gulf to the Persian Gulf. (See *The Age of Turbulence*, pp. 444–45, for a detailed description of the seminal shift in economic and hence political power.)

20. I exclude unexploited natural resources, such as oil reserves.

21. Peter Baker, "Lost Amid Scandal: A Workforce Bill," *Washington Post*, August 12, 1998.

22. The creation of the Interstate Commerce Commission in 1887 is the classic case of one market intervention creating competitive distortions that require still other interventions. Considering the huge advantages to productivity overall from these monopolies, I am hard pressed to argue, as I did in the 1960s, that the post–Civil War subsidized rails from the Mississippi to the West Coast were a wholly bad idea.

23. People who live in societies that do not believe in individual rights (for example, Mao's China and the Soviet Union) are taught that free markets are exploitive.

24. Fairness, as I note in Chapter 1, is a propensity of human nature that requires people to be judgmental. Without specifying the standards by which to judge what *is* "fair," each person, of necessity, sets his or her own value preferences.

25. See, for example, Peter Wallison's "Dodd-Frank's Liquidation Plan Is Worse Than Bankruptcy" (*Bloomberg,* June 11, 2012).

26. For an explanation of *ex ante* and *ex post,* see Chapter 7, note 20, page 360.

27. Kenichi Ueda and Beatrice Weder di Mauro, "Quantifying Structural Subsidy Values for Systemically Important Financial Institutions," IMF Working Paper, May 2012.

28. Wayne Passmore, "The GSE Implicit Subsidy and the Value of Government Ambiguity," *Real Estate Economics,* 33, no. 3 (2005): pp. 465–86.

29. To be sure, there was the Penn-Central bailout in 1970, but that episode gradually faded and was not considered as precedential.

30. Prior to the crisis, the yield spread between S&P ten-year BB+ industrial bonds and ten-year U.S. Treasury notes was less than 2 percentage points. In September 2011, the spread was more than 5 percentage points, though it had moved somewhat lower by early 2013.

31. On July 13, 2012, the firm revised that loss to $5.8 billion, noting that it could climb to upward of $7 billion depending on subsequent market conditions.

32. Two and a half years at the Council of Economic Advisers (1974–77) and eighteen and a half years at the Fed (1987–2006).

CHAPTER 12: MONEY AND INFLATION

1. Sovereign governments issue two types of currency granted "legal tender" status. The first is gold or silver coin, or paper money that can be

redeemed for specie at a fixed conversion rate. The second is paper money not backed by specie (fiat money).

2. The prohibition of the private holding of gold and gold clauses in private contracts effectively eliminated the dollar's historic tie to gold. The continuation of gold transactions between central banks until 1974 did not appear to engage the private marketplace or the fiat money price level.

3. In addition, if central banks ran into a surge of inflation, they were not required to restore the earlier *level* of prices.

4. It is true that these metals are attractive, relatively scarce, malleable, and fungible. But why this makes them more acceptable than other material with similar attributes has never been evident to me. But there can be no denying gold's universal acceptability. During the waning years of World War II, for example, only gold was an acceptable means of payment for most German imports.

5. Lying between gold and fiat currency are currencies redeemable in gold. That promise rests on a government's or a person's ability to fulfill the promise. The value of gold is perceived as intrinsic and does not require any further support.

6. Governments seem unable to hold the supply of fiat money in check. The lure of seemingly costless money has always been irresistible. It started with governmental "coin clipping"* and has progressed to printing money unrelated to the financing of economic activity.

7. Richard Nixon imposed wage and price controls in 1971 because prices were rising at an apparently politically intolerable 4.5 percent annual rate.

8. Milton Friedman, "The Counter-Revolution in Monetary Theory" (First Wincott Memorial Lecture, September 16, 1970).

9. I chose capacity instead of output because a unit M2 measure using capacity as its denominator behaves statistically slightly better than one using output (GDP). Moreover, unused capacity can be brought into a market to satisfy rising demand without prices rising inexorably.

The capacity of GDP is derived by first separating gross non-farm business GDP (76 percent of total in 2012) into industrial and all other. I obtain a first cut industrial capacity by dividing industrial GDP by Federal Reserve operating rates, and a first cut nonindustrial capacity by dividing nonindustrial business GDP by ISM nonmanu-

---

*Prior to the twentieth century, clipping the edges of silver and gold coins produced metal for resale, presumably without altering the face value of the coins.

facturing operating rates. The sum of the two, moderately smoothed, yields capacity for gross nonfarm business product. I assumed the rest of GDP (24 percent in 2012) operated at 90 percent of capacity and calculated its capacity by dividing gross nonbusiness GDP by 0.9. The total capacity was the sum of the nonfarm business and nonbusiness GDP.

10. Almost any financial asset whose market value can be determined—stocks and bonds, for example—can be exchanged for any good or service, and thereby create a price per unit. I am certain I can find an automobile dealer who would be willing to take as payment for a car listed at $29,000 a thousand shares of stock valued at $30 per share. But there is little doubt that convenience of payment is quite important to a transaction balance, especially because payments are increasingly being made electronically. Moreover, bypassing these modern electronic payment systems is becoming ever more infeasible.

11. Most foreign holdings of U.S. currency are held as a store of value and are not used to buy goods and services in the United States, and hence, one would presume, have little effect on domestic prices.

12. The choice of transaction balance should price all goods and services purchased in an economy, including imports, not just those that are produced domestically.

13. Associated Press, "Prices Rise on Greenspan's Remarks," October 28, 1991.

14. Cara S. Lown, Stavros Peristiani, and Kenneth J. Robinson, "What Was Behind the M2 Breakdown?" (Federal Reserve banks of New York and Dallas, July 1999).

15. The dummy variable in Exhibit 12.3 captures the extraordinary shift in U.S. financial markets (discussed earlier in this section) that, to this day, I find difficult to understand.

16. Money velocity can be seen as equal to nominal GDP divided by M2. Unit money supply is equal to M2 divided by real GDP. Given that nominal GDP is equal to real GDP times the implicit price deflator, the ratio of price to unit money supply is equivalent to money velocity. In my exhibits, the two series differ solely because (1) I use the more statistically significant "real capacity" as the denominator of unit money supply, rather than real GDP, and (2) I use the price of core personal consumption expenditures, rather than the GDP deflator, as my measure of price.

17. There are no capital charges levied on these sovereign funds. Hence,

their cost to the bank amounts to little more than electronic transfer fees.

18. Whether the claims banks have on the Federal Reserve are in the form of deposits or holdings of Federal Reserve notes does not affect the size of the set-aside. It is based not on the nature of central bank money but on the risk that the recipient of a bank loan will default. This is the reason that the ratio of M2 to the monetary base (the money multiplier) implies a set-aside that parallels the ratio of capital plus loan loss reserves to total loans outstanding surprisingly well (see Exhibit 12.5). I chose to use the balance sheet ratio rather than the more relevant income statement data (allowances plus new equity capital, as a ratio to gross loan extensions) because comparable data on loan extensions are not available. That the money multiplier was an unexpectedly low 3.7 in 1948, a relatively prosperous year, reflects the very large expansion of the monetary base created to help finance the war.

19. The proceeds of most new loans are spent almost immediately.

20. This is, of course, a stylized, simplified version of a much more complex lending process.

21. For example, given a 20 percent set-aside, $100 in reserves created by the Fed would ultimately lead to an increase in bank loans of $500 ($100 + 0.8 x $100 + 0.8 x $80 + 0.8 x $64 + ... = $500). The total increase in loans in our fractional-reserve banking system as a ratio to the Fed's initial injection of funds is called the money multiplier. It originally referred to the expansion constrained by legal reserve requirements. However, it works in much the same way when banks determine their own capital and loan loss set-asides.

22. There are a number of other temporary measures to absorb reserves, such as reverse repos and term deposits. But these efforts will become ever more difficult to sustain over time.

23. The money multiplier fell from 2008 to 2011, but most of the decline occurred in the few months immediately following the onset of crisis.

24. For these calculations, I assume that the size of Federal Reserve assets in mid-2013, at approximately $3.5 trillion, will remain unchanged through 2017; that U.S. currency held both at home and abroad will follow their recent trends; and that business capacity will rise at 2 percent per year.

CHAPTER 13: BUFFERS

1. Alan Greenspan, "Economics of Air Power"; the Conference Board *Business Record;* Vol. IX, No. 4; April 1952.
2. Roadbed maintenance for private railroads, for example.

CHAPTER 14: THE BOTTOM LINE

1. General Agreement on Tariffs and Trade.
2. Wheat exports soared to more than 300 million bushels in 1948.
3. The CBO estimates the comparable share of social insurance taxes paid in 2009 by the highest quintile at 46 percent.
4. The estimates of the savings rate of the upper quintile are notoriously flawed. Our major source is the annual Consumer Expenditure Survey. Data from the 2011 survey indicate a savings rate of 19.4 percent for all households. The Bureau of Economic Analysis estimates a savings rate of 4.2 percent.
5. Businesses are offsetting that decline by increases in business savings (undistributed corporate profits and depreciation) as a percent of GDP. The sum of household and business savings has remained trendless.
6. As I noted in Chapter 11, its struggle may have lessons for the United States.
7. When deficit spending first became a serious public issue in the 1930s, I recall it always being in the context of budget balance over a business cycle. But when it became obvious to previously fiscally prudent legislators that deficits do not always immediately create politically unpopular inflation, they abandoned the policy for a more flexible guideline of keeping the ratio of *debt* to GDP constant. In the context of the not-fully-funded benefits boom of the past near half century, it is apparent that such a paradigm, although economically sensible, does not work well.
8. I recall that when the yield on the ten-year Treasury note rose to near 9 percent in early July 1979, conventional wisdom was that the United States was not an inflation-prone society, and hence 9 percent—the highest level possibly ever—was generally deemed the peak in rates. By late February 1980, the rate had risen to almost 14 percent as the bond market collapsed.

INDEX